AMBITIONS
AND
REALITIES

AMBITIONS AND REALITIES

British Politics 1964-70

ROBERT RHODES JAMES

WEIDENFELD AND NICOLSON
5 Winsley Street London W1

64617

ISBN 0 297 99429 8

Printed by C. Tinling and Co. Ltd.,
London and Prescot.

For Sweet Aleck, with love

Contents

Contents

Page

Part One
Labour – The Language of Power 1964-79

Part Two
The Conservatives – The Leader and the Task
69

Part Three
The Conservatives – The Challenge
Of Powellism
147

Part Four
The General Election of 1970
215

Select Bibliography
309

Index
321

Preface

D ISRAELI's dictum that, 'the vicissitudes of politics are inexhaustible' has a particularly vivid application to the history of British politics in the 1960s. At the beginning of this decade the Conservative Party, victors in three successive General Elections, were triumphantly dominant; in sad contrast, the Labour Party was dispirited and disunited, and locked in vehement internecine disputes. 'The image of the Labour Party,' declared the authors of an independent study of the electorate in 1960, 'held both by its supporters and its non-supporters, is one that is increasingly obsolete in terms of contemporary Britain.'[1] But by 1963 the balance had completely changed. In October 1964 Labour displaced the Conservatives by the most narrow of majorities; in March 1966 it won a comprehensive victory; but in June 1970 it was swept out of office, the victim of the strongest movement towards an Opposition party in normal peacetime conditions in modern British politics.

This study is an attempt to examine these abrupt changes in political fortunes. It originated from a conviction that General Elections cannot be contemplated in isolation from their wider political, social and economic contexts. Recent studies, furthermore, offer surprisingly little between the extremes of what might be called 'The Making of the Prime Minister' school – which owes much to the work of Mr Theodore White in the United States – and the series of General Election studies conducted by Nuffield College, Oxford. Admirable though these very different approaches might be, it is evident that there is room for others. General Elections provide the most important opportunities for judgement and decision by a mass electorate, but it is very rare indeed that the issues and divisions between the competing factions are so clear that the result can be said to represent a definite choice between definite alterna-

[1] *Socialist Commentary*, May–July 1960 (quoted in S. Haseler: *The Gaitskellites*, (London, 1969) p. 144).

I

tives. Furthermore, the study of General Elections as isolated phenomena convert them into somewhat confused and meaningless incidents.

I should emphasize that I share (although not so completely) the scepticism of the late Iain Macleod about the all-embracing wisdom of political science,[1] if only for the reason that the phrase itself is perilously close to being a contradiction in terms. I must also confess that I regard the new subsidiary cult of 'psephology' with certain reservations. It would be absurd to underestimate the importance and quality of the work that has been done by political scientists in this country and in the United States over the past ten years, and which has thrown much light on areas which were previously unknown or ignored. In particular the recent study by Dr David Butler and Dr Donald Stokes[2] must be recognized as a pioneering work of substantial importance. It is necessary, however, to recognize the limitations of this approach. The increase in the size of the British electorate since before the First World War – from under eight million voters to nearly forty million – has had the result that, despite new methods of assessing movements of public opinion, improved techniques of political organization, and the revolution in the means of public communications, modern British electoral politics are more mysterious and perplexing than they were a century ago. Thus, when the results of elections are analysed, the observer, in attempting to comprehend the message of the silent multitude of electors, has to begin by accepting that it is impossible to know with any precision why people vote or do not vote. He can only examine certain episodes and movements that may furnish some clues, recognizing that the result of his enquiry can only be partial and unsatisfying.

It could be argued that to start from this assumption is an admission of defeat at the very outset. But in reality it is another approach to solving the mystery. The journalist is often obsessed by personalities, while there is a strong tendency in some academic students of politics to dismiss – or at least seriously to under-value – significant human factors, or to treat them in remote and clinical terms. The insistence by the political scientist upon firm evidence – usually statistical – to support

[1] 'The Private World of Political Science', *The Times*, 30 November 1969.
[2] David Butler and Donald Stokes: *Political Change in Britain* (London, 1969).

every claim and fact denies the argument that there are many things in British politics which are incapable of being fully quantified in a scientific manner. Not the least of the contributions of the General Election of June 1970 was that it made this latter point very clearly.

The student of contemporary affairs suffers from many disadvantages when he compares his situation with the historian of more distant events. He is very dependent upon personal accounts of events on which the archives will be closed for many years. He certainly lacks the advantages that accrue from the perspective that time brings. It is remarkable how disputes and events that attracted substantial public attention for weeks abruptly slip back into limbo, while other incidents which attracted little attention at the time are subsequently seen to have been of very considerable importance. The contemporary commentator is also to some extent a participant, and has difficulty in making fully objective judgements on the actions and motives of his contemporaries. As time passes, and as more evidence becomes available, it becomes more possible to separate the superficial from the profound, and to make a more fair and accurate assessment. Nonetheless, the contemporary commentator can make a valid contribution by beginning this long process.

This study has been very much a personal venture, and I have enviously noted the list of assistants who were involved in the Nuffield study of the 1970 General Election.[1] I cannot claim to have operated on such a lavish and thorough scale, but I hope that it may be accepted that there is a place in contemporary political literature – as there should be in contemporary politics – for the individual who takes his own line, in his own way, in his own time.

Many people have been most generous to me of their time and attention while this study was being prepared, but as all

[1] David Butler and Michael Pinto-Duschinsky: *The British General Election of 1970* (London, 1971). This was published after I had completed my study, but certain points made in it have been incorporated – and discussed – in the final version. No serious student of modern British politics should fail to acknowledge his debt to Dr Butler and his colleagues – even those who, like myself, have reservations about the approach, techniques, and philosophy of the Nuffield election series.

interviews and discussions were on a wholly confidential and non-attributable basis I accordingly cannot publicly thank all those who assisted me. I hope that they will accept a general expression of my gratitude. I have tried to be fair to those individuals whose actions I have described and on which I have made comment, and, while I would not expect all of them to accept all my judgements, I hope that they will appreciate that my intention has been to give an objective assessment. This hope applies with particular emphasis to those who were so helpful to me in my researches.

I am, however, able to make some public acknowledgements. I wish to express my gratitude to my colleague Mr Nicholas Deakin, for reading and commenting upon the sections relating to race matters; to Sir Michael Fraser, for permitting me to make use of the exceptionally extensive and well-catalogued presscutting archives of the Conservative Central Office and Research Department; and to Miss Julie Gooding, who gave me valuable assistance at the outset of the project. I must also particularly thank Mr Harold Wilson, who made available to me an advance proof copy of his memoirs; this was a kindness which was of very considerable value to me in the preparation of this study, which was completed some time before Mr Wilson's book was published. I, of course, bear the full responsibility for the judgements, comments, and conclusions contained in this study of British politics in the 1960s.

ROBERT RHODES JAMES

Part One

LABOUR – THE BURDENS OF POWER, 1964-70

ON 8 October 1959 the Conservative Party won its third successive General Election victory, securing the remarkable proportion of 49.4 per cent of the total votes cast, and gaining a House of Commons majority over Labour and the Liberals of 100 seats. In the four General Elections held since 1945 the Conservatives had steadily increased their Parliamentary representation from 215 to 365, whereas that of the Labour Party had fallen from 393 to 258. In 1945 Labour had won nearly 48 per cent of the total vote; by 1959 it was down to 43.8 per cent.

Here, in bleak statistics, was contained the drama of a remarkmarkable political transformation. In 1945 the Labour Party had won the largest majority enjoyed by a radical party since January 1906, and the Conservatives – in power virtually without serious interruption since the formation of the first Asquith Coalition in May 1915 – had suffered their heaviest defeat since the holocaust of 1906. The shock had been all the greater because, unlike 1906, the result had been wholly unexpected by both parties. To Labour, in its heady days of exultation, and the Conservatives, in their stunned despair, it appeared that an entirely new political and social situation had been created in Britain. As a result of the War, ten years had passed without a General Election, and it seemed that that tumultuous and terrible decade had made vehement and permanent changes in British society which had erased the old political cries and confederations. 'There was exhilaration among us,' Hugh Dalton subsequently wrote, 'joy and hope, determination and confidence. We felt exalted, dedicated, walking on air, walking with destiny.'[1] Yet, within five years, the overwhelming Labour majority of 1945 had been eliminated; in 1951 the Conservatives secured a slender Parliamentary majority; in 1955 they increased this to more comfortable proportions. By 1959 the

[1] Hugh Dalton: *High Tide and After* (London 1962), p. 3.

Conservative recovery was complete, and the confident prognostications of 1945 returned to mock the Labour Party and those observers who had heralded the permanence of its triumph and who had forecast a generation of Labour domination.

The Conservative revival and the decline of Labour occasioned judgements which were as sweeping as those of 1945. In 1960, contemplating post-war British political history, the dominant conclusion was that the British turned to radical parties and policies only in very exceptional situations. In normal times, the argument ran, the nation resumed its confidence in the Conservative coalition which had been, for nearly a century, the most powerful and consistent element in British politics and society. 'A middle-aged conservatism, parochial and complacent, has settled over the country,' one of the Labour Party's most promising young intellectuals lamented.[1] The possibility of the total collapse of the Labour Party and its replacement by a new radical coalition was generally regarded as a very real one. But, by April 1970, the Labour Party had been in office for five and a half years, and for four years it had enjoyed the first substantial Parliamentary majority that it had ever achieved in normal peacetime conditions. Speaking at Cardiff on 29 May 1970, the Prime Minister, Mr Harold Wilson, spoke of 'a feeling of national liberation, of a loosening of restriction on personal initiative, of a freedom of individual choice, combined with a national system of order and stability which makes us the envy of the civilised world . . . This is responsible government – financially and socially responsible.' This had been, almost word for word, the victorious Conservative message of 1959.

The story of British politics between 1959 and 1964 had been that of the abrupt decline of the Conservative Party and the resurgence of Labour. It was significant that the first preceded the latter, for it was not until 1962 that it was becoming clear that it was Labour, and not the Liberals or other parties, who was to be the principal beneficiary of the rapid disintegration of the Government that had won so convincingly in 1959.

The Conservative Party is a party of government. Its funda-

[1] C. A. R. Crosland: *The Conservative Enemy* (London, 1962), p. 127.

mental purpose is to obtain and retain political power, and to make use of that power to achieve gradual and ordered change in the context of the preservation of national institutions. If a party can be said to have a single credo, that of the modern Conservative Party was set out by Disraeli at Edinburgh in 1867:

In a progressive country, change is constant; and the question is not whether you should resist change which is inevitable, but whether that change should be carried out in deference to the manners, the customs, the laws, and the traditions of a people, or whether it should be carried out in deference to abstract principles, and arbitrary and general doctrines.

The causes of the success of the Conservatives in preserving themselves for over a century of fundamental social change cannot be swiftly analysed or related, but a major element has been an obsession with government, combined with a firm confidence that the British people at large are equally suspicious of 'arbitrary and general doctrines'. 'The English working man,' John Morley once remarked to Winston Churchill, 'is no logician, like the French "Red", whom I also know. He is not thinking of new systems, but of having fairer treatment in this one.'[1] It has been on this hypothesis that the Conservatives have consistently operated, and their success gives its own message. The Conservatives' ideology is power. They believe that they are more patriotic, more competent, more far-sighted, more sensible, more realistic and more flexible as a governing party than their rivals. Those rivals may mock these pretensions, but the self-confidence and single-minded determination of the Conservative Party to gain power and wield it responsibly must be accounted as its most important salient characteristic.

But what is the Labour Party for? Examination of its history – whether one dates it from the founding of the Independent Labour Party in 1893 or the establishment of the Labour Representation Committee in 1900 – discloses a fundamental imprecision about its purposes. Until 1917 Labour was a derisory appendage of the Liberal Party, but, even after it had achieved a separate identity and programme this imprecision remained. *Labour and the New Social Order*, published in 1918, formed the basis of Labour strategy for more than thirty years. But although

[1] Winston S. Churchill: *Great Contemporaries* (London, 1937.)

9

it established principles – the national minimum wage, democratic control of industry, the subsidization of social services by higher taxation, and the expansion of education and other social benefits for the people – the programme was vague on specifics. Although admirably suited for a crusade, this visionary and exciting programme had certain limitations in terms of practical politics. Indeed, part of the momentum behind the new party lay in this very fact, for 'practical politics' implied the old political order against which Labour was fighting. But there were already some Labour leaders – notably Ramsay MacDonald and Philip Snowden – who had been in the House of Commons for a considerable period, and who were convinced that a social crusade could only be effectively launched from a position of power – and power which had been won in the conventional manner by the winning of elections. The fledgling party found itself in office, but not in power, very soon, and its inexperience and the basic dichotomy of its outlook were swiftly and brutally exposed. The experience of 1924, of being unexpectedly put into office with Liberal support and then flung out of it when that support was withdrawn, did not assist in solving the essential dilemma; the traumas of 1929–31 confused the matter further. Was Labour a Democratic Socialist Party, aiming for substantial national support to implement Socialist philosophies and policies? Was it essentially a class party? Was it the party of protest and of pressure? Was it the party of the trade unions? Was it to be the natural inheritor of the principles of the Liberal Party or the defenders of Free Trade? Was it to be the architect of a new society?

Even by 1945, when Labour found itself – to the ill-concealed surprise of most of its leaders – with a massive Parliamentary majority, these issues had not been resolved. Very few plans had been made for the eventuality of office; on most questions the party had attitudes, but no very clear ideas on how to implement them.[1] Thus, although the 1945–51 Labour Government achieved a remarkable record of reform and change in very difficult circumstances, many of its supporters considered that it had shrunk from the fundamental far-reaching reforms which they desired from a Socialist Government. Indeed, to such critics it seemed that over a wide range of activities there was very little difference in substance between this Government and

[1] See, for example, E. Shinwell: *Conflict Without Malice* (London, 1955), pp. 172–3.

the Conservative Opposition. Not all members of the Labour Party shared this dismay. Hugh Gaitskell wrote of the group of young men who had gathered around him and Evan Durbin[1] in the 1930s that, 'they were equally devoted to democracy and personal freedom. They believed in tolerance and they understood the need for compromise. They were for the rational and the practical, and suspicious of large general ideas.'[2] This approach in effect rejected the conception of Labour as a doctrinaire party of the Left, and saw it as a responsible, socially-conscious rather than Socialist, national movement that was less interested in ideology than practical social reform within a moderate framework. But, it was argued against this approach, what was the Labour Party about if it was not interested in 'large general ideas'? This was not really a debate between Left and Right, or Anti-Revisionist versus Revisionist, although it was often depicted in such terms; it was the old debate about what the Labour Party existed for. When the 1945 Government eventually fell in 1951 the central question had not been resolved, and the situation was greatly complicated by the subsequent outbreak of personal and ideological rancours. Throughout the 1950s, staggering under a succession of failures and disappointments, the Labour Party seemed at times to have lost interest in gaining power, and increasingly resigned to an indefinite period of good Socialist Opposition. Not all members of the party regarded this situation with distaste. Better by far, it was argued, to go down to honourable defeat in a fine cause and vigorously defend that cause in honest opposition than to compromise the true principles of Socialism in a sordid quest for office, and subsequently to be forced to abandon them under the pressures of actually being a Government. The dilemma was posed – and answered somewhat hesitantly – by Mr Roy Jenkins in 1953:

Is it to be the job of the Labour Party to study the moods of the electorate so closely and to adjust its own position so nicely that it is able to be both the party of advance and the party of consolidation? Or is it to be its task to devote more time to leadership and less to an anxious study of the Gallup Polls, to offer the electorate

[1] Senior Lecturer in Economics at LSE; MP for Edmonton 1945–8.
[2] Introduction to E. F. M. Durbin: *The Politics of Democratic Socialism*, (London, 1940).

what it believes to be right rather than what it believes the electorate to want, and to take the political consequences of this? The conclusion of our argument is that the more courageous course is on the whole the right one.[1]

When Harold Wilson became leader of the Party in January 1963, following the sudden death of Hugh Gaitskell, it acquired a leader who was as dedicated as any Conservative to the achievement of power. He had the good fortune to succeed to the leadership at a moment when the Conservative Government was under heavy stress after twelve years of office, and when Labour could see the mirage of office rapidly assuming more positive indications. The deaths of Bevan in 1960 and Gaitskell in 1963 had symbolically marked the end of a period of Labour history that had been characterized by severe divisions. Gaitskell had determined to make Labour's appearance and policies more appropriate to modern trends, and in *Signposts for the Sixties* – published after the débâcle of 1959 – the first clear indications of this change had been seen. But the battles over the preservation of Clause Four of the Party constitution[2] and unilateral nuclear disarmament had revived the fundamental problem of whether Labour was to be a party dedicated to the pursuit of ideals or of office. Despite much courage and determination, Gaitskell's own attitude was somewhat ambivalent. It is fruitless to speculate on what might have happened had he lived, but it was evident that, despite his fierce belief in making Labour modern and relevant, and his own considerable contribution to that process, he lacked the complete urge towards power that his successor possessed. Few descriptions could be less apt than that of Hugh Gaitskell as 'a dessicated calculating machine'. He was a man of great warmth of character, with an interest in people as individuals that is, unhappily, rare in politicians. The political price that had to be paid for these personal qualities was that, politically, he bruised easily. He was not unafraid of controversy, but it

---

[1] Roy Jenkins: *Pursuit of Progress* (London, 1953). Quoted in A. Lester (ed.): *Essays and Speeches by Roy Jenkins*, pp. 197–209.

[2] 'To secure for the workers by hand or by brain the full fruits of their industry and the most equitable distribution thereof that may be possible upon the basis of common ownership of the means of production, distribution and exchange, and the best obtainable system of popular administration and control of each industry or service.' For a good account of this struggle see S. Haseler: *The Gaitskellites* (London, 1969), Chapter 8.

left its marks. There was in addition, a certain remoteness between him and the bulk of the Labour Party. Gaitskell's instinctive reactions betrayed his social and intellectual background; when he had time to reflect and consult, a different response emerged. Although he had been in the Labour Party all his adult life, one detected still a marked lack of understanding, and frequently of sympathy. It is significant that many of his closest associates and admirers doubted whether Labour would have won the 1964 General Election under Gaitskell's leadership. It is, furthermore, of more than marginal interest to note that whereas Gaitskell disliked Mr Harold Macmillan and abhorred all that he symbolized, his successor had a very different assessment of that complex politician's capacities and contribution.

Nonetheless, it was Gaitskell's principal achievement that, by 1963, Labour had taken a decisive step away from the attitude that had been put with particular clarity and vigour by Mr Richard Crossman in 1960:

> Those who assert that the sole object or even the main object of the Labour Party today should be to regain office seem to me to misconceive not merely the nature of British socialism but the workings of British democracy.[1]

Wilson's inheritance was a good one, but he unquestionably augmented it. Under Wilson's leadership in 1963–4 the decisive aim of the Party became office, almost at any price. Anything that seriously endangered this goal was disposed of or played down, and entirely new techniques of survey research and propaganda were carefully studied and skilfully harnessed to the main objective. The old concept of writing a good Socialist manifesto and trusting to the wisdom of the electorate was replaced by the new one of studying the market and preparing a prospectus that was likely to attract it. This was not a cynical or a defeatist attitude, nor was it a betrayal of the principles of the Party. It was an approach that frankly accepted that the defeats of 1951, 1955 and 1959 had had a cause, and that the Party had drifted away from political realities. It was also based on the not unjustified apprehension that a fourth defeat might well destroy Labour for ever. In the 1950s there had been

[1] Quoted in David Butler and Anthony King: *The British General Election of 1964*, p. 57.

a steady and ominous movement out of politics by some of the most promising men in the Party, and it was not unreasonable to anticipate that this drift would be accelerated after another defeat. There was, accordingly, a well-founded fear in the Labour leadership in the early 1960s that the Party was in a 'now or never' situation.

In 1960 Dr Mark Abrams had published the results of a private survey in *Socialist Commentary* that was subsequently published under the title *Must Labour Lose?*[1] Dr Abrams' association with the Labour leadership subsequently became close, and resulted in the establishment of the objective that Labour's policies must be directed towards a new category of 'target voter'. For the first time in British political history, the new techniques of survey research were applied to the processes of policy-formation.[2] It is not necessary to hazard what would have been Aneurin Bevan's views on this development; and apprehensions in the Party, although muted, certainly existed. But Labour advanced to the 1964 General Election with a programme and an approach that was deliberately designed to appeal to an electorate that had rejected the Labour alternative on no less than three consecutive occasions over a period of thirteen years. Although Wilson was an admitted admirer of the methods, style, and techniques of Harold Macmillan, it would be more relevant to emphasize that he was in close sympathy with the methods, style and techniques of the Conservative Party, and, above all, its relentless hunger for power.

The first step had been to make the Labour Party begin to think of itself in these terms as a governing party, rather than that of the party of conscience and social justice which could normally be expected to be in a noble but emphatic Parliamentary minority. This had meant some sacrifices of the principal cries of the 1950s, and particularly in a significant muting of emphasis on nationalization. At the time the Conservatives were in such disarray, and the Labour Party apparently so marvellously united, that the voices of the doubters were faint; but the discordant mutterings could be heard. Thus, although Wilson's own deliberate concentration on the challenges of science and technology and on responsible administra-

[1] Mark Abrams: *Must Labour Lose?* (London, 1960).
[2] Butler and King: *op. cit.*, pp. 69–71.

tion of the economy had a considerable general appeal, it was a puzzlement to many Party stalwarts.

This emphasis on science and technology tended to be dismissed then and later by Wilson's critics as an example of 'gimmickry',[1] but an examination of Wilson's speeches throughout the 1950s demonstrates that this was not a suddenly developed new theme, appropriate for elections. Wilson was genuinely convinced that British industry was being held back by bad management and amateurism, while sufficient opportunities were not being given to younger technicians. His attacks on 'old school tie' cliques, absentee or incompetent company directors, and businessmen more interested in expense-account luncheons than work, represented a genuine contempt for practices and traditions which he considered inefficient and unfair. But he also believed that a modernized industrial society in which men rose by merit alone would effect a far more profound long-term social revolution than the standard doctrinaire Socialist approach to social equality. He was not unaware of the fact that the Conservatives had polled very heavily in the rising white-collar worker group in 1959, and there was unquestionably a significant political motive in his vigorous espousal of Labour's commitment to industrial modernization and restructuring; but it would be wrong to conclude that the political motive was the only one.

This approach had a particular force and interest because it actively encouraged and sanctified personal endeavour and success within the capitalist system, something that no Labour leader had ever expressed so clearly or emphatically before. The new heroes were men of the calibre of Sir Donald (later Lord) Stokes, Mr Peter Parker, and Mr Arnold Weinstock. Success on sheer merit, instead of being regarded as vaguely anti-social, was now lauded and rewarded. One of the most powerful and attractive features of the Conservative philosophy was thus neatly appropriated.

The second step in Wilson's strategy was to convince a significant proportion of a sceptical electorate that the appearance did not belie the reality, and that Labour was a viable and responsible alternative to the Conservatives. The Labour theme

[1] Sir Alec Douglas-Home described Wilson in the 1964 campaign as 'a slick salesman of synthetic science'; not surprisingly, his tongue stumbled over this appalling prepared alliteration.

in the 1964 Election was that the Conservatives were the party of the past, whereas Labour was concerned by the future. 'We seek to create an open society in which all have a vital and vigorous part to play . . . For if the past belongs to the Tories the future belongs to us, all of us.' This theme was best expressed by Wilson himself, whose performance during the campaign was a remarkable personal triumph, marred only by one major tactical error – when he implied that strikes during elections were deliberately contrived on behalf of the Conservatives – and by a faulty strategy which ended the Labour campaign three days before polling day. But despite massive Conservative disenchantment, Labour only won the 1964 Election by a fraction, and with a vote that had actually declined on its 1959 total. The narrowness of that victory demonstrated that Labour was not yet fully accepted in its new presentiment.

To establish this was the principal task of the 1964–6 Labour Government, a task made even more difficult by the fact that only Wilson himself had been a Cabinet member, and only two of his colleagues had had senior Ministerial experience.[1] It was suddenly evident what thirteen years in Opposition can do to a Party. Wilson's situation was in this respect only marginally better than that of MacDonald in 1924, and infinitely more difficult than that of Attlee in 1945. To convert this group of inexperienced Ministers into a presentable national government was the primary task of the new Prime Minister, and to this end he seized every conceivable opportunity for eliminating the picture of Labour as a sectional party and himself as a sectional leader. The first clear indication of the success of this operation was Wilson's admirably phrased and sensitive television tribute on the death of Sir Winston Churchill in January 1965. In Parliament he dealt with the Conservatives with a robust aggression and tactical skill; on the larger stage his rôle was that of the National Leader.

In this development he was considerably assisted by his opponents. When Sir Alec Douglas-Home resigned the Conservative leadership in July 1965 and was replaced by Mr Edward Heath, Wilson's advantage was considerably increased. For the first time since 1911 the Conservative leader was not a former Prime Minister. To the public at large, moreover,

[1] Mr James Griffiths and Mr Patrick Gordon Walker.

Heath was as obscure a figure as Bonar Law had been in 1911, and was certainly less well known than Mr Reginald Maudling or Mr Iain Macleod, or than Gaitskell had been in 1955 or Wilson in 1963. Home had been Prime Minister, and had become in a short time a genuinely national figure; his successor was a much less well-known quantity. By the end of 1965 Wilson had definitely established himself as The National Leader, and the Labour Party as The Government. In addition, the Conservatives had found the process of turning from Government to Opposition a very difficult transformation, and were still involved in 're-forming under fire' – to quote Lord Blakenham's words – when Wilson dissolved Parliament in March 1966. On the cry that 'You *know* Labour government works', Labour rode to a decisive victory.

It was a remarkable exercise in political *legerdemain* and in stealing the clothes of the other side – less in the sense that Labour had taken over Conservative policies (although in some areas it had indeed done so) than in that it had absorbed the Conservative concept of a political party's essential purpose. The agonized debates of the late 1940s and the 1950s seemed very far in the past.

It is necessary to be cautious of regarding personality as being everything in politics, and, in particular, of leaders as a major factor in British elections. This distortion has been present in British political writing since the Disraeli – Gladstoned uels of the 1860s and 1870s, but it hardly stands up to serious analysis. Can it be seriously claimed that British electoral politics revolve around the personas of the opposing leaders? That, in 1895, the issue hinged upon public estimation of Salisbury and Rosebery? or, in 1906, of Balfour and Campbell-Bannerman? or MacDonald and Baldwin in 1923? or Attlee and Churchill in 1945? Even a swift glance at these elections and their contexts exposes the flimsiness of this approach. But recent political commentators, and many politicians, have become obsessed by the relative capacities and popularity of party leaders as though the whole fate of a substantial national confederation depended utterly upon the statements, speeches, impressions and appearances of one individual.

Personality in politics is indeed crucial, but in a considerably more complex and subtle manner than simply the personification of a party with its leader of the moment. The myriad factors that lead people to vote as they do defy scientific analysis, but examination of modern British politics leads to the inescapable conclusion that the personalities of the respective individual leaders are of much less importance than they are, for example, in the United States. Occasionally a political figure acquires extreme admiration or pprobrium, but even in these very rare instances it is not possible to link actual voting directly with these phenomena. The decisive factors seem to be the collective personality of a party – a personality which covers tangible and intangible elements, actual policies and implied attitudes. Thus, to see British electoral politics in purely personal and 'Presidential' terms makes good drama but inadequate history. Nonetheless, Wilson is so crucial a figure in this period that his personality and career merit closer attention.

For a political historian, perhaps the most difficult of all his tasks is to attempt to draw, in swift delineaments, the portrait of a public man. The difficulties are severe enough when the historian has to hand the public and private papers of his subject, and has the further advantages that time lends to a fair evaluation; when the subject is a contemporary, the problems are substantially magnified. Furthermore, we are seldom able to achieve real detachment and objectivity about our contemporaries, and in recent political history perhaps only the portraits of their contemporaries by Bryce and A. G. Gardiner have really withstood the test of time. Nonetheless, if politics is to be seen as something that is more complex and fascinating than a procession of events happening without apparent cause, the student of contemporary politics cannot avoid the necessity of attempting to draw the portraits of the leading political personalities. Politics is a very human business, and to ignore the importance of personality is to transform the study of politics into the study of something else and results in a distortion which is as serious as that given by over-emphasis on personality.

Harold Wilson first attracted attention when he became

President of the Board of Trade at the age of thirty-one in 1947; he had been appointed a junior Minister on his election to Parliament in 1945, and had the remarkable distinction of never sitting as a back-bencher throughout his political career. He had previously been an Oxford don, a civil servant, and had been involved in the preparation of the Beveridge Report. He was, at that time, a somewhat unexciting figure, and his speeches were lacking in power or originality.

Wilson's most distinct achievement was his much-advertised 'bonfire of controls' at the Board of Trade, but public dissatisfaction with those restrictions that remained was considerably greater than gratitude for those that had been removed. After what was regarded by many of his colleagues as his equivocal attitude to the devaluation of the pound in 1949, his stature fell, and his resignation with Bevan over the issue of the imposition of prescription charges in Gaitskell's first (and last) Budget in 1951 was not universally interpreted with charity. Perhaps these suspicions of Wilson's motives were unjust, but the fact that they had begun to develop so early in his career was not without significance.

At this stage he was already, and has always remained, a curiously solitary figure. In politics he has made very few friends and very many enemies. There is about him a reserve and a felinity that renders his frequent references to his Yorkshire ancestry – with the implications of dogged industry, determination, and straight talking – peculiarly obnoxious to those who love him not. In the early 1950s his association with Bevan won him important new adherents on the Left, but many of these were dismayed when Wilson took Bevan's place on the Parliamentary Committee (the equivalent of the Shadow Cabinet) when Bevan clashed sharply with the Party leadership and was expelled in April 1954. Wilson aroused that most potent of all political disadvantages, that of mistrust. Gaitskell worked with him, but without enthusiasm; many of those close to Gaitskell viewed Wilson with unconcealed emotions of aversion which reached their height when Wilson openly challenged Gaitskell for the leadership of the Parliamentary Party in 1960.[1] But when Gaitskell died suddenly in January 1963 Wilson was unquestionably the best qualified successor; it is also very probable that, had a viable 'Gaitskellite' alternative been

[1] The voting was 166 for Gaitskell, 81 for Wilson.

available, Wilson would not have been elected.[1] But he was by no means the first, nor will he be the last, party leader who has been chosen *faute de mieux*.

By the time he reached the leadership Wilson had become, by sheer industry rather than through natural ability, a very formidable debater and public speaker, and he had developed a style in which pungency, wit and calculated phraseology were excellently combined. As 'shadow' Chancellor of the Exchequer under Gaitskell his speech in the annual Budget debate had become one of the events of the Parliamentary year, and his appearances at the Party conferences had become increasingly impressive. Most politicians, to a greater or lesser degree, attempt to ingratiate themselves with their opponents, and to follow the dictum of Sir William Harcourt that a public man should have it as his objective, 'to stand well with the House of Commons'. Wilson's deliberate tactic was to make himself as keenly disliked as possible by the Conservative Party, in which enterprise he was wholly successful. For a moment in 1957, after insinuations about a 'leak' of the announcement of an increase in Bank Rate had been decisively and indeed contemptuously disproved, it seemed that he had gone too far; but he refused to apologize or withdraw, and delivered a speech of such belligerence and spirit in the Commons that the balance of advantage from the episode was neatly reversed. The Conservatives never forgave him, and their angry abuse of his political and personal character can hardly have harmed his position in the Labour Party. In the 1950s he was not generally regarded in the House of Commons as a politician of any real weight, and there is something to be said for the argument that the deaths of Bevan and Gaitskell, and the decline and retirement of Macmillan, made Wilson look a much more formidable politician and debater than in fact he was; but it was also the case that Wilson's own development as a speaker and political tactician in this period was very considerable.

It would be incorrect to describe Wilson as a great debater. What he became in the 1960s was an acute exploiter of the weaknesses of his opponents. He could also demonstrate a venom in debate which upset and frightened those who contended with him. It was said by Margot Asquith of Lloyd George that

[1] On the second, and final, ballot the figures were: Wilson 144, George Brown 103.

he could not see a political belt without hitting below it, and Wilson's victims considered that the description was not inapposite to his dialectical technique. He is not, in debate, the possessor of a bludgeon, like Gladstone; nor does he possess the merciless coldness of a Joseph Chamberlain. He is more like the sadistic collector of butterflies who thrusts the lethal pin into his victim and then watches, with exquisite pleasure, the doomed creature thrashing wildly and unavailingly in its agony. His eyes, his demeanour, the curl of his mouth, arouse in his opponents emotions of unease and apprehension which disconcert them as much as the sight of Gladstone's terrifying eyes unnerved Conservatives in the 1880s. Thus, although Wilson could not be described as a great Parliamentary debater, he became unquestionably a most formidable, dexterous, and alarming Parliamentary personage.

It is a persistent comment on Wilson that he has – in the best sense of the phrase – a journalist's mind. The description has a certain literal accuracy, for he has a keen understanding of the processes of journalism, and the pressures to which newspapers and their servants are subjected. Most Conservatives tend to regard journalists – unless (and sometimes even then) they emanate from *The Times* or the *Daily Telegraph* – as odious necessities, on whom stories can be planted, to whom press conferences may be delivered, of whom practical use may be made. The Labour Party's attitude to the capitalist press is one of mild paranoia. Wilson, by his courtesy and considerateness to journalists, and by putting himself to considerable inconvenience on their behalf, built up a cadre of genuine admirers in this profession between 1963 and 1966. In their gratification and enthusiasm some of them failed to see that they were being very skilfully exploited.[1]

But Wilson's mind can be described as journalistic in another, and more profound, sense. The House of Commons has an extraordinarily ephemeral time-scale, in which Today's Speech is vital and Yesterday's – unless outstanding in one sense or the other – is totally forgotten. If, to this obsession, another is added – that Today's Headline is vital – the politician is on a course that may bring him much immediate advantage but which will leave him eventually bereft. Wilson has, rightly, been accredited with the comment that in politics a week is a long

[1] See p. 44.

time, but this approach is only relevant in the context of an interpretation of politics which is dominated by tactical considerations. This approach brought Wilson considerable dividends in the particular circumstances of 1963–6, but it lured him to misfortune. If Labour had won a reasonable majority in 1964 Wilson would have been able to make strategical plans for at least the middle distance; in the event, he necessarily had to live from day to day, and the experience was so exhilarating and his methods so successful that Wilson became persuaded that government could be effectively conducted under these conditions and on these terms. In 1963–4 the task was to win the Election; in 1964–6 it was to seize the headlines and harry the Opposition; but when, in April 1966, Labour had acquired a real majority, this *ad hoc* and dramatic method of conducting government had become fatally established.

Wilson is a professional politician, a man who has devoted his entire life to the profession of politics. His approach to all issues is political. Whatever the issue may be, whereas other politicians would see it in economic, social, military or international terms, Wilson's instinctive reaction is to interpret it in political terms. Although in certain situations this approach has its strength, it also closes other avenues which could be more profitably explored. Thus, his solutions to problems are almost invariably political solutions, and it is a curious characteristic that, in an age when many politicians have become increasingly sceptical about the value of the straightforward political approach to complex subjects, Wilson firmly retains his faith in it. His opponents and critics persistently missed the point when they labelled his responses as 'gimmickry' or 'instant government'; the real point was that Wilson's responses to situations were usually immediate, and almost invariably political. This approach, in 1963–6, was of considerable benefit to Labour. Afterwards, its limitations became increasingly evident.

It would be wholly wrong to portray Wilson as a man of no principles and convictions, but it is, significantly, difficult to detect many major consistent strands in his career. His approach has always been pragmatic, and his interest in political theory and ideology has never been particularly marked. His knowledge of the complex grouping known as the Labour Party became very substantial, and he possessed the one attribute which Gaitskell never acquired – an instinctive feeling for what the party will accept. This instinct is not infallible, but it is usually acute. His approach to Labour Government can hardly be described as a philosophy, but it was certainly clear and coherent. It operates firmly within the accepted constitutional framework. It fully accepts the established machinery of government, which it is prepared to vary, amend, and adapt, but not to change radically. It is cautious, behind a façade of radicalism. It believes that the job of a Government is to govern. It is a very middle-class, middle-of-the-road, mildly reforming Government, determined to be respectable. The manner in which the 1964–70 Government developed faithfully reflected Wilson's own political personality and approach.

Wilson is a man of so many parts that it is difficult to determine which is the dominant one, but it can be justly asserted that he is a kind man, a somewhat reckless man, a lonely man, and an unconfident man. The last adjective may appear absurd to those who have endured his cockiness and apparent egocentricity, but the emphasis should be placed on 'apparent'. Few politicians of the past century can have been so personally obsessed by, and so ready to quote, his own speeches, or to regale his audiences with his past achievements. All politicians have a strong tendency – to which some succumb more readily than others – to gloss over failures and emphasize successes, but few have a capacity equal to that of Wilson to turn actual disasters into retrospective triumphs. Observing him in action, this commentator was reminded of Macaulay's comment on the Younger Pitt:

> While his schemes were confounded, his predictions falsified, while the coalitions which he laboured to form were falling to pieces, his authority over the House of Commons was constantly becoming more and more absolute . . . Thus, through a long and calamitous period, every disaster that happened without the walls of Parliament was regularly followed by a triumph within them.

It is possible to regard this feature of Wilson's political personality in rather more severe terms than as evidence of a fundamental insecurity and lack of confidence, but it is Wilson's compulsion to build his achievements into an infinitely greater edifice than is acceptable which is so interesting. A confident and secure man, to take one example, is prepared to admit error. There is a very substantial difference between the Disraelian dictum of 'never explain, never complain' and a complete refusal to acknowledge a mistake. Wilson's sensitiveness to criticism, his refusal to admit error, his eagerness to draw attention to his own achievements, and the fact that he is a walking compendium of his own speeches, point less to a vain man than an unsure one. This lack of confidence can be clearly seen in his rhetoric, where the compulsion to coin phrases which give the impression of the stamp of personal authority over events over which he has in fact no control is very noticeable.[1]

Wilson is obsessed by his own record and by proving his own prescience, as though he were surrounded by people whose only objective was to prove the contrary. It might have been thought that the Premiership would have lessened this strong personal preoccupation, but it did not. This phenomenon demonstrated very clearly that Wilson's insecurity was of that nature that cannot be assuaged with success. To become Prime Minister is, after all, *the* summit for a public man; in Wilson's case, the interesting feature was that it was not enough. His enjoyment of the office – an enjoyment which at times was very endearing – was significant. And his dark and deep suspicions of all possible competitors demonstrated how dearly he loved his prize and how unsure he was of its permanence. It should be recalled that Wilson was in 1966 a man who had known no major misfortune throughout his life. He had moved inexorably from step to step, with checks which were so trivial that they could hardly be accounted. Nothing of any major importance had ever gone wrong for him, and fortune had certainly aided him lavishly at several crucial moments. Nonetheless, he still resembled a man who had been cruelly buffeted, and who perpetually looked over his shoulder with manifest nervousness. He was neither arrogant, nor self-assured, nor complacent. Despite his many qualities and considerable achievements, he resembled the self-made entrepreneur who knows that this excellent fortune cannot last.

[1] An example of Wilson's 'tough' style at its most inappropriate was his speech to the Economic Club in New York in April 1965, which included the phrase: 'Given the response of which our people are capable, be under no illusions; we shall be ready to knock hell out of you.' Wilson has subsequently described the reception to this speech as 'tumultuous' (Harold Wilson: *The Labour Government, 1964–1970*); the judgement of other observers was that the Economic Club, whose membership is notably hard-headed, experienced, and intellectually sophisticated, was not impressed.

Wilson's political character has – in the very best sense – a certain feminine quality. He is exceptionally sensitive to atmosphere, his immediate reactions can best be described as intuitive; and he has a remarkable confidence in snap estimates and evaluations. His quickness in discussions or debate is something more than cleverness, and some of his judgements – as, for example, his early recognition of Mr Enoch Powell's charisma at a time when it was customary to regard that politician as a melancholy eccentric – have been very acute. His real foundation is neither intellect, nor application, nor experience, but intuition. To seek a comparable politician in recent political history, one again thinks of Lloyd George. The differences between the two men are very substantial, but the similarities are worth remark. Both were rootless men, who lived on their wits, who had no real base, and who had no interests outside politics. And each interpreted the word politics in a highly personal sense.

No one who has had any close association with Wilson should challenge the assertion that he is a kind and a humane man. He goes to some trouble to conceal his real kindnesses, and he is jealous of his false reputation for ruthlessness. In fact, it is one of his most serious weaknesses as a public man that he is too kind to those to whom he regards himself beholden. Some of the worst appointments which he made in 1964 were the consequence of remembrances of past kindnesses and support. This was endearing in the man, but less admirable in the politician. Again, one may note that a truly confident man does not behave in this manner. Wilson did not owe many political debts when he became Prime Minister, but those he had he repaid with a lavishness and generosity that was neither in the Party nor the national interest.

Intellectually, Wilson is a surprisingly limited man. He picks up phrases and trends very quickly, but he is less interested in pursuing them to their source. His mind does not contain those elements of query and penetration that are essential to a great leader. Both he and Heath are serious, lonely men, dedicated to their careers, who have risen through the Westminster maelstrom. But Heath lacks Wilson's imagination and quickness, and Wilson lacks Heath's thoroughness and relentless attention to detail. Wilson's mental agility often tempts him to laziness; Heath, with a much less nimble mind, has to plod doggedly in order to reach conclusions and find solutions. But these, once reached, are adhered to with far greater tenacity.

Wilson has been described by one observer as a 'clever, egocentric, decent, small man',[1] a description that is neither flattering nor comprehensive. But it must be admitted that there is some truth in it. His obsession has always been with impressions rather than with results, with the fine speech he would make in announcing a policy rather than in the effectiveness of the policy itself. On occasion it has not been difficult to assume that Wilson's attitude to politics has not been dissimilar to that of Duff Cooper towards poetry;[2] it is best to succeed in one's time, to enjoy those fruits, and not to sacrifice oneself to abstract and indefinite expectations of recognitions. There is, after all, much validity in the question posed and answered by the Irish politician: 'Why should we trouble with Posterity; what has Posterity ever done for us?' But one of the most interesting features of Wilson's political character is that he desires both immediate recognition and eventual salutation – desiring to be Disraeli and Peel at once. To be, in short, the successful and the triumphant, and also the mourned and the revered. Wilson's approach to politics has always been that of the man before his time who wishes to be recognized in his time. Thus, the immediate rewards for which he worked are only part of what he wishes to achieve.

The other interesting aspect of Wilson's character is that he has a strangely un-inquisitive mind, and an impatience with essential detail and preparation. His ideas and instincts are often very sound, and, which is much more important, very imaginative; but he rarely carried them through in terms of practical action. He established, rhetorically, a great deal; the practical consequences were usually considerably more meagre. The journalist in him was more interested in the appearance than the substance, and the politician in him was more interested in the political rewards than in the practical consequences. There was a good example of this after the 1955 General Election, when his report on the Party organization to the National Executive declared that, 'compared with our oppo-

---

[1] David Watt, *Financial Times*, 29 May 1970.

[2] 'I cannot think that the muse thrives upon ease and prosperity, but I would rather have been a happy man than a famous poet.' Duff Cooper: *Old Men Forget* (London, 1953), p. 38.

nents we are still at the penny-farthing stage in a jet-propelled era'. The substance of the report, however, was unimpressive, and it neither furnished a proper diagnosis of the weaknesses in the Party machine nor did it propose any serious effective changes.

Whereas Wilson gives the impression of being a very relaxed man, in fact he is extremely tense. Since 1945 his has been essentially a one-man performance, and the emotional and physical strain which this imposed on him on his long climb to the Party leadership can only be guessed at; but it must have been very severe. Politics, it has often been remarked, is a very brutal occupation; in the Labour Party it can be lethal. It can hardly be denied that Wilson's personal contribution to the Labour victory of 1964 was very substantial; in 1966 the Labour triumph was essentially Wilson's triumph. He was the Labour Party's leader, producer, stage-manager, author, and director. Although he relished this comprehensive task, the physical and mental cost must have been heavy, both on himself and his Party. In the public view, and in his own view, the Labour Government was the Wilson Government. There was a certain irony in the fact that the man who had in the Macmillan era derided the cult of personality was himself its most remarkable exponent in this period. And thus, for over five years, he wielded a personal authority that although often challenged, few party leaders outside wartime conditions have enjoyed in recent British politics.

The circumstances under which Labour took office in October 1964 were not hopeful. The narrowness of the election victory had been an unpleasant surprise; most of the new Ministers had no experience of office; and the new Administration had then taken over at a moment when the economic situation was bleak and lowering.

The fundamental problem of the British economy since the War was that attempts to increase growth have resulted in higher imports, a balance of payments deficit, a crisis of international confidence in the pound and a subsequent deflation – the classical cyclical process derided by Wilson in his Opposition days as 'stop-go'. With the wisdom of hindsight it can be argued that the restraining measures of 1955–8, designed to curb inflation but doing so at the expense of growth, were principally responsible for the subsequent difficulties. The establishment of the National Economic Development Council in 1961 and the renewed emphasis on growth could not immediately overcome the unfortunate effects of the 1955–8 stagnation in industrial production, investment, and capacity. Maudling's attempt in 1963 to increase the pace of growth led directly to the 1964 balance of payments deficit – a deficit which Maudling himself had anticipated in his 1963 Budget speech, but which was on a far greater scale than anyone had expected. It is also fair to point out that Maudling's growth policies were generally supported at the time – and only criticized by Labour spokesmen as not being sufficiently ambitious.[1] But the fact remained that when Labour took office in October 1964 the British economy had reached stage two of the cycle, with a balance of payments deficit which was now anticipated at £800 million for the year.[2] Stage three was clearly imminent, and the dilemma was whether the Government could take direct action by devaluation or deflation.

This was self-evidently a gloomy inheritance and a serious situation; it is, however, arguable that it was made even more serious by the immediate actions of the Government, and what was perhaps even more significant, the manner in which they were taken. In the frenetic activity at the outset of Wilson's 'first hundred days' it was difficult for observers to detect any philosophy. A White Paper on *The Economic Situation* was published on 26 October, which showed clear signs of hasty preparation and curious priorities. The imposition of import surcharges that the White Paper announced was a reasonable step; the failure to consult the European Free Trade Association (EFTA) – while the United States was consulted – seemed to denote a somewhat amateurish touch. The surcharges were, furthermore, technically illegal. Wilson's double posture of emphasizing a crisis situation on the one hand and pressing on

[1] See, in particular, speeches in the Commons by Wilson, Jenkins and Callaghan, on 3, 8 and 15 April 1963, respectively.

[2] Subsequent re-evaluations of the actual deficit for 1964 have varied very considerably. A recent Conservative estimate is £747 million (Brian Reading: *The Great Mess Myth*, Conservative Research Department, May 1970), but other independent estimates have been considerably lower (see *National Income and Expenditure*, Central Statistical Office).

with the Government's policy of increased expenditure on social services on the other also did not carry conviction. And there were early indications that the relationship between the Treasury and the new Department of Economic Affairs was not going to work.

The original intention was that the DEA, in Wilson's own words, 'would be concerned with real resources, with economic planning, with strengthening our ability to export and to save imports with increasing productivity, and our competitiveness in domestic and export markets'.[1] Unfortunately, no clear allocation of functions between the DEA and the Treasury was made before the Election, and when the DEA surfaced officially it was discovered that it had acquired responsibility not only for prices and incomes – which was to become its prime obsession – but for matters concerning overseas economic policy. This was a significant overlap with both the Treasury and the Board of Trade, and caused considerable subsequent difficulties. The 'creative tension' that Wilson had hoped to see between the DEA and the Treasury never developed; there was certainly tension, but it was not invariably creative. The DEA was a good concept which failed because the practical problems of the division of responsibility were inadequately considered, because the eventual 'concordat' went beyond the original concept, and because the DEA – under George Brown's vigorous leadership – increasingly concentrated on prices and incomes questions.

The precipitate announcement which strongly implied that the Anglo-French Concorde supersonic aircraft project was to be abandoned was clearly made before the legal and international implications had been properly examined; this was all the more curious because the Treaty which established the project had been publicly examined and commented upon adversely by the Estimates Committee of the House of Commons in 1963. The project could not be unilaterally abrogated, and the Government's competence came under further hostile scrutiny.

Thus, while there was a great amount of energy and tough talking in Whitehall, the impression created abroad was of an Administration which did not really know what it was doing. In retrospect, it can be said that several of the decisions taken

[1] Wilson: *op. cit.*, p. 3.

by the Government were sensible; but their context and circumstances were less impressive at the time. The fundamental choice before the Government was between devaluation and deflation. The first was ruled out emphatically by Wilson, but the second was not taken. The Government failed to realize that its belief in a third choice – that of rather vaguely described 'direct action' – was a chimera. The announcement in the November 1964 Budget of forthcoming Corporation and Capital Gains taxes further alarmed the foreign exchange market. Within a month the Government had succeeded in arousing the apprehensions of everyone with a substantial stake in sterling. The balance of payments deficit in itself was a matter for legitimate concern; this concern became much greater when foreign holders of sterling attempted to comprehend the real thrust of the activity in Whitehall. On 16 November Wilson declared in a speech at the Mansion House the determination of the Government to 'keep sterling strong', which was assumed to be the precursor of an immediate increase in Bank Rate. Nothing happened, and by the 19th the pressure on sterling became intense. Bank Rate was raised from 5 to 7 per cent on the following Monday (23 November), but in circumstances that gave an impression of panic. The Government was thus plunged into a massive crisis from which it was extricated only by a substantial international provision of $3,000 million of short-term credits.

The position of the Governor of the Bank of England, Lord Cromer, was particularly difficult. It is evident that he fully shared the widespread and mounting unease in international banking circles at the competence of the new untried Government. He was also a close and crucial participant in the Government's attempts to maintain sterling. His problems cannot have been eased by his personal relationship with Wilson, who at one stage dramatically informed him that to accept the requirements for the restoration of international confidence would be 'to ring down the curtain on parliamentary democracy'.[1] Cromer appears to have worked loyally with the Government, and he certainly played a major rôle in the international operation which shored up the pound in the 1964 crisis; but it was clear that the Governor and the Government did not have a complete mutual confidence. And there was a

[1] Wilson: *op. cit.*, p. 37.

general disposition in the international monetary world to have more confidence in the capacities of the Governor than in those of the Government.

It was this early fall of international confidence in Labour's competence that essentially created the crises of the next three years. In each case the activating cause was different, but it is highly doubtful whether the consequences would have been as serious if this confidence had existed. The greatly improved situation in 1968–70 was the result less of actual measures than of restored confidence in the Labour Government's professional capacities. As will be seen, the personal part played in the process by Roy Jenkins was very substantial.

It would be superficial and unfair to allege that the Labour Government talked itself into a major economic crisis in October–December 1964. The foundations for that crisis had been laid beforehand. It is, however, fair to state that the manner in which the new Government behaved in its early weeks, and the crisis atmosphere in which Wilson appeared to enjoy operating, made a bad situation very considerably worse. At the time, and subsequently, Ministers blamed a malignant group of 'international speculators' for their troubles, whereas in fact they had themselves helped to erode national and international confidence in their competence to the point when sterling appeared to be a highly dangerous commodity. Until the middle of 1968 the shock given to international confidence in sterling by the first weeks of the new Government was such that the British economy became peculiarly vulnerable.

The actions and approaches of the 1964–70 Labour Government were, from its outset to its end, dominated by the state of the national economy. It assumed office with a substantial balance-of-payments deficit, and its entire existence was overshadowed by the need to create a substantial surplus. To do this was its evident public duty, but gradually the economic situation became *the* overwhelming priority, *the* vital subject, *the* challenge confronting Ministers. The lives of Ministers revolved around the trade figures and the standing of the pound sterling in the international market, until the obsessions of Downing Street became the obsessions of the nation at large. It was like receiving daily bulletins from an ailing relative over a number of years. And the reports were rarely non-committal. Either the patient was blooming, and had even recovered, or he was at death's door. The drama was characteristic of Wilson, but it gradually assumed such a dominant position that, in comparison, other problems of hardly less magnitude seemed to shrivel into nothingness.

One does not have to be an intellectual purist, far removed from the harsh political realities, to make the point that the 1966 General Election was won on a false prospectus. For it was claimed that the patient had made a full, complete, and glorious recovery from the near-mortal condition in which he had been discovered in October 1964; the doctors were not disinclined to minimize their contribution. The assurances given by the Chancellor of the Exchequer, Mr James Callaghan, on future taxation on 1 March 1966, on the state of the economy, and the balance of trade situation, were swiftly reversed after the Election.[1] As soon as the Election was safely won, the very Minister who had told the House of Commons in March that 'the best guidance that I can give the House, at this stage, is that I do not foresee the need for severe increases in taxation' was, a month later, announcing tax increases of £375 million, and making it plain enough that the confident pre-election trade forecasts had been excessively optimistic. Indeed, the Government barely had time to congratulate itself and its leader on their electoral triumph when it was plunged into the first of the economic crises that haunted it until the end of 1969. The vigil beside the patient's bed had begun again.

The first post-Election Budget announced the introduction of the Selective Employment Tax, whereby the often-discussed payroll tax was given an unexpected new dimension. The creation of Professor Nicholas Kaldor, SET was designed to achieve two purposes simultaneously; to bring in substantial new revenue (£315 million in the first year alone), and – more important in Professor Kaldor's original concept – to encourage the movement of employees from 'service' to 'manufacturing' industries. For, in the case of the latter, the tax would be

---

[1] Wilson has claimed that the differences between Callaghan's pre-Election and post-Election forecasts were 'strictly based on Treasury advice' and constituted 'an honest, non-political assessment' (Wilson: *op. cit.*, p. 228). It will, of course, be a considerable time before this claim can be confirmed by examination of the relevant documents. The most that can be said at this stage is that the circumstances of the March and April pronouncements were such as necessarily to arouse suspicions of exactly how 'non-political' the interpretation of the first economic assessment was.

refunded to the employers. The Labour Party, taken aback by this unexpected novelty, was manifestly uneasy about the impact of the tax on service industries, and in the heated debates that followed the Government was forced to amend some of the categories, charities and farming being the most conspicuous examples.

The weakness of SET was, however, that it appeared to be – and indeed was – an alternative to the comprehensive deflationary Budget which was generally considered necessary. Here, the pre-Election promises not to increase taxation came home to roost. SET was – and was seen to be abroad – as a compromise between economic requirements and domestic political considerations. Its impact on the international position of sterling was, accordingly, bad. As Mr Brittan has rightly written: 'Whatever its longer-term merits or defects, SET was a singularly ill-chosen measure for the particular needs of the 1966 Budget.'[1]

Furthermore, the passage of SET was taking place simultaneously with a serious seamen's strike which lasted for forty-seven days, and which Wilson ascribed to a 'tightly knit group of politically motivated men'. The strike was clearly not helpful, but it was not in itself responsible for ominous trade figures for the early summer, which threw very heavy doubt upon Callaghan's confident forecasts. A Prices and Incomes Bill, which required advance notification of wage claims and price increases and established a Board with powers to defer awards while the merits were being examined, precipitated the resignation of the Minister of Technology, Mr Frank Cousins, on 3 July. Cousins had been brought into the Government by Wilson in 1964, and his lack of Parliamentary experience had been very evident; but before he quit the House of Commons he developed an astringent back-bench style that discomfited Ministers.

This first warning of the clash between the Labour Government and the Trade Unions was overshadowed by a run on sterling that was unchecked by the raising of Bank Rate, and which resulted in a hurried imposition of restrictions on the evening of 19 July after Cabinet discussions bluntly described by one Minister as 'chaotic', and in which it was clear that there was a developing split between those Ministers who

[1] Samuel Brittan: *Steering the Economy*, p. 212.

favoured deflation, and those who argued that the price to be paid for maintaining the pound sterling at the $2.80 parity rate might be excessive. Wilson was not, at that stage, a 'deflationist', as he seems to have been clinging to the hope that there was still another alternative to the devaluation/deflation choice. He was at that moment also very concerned over preparations for a visit to Moscow, but whatever the immediate causes, the fact remained that action was taken much too late, and had to be much more severe than if it had been taken earlier.

The 'July measures' included a six-month wages and prices freeze; a £50 foreign travel allowance limit; a 10 per cent surcharge on surtax for the year; 10 per cent increases on the duties on tobacco, wines, and spirits; higher postal charges; the extension of building controls; and cuts in expenditure on the nationalized industries, local government, foreign aid and Defence. George Brown, whose empire at the Department of Economic Affairs was already crumbling, resigned, de-resigned, resigned again, and finally de-resigned.

The problem of the DEA-Treasury relationship was that the former was dedicated to the 25 per cent growth laid down in the National Plan and the 1966 Labour manifesto, and it became gradually convinced that this goal was unattainable without devaluation. Brown himself became convinced that further deflation would destroy his objective, and accordingly accepted the lesser evil of devaluation. This was the background to the angry debates in the Cabinet over the July 1966 measures, and to Brown's subsequent movement to the Foreign Office. The combination of the Treasury and the Prime Minister had been too formidable.

Brown subsequently moved from the sadly moribund DEA to the Foreign Office. Labour majorities in the Commons slumped; by-elections and opinion polls revealed a violent reaction against the Government in the country. And this was less than four months since the Election!

In a sense, Labour never really recovered from these initial shocks. The announcement that the Government, abandoning its implicit position in the 1966 Election campaign, intended to apply for membership of the European Economic Community was followed by the abortive talks in December on HMS *Tiger* with the Rhodesian leader, Mr Ian Smith. At this conference

Wilson's proposals for a settlement in effect represented a complete abandonment of the principles for a settlement which the Conservatives had enunciated and which the Labour Government had endorsed.[1] The circumstances of the meeting – a secret rendezvous in a British warship in the Mediterranean – seemed excessively dramatic and pseudo-Churchillian, but when the British proposals were disclosed they seemed to have a flavour more reminiscent of Munich. The Commonwealth Prime Ministers' Conference in September had demonstrated clearly that Commonwealth impatience with the British was rapidly approaching the point when the Rhodesian question would be taken to the United Nations for the imposition of mandatory sanctions. It was to head off this alarming possibility that Wilson attempted to settle with Smith on terms which gave the Rhodesians almost everything they wanted in return for assurances which appeared to meet the Six Principles. It was a clever operation, but transparently obvious. It was fortunate for Wilson that the Smith regime would not accept even these terms, and Wilson was able to cover himself from his vexed supporters by a vehement attack on the Conservatives for being supporters of the Smith regime. This tactic followed the lead set by Wilson in 1965. Whenever the Rhodesia issue arose the divisions in the Opposition ranks – skilfully exploited by Wilson – became glaringly apparent, and Heath's repeated attempts to maintain an agreed line were not successful. In these circumstances it was not difficult for Wilson to divert the worries of the Government back-benchers into derision of the Conservative leader, and every time he did this the difficulties of Heath increased. The performance of the Opposition Front Bench may not, as Wilson claimed, have 'made Pontius Pilate, by comparison, appear one of the decisive figures of history', but it was certainly not impressive. But Wilson's repeated condemnation of the Opposition for playing party politics with the Rhodesian problem may be regarded with a certain degree of cold scepticism.

[1] The original Five Principles had been established by the Conservatives, and consisted of unimpeded progress towards majority rule; guarantees against retrogressive legislation; immediate improvement in the political status of black Rhodesians; the ending of racial discrimination; and acceptability to Rhodesians as a whole of any settlement. To this Labour added a sixth – that there was to be no oppression of one race by another – which was somewhat superfluous. For further discussion of the Rhodesian episode, see pp. 61–2 below.

This episode, coming as it did on top of the unexpected announcement of the EEC application, re-opened many wounds in the Labour Party, and the mistrust of Wilson personally, dormant since 1963, began to revive. This restiveness was not allayed by a speech by Wilson to the Parliamentary Party that contained the warning that 'Every dog is allowed one bite, but a different view is taken of a dog who bites all the time. If the dog bites because he is vicious something happens to the dog. He may not get his licence renewed when it falls due.'

Not the least of Labour's problems was the continuance in office of personal antipathies which had soured the Party in the Opposition years. One of the most conspicuous peculiarities of the Labour Party is its disinclination to keep such feuds to itself, thereby presenting its opponents with material that could be actively exploited. There are probably no fewer personal bitternesses and intrigues in the other parties, but neither can match the Labour Party in its eagerness to make them public. The Conservatives keep these matters to themselves; the Labour Party does not. The commentator can, accordingly, be misled about the respective morale of the two major parties. Nonetheless, the Labour Party in office was no more George Lansbury's 'happy band of brothers' than it had been in Opposition, and, in particular, the seething animosity between Wilson and Brown was not abated.

These events, which reduced Wilson's personal standing in the Party, were swiftly followed by others. It was becoming evident that one of Wilson's principal characteristics was that, like Sir Stafford Northcote, he was 'always seeing blue sky'. It appeared that the patient, the economy, had been dramatically revived and indeed cured by the July measures. Bank Rate was cut, the restrictions on central and local government spending were reduced, and limitations on hire-purchase and other consumer spending were relaxed. The 'severe restraint' inaugurated in July 1966 was of short duration. In the 1967 Budget Callaghan gave good predictions of the balance of payments situation, declaring that the ship of state was 'back on course', and that the motto for the future was 'steady as she goes'. These confident forecasts were relentlessly disproved, and it was now apparent that the electorate was sharing the scepticism with which the international financial market was viewing

Government predictions. By-elections were disastrous, and in April the Conservatives won the Greater London Council elections in a landslide. One had to be at least middle-aged to have been in a position to remember when the Tories had last ruled the national capital. At the end of August Wilson announced that he would take charge of the Department of Economic Affairs, with a position comparable to that of Churchill during the War, when he had been Minister of Defence as well as Prime Minister. This intelligence came in the course of a press conference.[1] On 8 September, at Newport, Wilson claimed that the nation's overseas payments had 'reached a position of basic balance and growing strength'. But within a very short period the autumn trade figures mocked the Government's glowing assurances, a run on the pound began, Bank Rate had to be hastily jerked up once again, and we were back at the death-bed scene.

Sterling had become virtually the last element that gave British Governments an illusion of being internationally indispensable. But in reality the sterling area's base had become too narrow, and Britain's inadequacies as a source of capital and technology had become more and more evident in the 1950s. The sterling crisis of 1957 was of particular interest and significance because it occurred at a time when the British economy appeared to be in a good condition; the ominous implications were spelt out by Andrew Shonfield in his book *The British Economy Since the War* and in the Radcliffe Report on the working of the monetary system, published in August 1959.[2] The evidence was clear that the cost to Britain of maintaining sterling was unacceptably high, and that sterling itself was a seriously over-valued and faltering commodity. The events of the early 1960s – and particularly the British involvement in the Malaysia–Indonesia confrontation, which at one point was costing the British taxpayer over £1 million a day – had only worsened the situation. Thus, when Labour came into office the position of sterling in relation to other currencies was unreal, and could only be maintained by heavy international borrowing and drastic cuts in capital investment at home. In

[1] The conclusion of this responsibility was somewhat less well publicized. It was announced in a brief reply by Wilson to a supplementary question in the Commons asked by Heath on 11 April 1968.
[2] Cmnd 827, 1959.

short, the decision to support the pound was a massive hindrance to the British economy as a whole, and was particularly damaging to the growth prospects. There is strong evidence that the United States Government actively encouraged the British in this course, and that the latter were willing to pursue it at a cost that brought Britain, by July 1968, to a condition of technical bankruptcy.[1]

From the beginning of his Premiership, Wilson had regarded devaluation as unthinkable, and mention of the word itself was strictly forbidden. He regarded it, as he expressed himself in 1963, as 'a lunatic and self-destroying operation'. Although this alternative had been raised in the July 1966 crisis it had never been seriously considered, and both Wilson and Callaghan had committed themselves strongly against it. This reaction was pre-eminently personal, political, and psychological. Wilson believed that the 1949 devaluation had destroyed the Attlee Government, and that for Labour to become 'the Devaluation Party' would be a political albatross for all time. But there was something else evident in his attitude, which is less easily definable. It was as if his political masculinity, at home and abroad, was at stake, and that the preservation of the pound sterling at the $2.80 parity was the symbol of his capacity as a national leader. 'A second devaluation', he had said in the Commons in July 1961, 'would be regarded all over the world as an acknowledgement of defeat, a recognition that we were not on a springboard but on a slide.' The matter had become emotionally comparable to the return to the Gold Standard and the pre-war parity in 1925, and it was conspicuous that Heath's speeches on the issue rivalled those of Wilson in their insistence on the vital importance of the maintenance of the pound at $2.80, virtually regardless of the consequences. There were few prospects of the matter being discussed rationally, but what chances there may have been were destroyed by the emphasis placed by both Party leaders on the symbolic significance of $2.80. Quite apart from any other consideration, it was clear enough that devaluation would be followed by a howl of patriotic fury from the Opposition and the Conservative Press. The decision not to devalue in the immediate post-

---

[1] See Susan Strange: *Sterling and Foreign Policy* (London, 1971), also Brian Johnson: *The Politics of Money* (London, 1970).

election economic crisis of 1964 had been made principally on political grounds. As Wilson subsequently wrote: 'There would have been many who would conclude that a Labour Government facing difficulties always took the easy way out by devaluing the pound ... So devaluation was ruled out by a deliberate decision.'[1]

Wilson's problem – and his error – was that he had so outflanked Heath in patriotic posturings on this matter that he had left himself no real room for dignified retreat. For, by November 1967 the Great Unmentionable had to be undertaken.

The decision itself was taken too late, in the wrong context, for the wrong reasons, and at the wrong time. A deliberate and calculated devaluation – as in 1949, or the French devaluation in 1969 – is one thing. A forced devaluation is quite another. And in 1967, in marked contrast with 1949, the political mechanics were bungled. This was principally the result of one of the most expensive errors of judgement ever committed by a British Prime Minister. On 15 November, in answer to a private notice question by Mr Robert Sheldon, Labour MP for Ashton-under-Lyne, in the Commons asking whether the Government was negotiating another loan to buttress the sagging pound, Callaghan refused to comment. There are occasions in politics in which a straight lie is not only defensible but is in the national interest, and this was one of them. Iain Macleod, who was rightly convinced that the devaluation machinery was already far advanced, had expected Callaghan to deny this with virtuous vigour as Cripps had done in 1949. To his astonishment and dismay, Callaghan let the opportunity pass, with the result that there was a panic selling of sterling. Devaluation accordingly took place in the worst possible circumstances. A few days later Callaghan resigned, was moved to the Home Office, and was replaced at the Treasury by Roy Jenkins.

[1] Wilson: *op. cit.*, pp. 6–7. Wilson has made the point that 'a contingency plan for devaluation of sterling had been long in the Treasury files – *indeed it had been there when we took office*', *op. cit.*, p. 444. The implication is that the Conservative Government had been contemplating devaluation. It would be as reasonable to cite that, as Labour found contingency plans for a nuclear war prepared by the Ministry of Defence, the Conservatives were expecting a nuclear war. So far as this commentator has been able to discover, no serious consideration had been given to the possibility of devaluation by the Conservative Government; there were contingency plans available, as there were for a wide variety of possibilities.

The devaluation of the pound, and the manner in which it had been done, was very harmful to the reputation of the Government. Ministers were justified in pointing to the Middle East crisis of June 1967 – and particularly the closing of the Suez Canal – as a major contributory factor to the devaluation crisis. But that event, serious though it was in its effects on the balance of payments and related matters, was only a contributory factor. As Mr Brittan has pointed out, 'The sharp turn round in the sterling market occurred, in fact, in the middle of May – about three weeks *before* the Arab-Israeli war.'[1] The real cause was the renewed lack of international confidence in sterling as a commodity; in this calculation many factors played a part, and not the least of them was a revival of lack of confidence in the capacity of the Government to solve its economic problems. It can be argued that this emotion was unfair and inaccurate; it is difficult to argue that it did not exist. To quote Mr Brittan again:

The really serious mistake of the Labour Government, after both the 1964 and 1966 elections, was to refuse to admit that a choice between devaluation and relying on unaccompanied deflation had become necessary. The result was an eventual devaluation, which in all but the technical sense was forced, at the worst possible time internationally, when resources not only of foreign exchange but of confidence, patience and credibility had all been nearly exhausted. Trying to get the best of both worlds, the Government succeeded in achieving the worst.[2]

In his post-devaluation television broadcast Wilson inserted a passage which was not quickly forgotten:

Tonight we must face the new situation. First, what this means. From now on the pound abroad is worth 14 per cent or so less in terms of other currencies. It does not mean, of course, that the pound here in Britain, in your pocket or purse or in your bank, has been devalued. What it does mean is that we shall now be able to sell more goods abroad on a competitive basis.

Wilson has argued with justification that this was a straight statement of fact. But for once he had misjudged the impact of an arresting phrase which was virtually bound to be quoted

---

[1] Brittan: *op. cit.*, p. 225.
[2] *Ibid.*, p. 188.

against him out of context, with damaging results. And this is exactly what happened.[1]

This was not destined, however, to be the last of the difficulties which 1967 provided for the harassed Administration.

One of the most curious, and historically interesting, episodes at this time concerned the sale of arms to South Africa. These sales, banned by the Labour Government in 1964, had continued until 1967 in the form of the fulfilment of existing contracts; but in the late summer of 1967 the South African Government made a formal request for the resumption in full sales on the normal willing buyer–willing seller relationship.

The Government had taken up a firm moral position on this issue at its outset, but there were indications that this position was not, in fact, as firm as it was publicly paraded. The South African Government's purpose was political rather than military, as it could obtain – and was obtaining – excellent equipment from other countries, notably France. Furthermore, there can be no doubt that the South African Government would not have made the approach without having some confidence that it would be welcomed in certain Government quarters in Britain.[2]

The exact line-up of Ministers on the question remains a matter of controversy, but it can be stated firmly that Brown and Healey were the most vigorous proponents of ending the ban, that Callaghan was sympathetic to them, and that Jenkins would have welcomed any act that would have assisted the

---

[1] An interesting parallel may be drawn with Macmillan, who did not in fact coin the phrase 'You never had it so good' – it was first used in the American Presidential Campaign of 1952 – and was quoted in the 1959 Election campaign in a derogatory context. It was however, seized upon, and became identified as the *leit-motif* of the Conservatives' 1959 campaign.

Wilson has stated that it was Crossman who urged him 'almost to exult in our decision' in his television broadcast (*op. cit.*, p. 463). He also makes the point that the Treasury draft contained the phrase, 'It does not mean that the money in our pockets is worth 14 per cent less to us now than it was this morning' (*op. cit.*, p. 463). Wilson's claim that the phrase was grossly misrepresented by his opponents is fully justified.

[2] On this point see Lord George-Brown: *In My Way*, p. 172, which specifically states that the 'nod and wink' communication to the South African Government 'was done wholly with the knowledge of the Prime Minister'.

balance of payments problem. This was a very formidable group, and it was backed by at least three other senior Cabinet Ministers.

Wilson had invested considerable personal capital in the moral issue that was at the heart of the controversy. Some of his Cabinet colleagues were sceptical about the depth of this moral commitment, but in the immediate post-devaluation situation – the issue reached its climax in December 1967 – to ask another major public *volte face* from the Prime Minister would have been to ask a great deal. In any event, Wilson refused to consider the possibility. In answer to a Parliamentary Question on 14 December before the Cabinet had in fact reached a decision, he stated that the Government had no intention of changing the 1964 policy. He added that an announcement had been postponed because Brown was delayed by fog in Brussels, where he had been attending a NATO meeting, and the answer contained the clear implication about what Brown's position was.

Behind this public statement and its significance there lay something else. An Early Day Motion calling on the Government to support the arms ban had received a large number of Labour signatures, and the Chief Whip – Mr John Silkin – had certainly not discouraged Labour MPs from signing. Ministers drew the obvious conclusion that the Chief Whip would not have acted in this way without the Prime Minister's cognizance and approval. Some believed that Wilson had in fact initiated the entire exercise. Wilson has emphatically denied the repeated allegation that he in any way encouraged – or even knew about – the back-bench Motion, and he has emphasized that Silkin's action in approving it as representing declared Party policy was natural. We may therefore regard it as one of those fortuitous episodes which from time to time ease the burdens on the shoulders of heavily pressed Prime Ministers. Thus, the discussion in the Cabinet on 15 December was acrimonious and the compromise arrived at – the maintenance of the ban for the time being only – was clearly a defeat for Wilson. By the following Monday, however, the situation had changed. Wilson's public position – which he had re-stated on the 14th – was so evident that his authority would be destroyed if he had to make an announcement on the lines agreed by the Cabinet. The Cabinet agreed to an unconditional ban. In fact, the sales of equipment under existing contracts continued, and other devices were found whereby the ban could be publicly maintained and surreptitiously circumvented.[1]

Some Ministers – of whom Brown was, understandably, the most notable – were greatly angered by Wilson's conduct throughout this affair. In particular, they claimed that the great moral principles at stake had manifested themselves somewhat late in the day. But it could also be argued that Wilson's political sensitivity had been much more acute than theirs – a fact which they may have appreciated more closely in the summer of 1970 when the announcement by their successors to resume arms sales to South Africa aroused a storm of protest which was by no means confined to the Labour Party. The Conservatives, furthermore, could claim that this undertaking had been contained in their election manifesto; Labour would have had to renege on their commitments. It is by no means inconceivable that to have done so would have brought down the Government, which was still reeling from the devaluation crisis.

Another significant aspect of the incident was the critical interpretation of Wilson's tactics by some of his Cabinet colleagues with the clear implication by some that they had been double-crossed by the Prime Minister. But should a Prime Minister tamely acquiesce in a movement towards a collective Cabinet decision which he believes to be wrong? And, if he is in danger of being over-ruled by the Cabinet, can he not be made to make use of his other powers – and particularly that of being Leader of his Party? A sober evaluation of the episode leads to two conclusions: the first is that Wilson out-manoeuvred an important element in his Cabinet on an issue which he regarded – whether from moral, political, or even personal motives – as crucial to himself and the future of his Government. And the other conclusion is that he was right to do so.

But 1967 was not to end without another blow to the Government's position. In December, the EEC application was curtly vetoed by de Gaulle. Thus ended the year!

The events of 1967 had revived the apprehension that the Government had no real aims or objectives beyond an obsession with the balance of payments and to prove that it really could

[1] Wilson: *op. cit.*, p. 471.

govern – what Dr Michael Lipton has described as 'the competence mandate'.[1]

One indication of nerviness was the breakdown in relations between the Government and most of the Press and television. The cosy relationship of 1963–5 had shown signs of strain in and immediately after the 1966 Election, when Wilson's suspicion of the BBC's impartiality became public. In 1966 and 1967 the situation became much worse, to the point when the complaints of Ministers of the bias of the Press were matched by complaints made by the Press of the lack of candour demonstrated by the Government. It was at this time that the phrase 'the credibility gap' was being heard in the United States in relation to President Johnson's methods of communication, and the phrase was increasingly quoted with reference to Wilson. These charges and counter-charges were not confined to the Government. The Conservatives had bitter recollections of the treatment meted out to the Macmillan Government in its last year by Fleet Street, and the observer was increasingly conscious of an ever-worsening relationship between politicians of all parties and journalists. In the context of 1966–70, however, this deterioration undoubtedly hurt the Government more than the Opposition. While the most extreme complaints of Ministers need not be accepted in full, no dispassionate observer could fail to accept the validity of the general charge that the Government was harshly treated in the national Press, which remained overwhelmingly pro-Conservative. Nonetheless, there was some strength in the argument that this situation would not have arisen without good cause, and that Downing Street could not evade all the responsibility.

But, in retrospect, we can see that the Government had turned the corner. Callaghan's period at the Treasury could hardly be described as distinguished, but the fact that his successor was Roy Jenkins was to be of very considerable significance in the fortunes of Labour. Jenkins has a subtle mind, with which goes a certain fastidiousness which does not arouse very great political apprehension in others. His approach to politics is somewhat detached and sardonic, and although he works, thinks, and reads hard at his profession his general demeanour is reminiscent of Churchill's celebrated description of Balfour as 'a powerful cat walking delicately and unsoiled

[1] Tyrrell Burgess (ed.): *Matters of Principle: Labour's Last Chance.*

across a rather muddy street'. He has always aroused in his officials an exceptional respect and affection, and perhaps the most remarkable example of this was to be seen in his relationship with the police when he was Home Secretary, at a time when he was courteously rejecting almost all of their insistencies and pursuing policies that greatly dismayed them.

The great unresolved question about Jenkins was whether he possessed real political courage. Although he did not have a substantial personal following in the Labour Party, he had been one of the major successes in the Government, first at the Ministry of Aviation and then at the Home Office. Although a more critical closer examination of his record may reveal a certain absence of personal decisiveness, this was very effectively covered by an impressive aura of authority and determination. It was certainly the case that the major libertarian reforms, undertaken while Jenkins was Home Secretary were (with the notable exception of the 1967 Criminal Justice Act) brought forward by back-benchers, but whereas some observers considered this strategem showed a certain lack of political courage, others (and in this commentator's opinion rightly) detected Jenkins' skilful manipulation of the political machine and political realities to gain his desired ends. Even if these measures – particularly the amendment of the law relating to homosexuals and abortion – were not 'planted' by the Home Secretary, they were certainly warmly supported by him and the degree of assistance given by the Home Office to these measures in the form of encouragement, expert advice and Parliamentary time was very considerable. The result, whatever the stratagems were, was that the Home Secretary had deliberately gained all his desired objectives without involving the Cabinet in needless worryings and without exposing the Labour Party to harsh accusations of being formally identified with queers and loose women; it would be to under-estimate Jenkins to believe that all this had been secured fortuitously.

Jenkins' tenure of the Treasury falls into three distinct phases. The first was a nightmare one, when he arrived at the Treasury almost literally on the morrow of devaluation to discover what has been rightly described[1] as 'a situation of chaotic vacuum'. The circumstances of the devaluation had shaken national and international confidence to the point when there was serious and

[1] *The Economist*, 6 June 1970.

widespread speculation about a second devaluation. Jenkins, although well versed in economic matters, had not been a member of the Cabinet's economic committee and had not been closely involved in economic policy. This gave him the advantage of not being associated with the fiascos of 1964–7, but it also meant that he had to start from scratch. Not surprisingly, his first weeks at the Treasury were uncomfortable for himself and the Government. Within two days he was plunged into a major humiliation when he rashly assured the Commons that the Letter of Intent written by Callaghan to the International Monetary Fund had contained no conditions on the loan to tide sterling over the post-devaluation period; in fact the latter had contained certain undertakings to the IMF which were palpably conditions, and this fact was bound to be revealed. This was an embarrassment; what was far more serious was the discovery of a virtually total absence of real post-devaluation planning, a rock-bottom confidence in the British economy, and a general condition of what can best be described as the economic jitters. It was quite clear that, unless a drastic check were applied, another forced devaluation was a real possibility, which the Government could hardly have survived. No modern Chancellor of the Exchequer has entered his inheritance under such grim circumstances.

With the wisdom of hindsight, it can be seen that it would have been best for Jenkins to follow one of two courses; either to have introduced an immediate 'holding' Budget while he worked on his longer-term plans, or to have brought in a full Budget at once. It was clear that domestic demand would have to be curbed, and it was also clear that it should have been done as part of the immediate post-devaluation strategy. In the event, he issued stern warnings about what would be in the March Budget. The error was perhaps even more serious psychologically than economically – although the economic consequences in delaying curbs on domestic demand and thereby shifting resources towards exports were serious enough – but it was symptomatic of Jenkins' very unsure touch in this period.

Jenkins had one advantage denied to his predecessor. Circumstances rather than intention had created a rational economic policy with the abandonment of the expensive support for sterling and the announced withdrawal of military bases from the Far East and the Persian Gulf. This very belated recognition of the reality of Britain's position to the world was perhaps the most significant contribution of the Wilson Government.

After this weak start, Jenkins moved gradually towards containing domestic consumption within reasonable limits, and increasingly towards control of the money supply. Before Jenkins' arrival at the Treasury no Chancellor had received daily information of the operations of the Bank in the money market. Jenkins was also willing to attack Labour shibboleths when necessary. He refused demands for a wealth tax, and in his first Budget speech envisaged a simplified tax structure with lower rates and fewer special exemptions. Those who decry the rôle of intellect in politics would be wise to avert their eyes from Jenkins' tenure of the Treasury. Mistakes were certainly made, but the Chancellor saw where he was going; and he understood the fundamental realities. In a situation of such volatility, when so much depended upon confidence in the capacity of the British to weather the storm, Jenkins' own personality was a major factor. Neither Wilson nor Callaghan had been able to establish this confidence, but the fact that Jenkins was a new man, of manifest ability and public caution was of considerable psychological importance. While it would be unwise to exaggerate this factor, and important to emphasize that international financiers are more impressed by realities than appearances, it was an element in the situation which should not be lightly dismissed. The international financial community had been unnerved by what it regarded as an absence of practical common sense in the handling of the British economy since October 1964, and wearied by rhetorical claims which clearly had no basis in fact. Jenkins' approach, accordingly, was encouraging and refreshing, and gradually inspired a greater confidence in the British ability to restore their ailing economy. The fundamental situation remained bad, but the fact that subsequent monetary crises were – at a heavy cost – resisted with international assistance owed a great deal to the gradual restoration of international confidence that further devaluations could be at least postponed and the chronic balance of payments crisis resolved. In this gradual process, Jenkins' own personality played its part, and must be acknowledged.

Jenkins' task was not made any easier by the hostility of the Opposition. This was partly the result of personal animosity towards Wilson, partly occasioned by the feeling that the Government was on the point of collapse, and partly by a general scepticism about Government claims and assurances. Furthermore, the Opposition's hostility to a statutory prices and incomes policy was now firmly established. The new Prices and Incomes Act of 1968 envisaged a $3\frac{1}{2}$ per cent ceiling for wage, dividend, and salary increases, and gave the Government delaying powers for up to a year. This revival of the lapsed provisions of 1966 was a holding operation, but it was strongly opposed by the Conservatives and from the Labour benches. By this stage it had become almost an article of faith that a statutory prices and incomes policy 'did not work'. In fact, it did achieve a considerable success, but the pressures on Jenkins not to seek its renewal in April 1969 were too strong. It was not surprising that in this situation the prices and incomes provisions were, although nominally retained, in fact abandoned by the April of 1969. It would have been far better, if such a course had been politically feasible, to have raised the ceiling and to have made the phasing-out of controls more gradual. The subsequent 'reactivation' of the controls, to provide for a three-month delay, later in the year made this point, as did the December White Paper on 'Productivity Prices and Incomes Policy After 1969'.[1] But the vehemence of Labour opposition to this reactivation – which was passed in the Commons on 17 December by a majority of only 28 – emphasized the strength of the forces against which Jenkins had had to contend. This decision substantially undermined the hard-won gains of Jenkins' policies, and opened the way for the rapid upsurge of wage demands over the following year. These provided Labour with its electoral opportunity in the spring of 1970, but paved the way for the erosion of real wages and the leap in inflation which, by the middle of 1971, constituted a serious situation. And it is fair to emphasize that the Conservatives played their part in the Government's decision of April 1969.

By this stage it had become axiomatic in the Conservative Party and in the bulk of the Labour Party that central control of wages and prices was unworkable. Certainly, it can be argued with justification that the record of the 1966 Prices and Incomes Act was not impressive. But the alternatives to some form of central control were well set out by Jenkins in the debate of

[1] Cmnd 4327.

17 December 1969. However, by this stage the credibility of the exercise had been compromised, and it died unmourned. But it is probable that economists will devote more attention to the imperfections and inconsistencies in the Labour Government's handling of the matter than to the simple declaration that the episode proved that a statutory prices and incomes policy is an impossibility.

This was essentially a political decision, whose background will be described later, and it was one that was to undermine the limited but real economic recovery that Jenkins had presided over with increasing confidence and capacity. For Jenkins had quickly realized the severe limitations under which a modern British Government has to operate. It is fruitless to lament that things are not as they are, and equally futile to attempt to change fundamentals by rhetoric or legislation. The politician has to work with what he has, good or ill. And the more he looks at his predicament, the more he is aware of how limited his powers really are.

The problems of managing the economy provide perhaps the best example of this situation. A Government cannot, in reality, 'manage' a complex mixed economy. The real task is that of steering it, and here the prime tasks of the Government are to control domestic demand, to keep the economy in external balance, and to finance the expenditure of the State. It can assist and encourage certain industries and can stimulate sensible capital investment; but it is ultimately reliant upon industry to manufacture the goods at a price and of a quality that will be attractive to purchasers. What a Government must do – and what the Labour Government conspicuously failed to do in 1964–7 – is to recognize those strategic priorities in which its actions can make a beneficial contribution. Thus, although the Government possesses certain powers, it does not have the ultimate control that can be described as 'management'. There are some powers – of which import surcharges and export subsidies are good examples – which are internationally illegal. There are others which are politically impossible, or at least very hazardous. The power of direction that a British Government possesses are very limited, and it is to a very large extent dependent upon factors outside its immediate control for the success or failure of its policies.

This dilemma is not confined to industrial matters. The

pattern of change in the population of the United Kingdom provides another example.

In the period 1951 to 1968 the total population increased by 7.2 per cent (50,573,000 to 55,388,000). In these years Britain had achieved both a younger and an older population, for whereas in 1951 there were just over $14\frac{1}{2}$ million people under the age of 19, in 1968 there were over 17 million; yet, also in the same period the total number of women over 60 and men over 65 had jumped from 8.6 million to over 11 million. Meanwhile, the total number of women between 20 and 59 and men between 20 and 64 had risen by only some 600,000. It would be superficial to regard the under-20 group and the over-65 group as being wholly dependent on the 20–64 group, yet the fact is that the proportions of the young and old population have risen sharply, and these groups are those on which the bulk of social service expenditure is concentrated. The burden upon the other group – the one that has been virtually static in size in this period – has accordingly grown very substantially. Current expenditure on goods and services at constant prices in this period rose by 49 per cent on health and 103 per cent on education.[1] Thus, throughout the 1950s and early 1960s the cost of maintaining an elaborate system of social services became an ever-heavier load on the shoulders of the working population. Thus also, so long as there was a determination to increase the quality of the social services by the two political parties – and particularly by Labour – this burden on the wage and salary earner was bound to become even more severe.

Thus, by the 1960s both political parties were trapped in a situation over which they had little control, and which was bound not only to continue but possibly to get even worse (from the strictly economic point of view). The money for the services had to be found, and had to be found from the active, healthy and productive members of the society. It had to be found in direct taxation, indirect taxation, taxation on industry, taxation on death, and taxation on employment. However the devices were arranged, the result was an inevitable general and substantial increase in the amount of money that was being taken from the pay-packets of the productive citizen and the profits of the productive firm. The result was wage demands

[1] *Social Trends*, No. 1 (HMSO, 1970), pp. 13–15.

from the former, and the establishment of higher prices by the latter.

The most depressing – and indeed alarming – feature of public expenditure in the 1960s was the lack of practical results in relation to greatly increased expenditure. Between 1959–60 and 1969–70 public expenditure on housing (including subsidies and improvement grants) rose from £426 million to £1,089 million, but the housing problem remained implacably unsolved. Expenditure on education in the same period rose from £916 million to £2,513 million, yet the results for this vast increase in cost seemed relatively meagre. The cost of the national health service rose from £827 million to £1,931 million, yet at the end of the decade the crisis in the health service remained unresolved. Almost every area of public expenditure presented the same story. Despite the injection of substantial amounts of money, the basic situation seemed unchanged. The complaints of 1959–60 were still valid in 1969–70, and this in spite of a massive injection of public money on scales that were not conceived of in the 1950s.

The villain was not entirely inflation – although this played a very considerable part. A major contributory cause was the dispersal of responsibility between the central and local governments, and, consequently a breakdown in what may be described–albeit imprecisely–as the cost-efficiency machinery. The financial controls were still rigorously applied, but the judgements of value-for-money were too often at fault. This commentator recalls contemplating the erection of a school in Lancashire over a period of nearly two years in the late 1950s. It was questionable whether the school was really needed in the first place, but what was patently obvious was that it was built in the wrong place, of the wrong materials, and on the wrong site. The final cost was more than double the original estimate, and this expenditure and effort were for what was in effect a village school, for approximately 300 children, who had, furthermore, to be transported to it from afar by elaborate (and costly) bus services. This ugly monstrosity, which defiled a hitherto beautiful village, turned out to be impracticable for its task without substantial subsequent changes. Meanwhile, also, the salaries of qualified teachers remained low. Even if the school had been necessary, it was certainly not justifiable in educational terms that really matter – the quality of the education being given.

Education is a good example of the problems which are created by the existence of large and, in some fields at least, semi-autonomous local authorities. The case for the introduction of the comprehensive system was, in this commentator's judgement, overwhelming. But between the Labour objective to reorganize secondary education on comprehensive lines and the practical achievement there was an enormous gulf. The famous Circular 10/65, issued by the Government in 1965 to all education authorities, was attacked by Conservative councillors as an attempt to impose the comprehensive system. In fact, it was a relatively mild document. The postponement of the extension of the school-leaving age in January 1968 was a serious setback to the concept of an overall education policy that encompassed primary schools, the comprehensives, and higher education. What was perhaps even more serious was that whereas universities were hardly affected by the cut-backs (proportionately, that is) the new polytechnics were. The one project that was never seriously affected was the Open University – originally called 'The University of the Air' – whose purpose was to bring higher education advantages to the masses by means of television and private reading. This was one of Wilson's favourite projects, and it became almost sacrosanct when economies in education were involved. It is very doubtful whether the project really merited this degree of priority. With the exception of the establishment of the comprehensve principle – and it is questionable whether this would not have been established in any event by a Conservative Government eventually – Labour continued to attempt to operate a system which, although administratively competent enough, lacked direction, sensible priorities, and balance. One of the most significant features was the deliberate refusal to harm the private sector. The removal of the charitable status of the private schools would have dealt them almost a mortal blow, but when the issue arose the Government passed the matter to the Public Schools Commission!

Regarded as a whole, the villain was a system that involved blurred local and national responsibilities and which was often incapable of common sense. Virtually every community in

Britain could relate stories of lavish expenditure for little identifiable gain in *real* terms. One was presented with the spectacle of a nation pouring its economic life-blood – its capital in money, ability, and resources – into what were not futilities, but which were not essentials. Both political parties became enraptured by the expenditure of funds and the creation of new edifices, without analysing how the funds were being expended in terms of real gain or whether the new edifices were necessary, or desirable, or useful for their task. Labour had been right in stating that what was needed in 1964 was a national plan. The resultant National Plan of 1965, however, missed the point entirely; its collapse pushed Labour away from the concept itself, and back into the *ad hoc* system of clashing priorities and confusions of the 1950s.

Labour had unquestionably inherited a mess. The British system of control of public expenditure – both in the Treasury and in Parliament – was created and perfected in the nineteenth century. For the purpose of the time it was adequate; but, as the twentieth century proceeded on its roaring way it was ever more evident that something radically new was needed. Nothing radically new was provided. The concept of the DEA was promising, but proved unworkable, and not least because the prior planning had been inadequate. 'I think it is a pity that we didn't produce a blue-print setting out precisely what we were trying to achieve,' Brown subsequently wrote: 'That would have been a valuable exercise in itself, and a useful source when some of our ideas were questioned later. But everybody was always so busy that things just didn't get done in that way.'[1] The basic structure was amended, and tinkered with. Certain cautious new departures were ventured. New techniques were introduced, and new expertises developed. But these remained only palliatives to the essential problem, which was how to run a twentieth-century system on nineteenth-century methods.

Labour had given some promise of understanding this problem, and of having ideas on how to meet it. In the event it was evident that Ministers neither understood it nor had anything of major originality to contribute towards its solution. It had been hoped that the Parliamentary structure might itself be revolutionized. Richard Crossman was a most inventive and

---

[1] George-Brown: *op. cit.*, p. 96.

imaginative Leader of the House of Commons, but his proposed reforms could have had no real effect without a genuine and radical support from his colleagues, which never came. But Parliamentary reform was in itself only a small part of the whole problem. What was created was a skeleton of a fine new building of Parliamentary involvement, control, and expertise, but nothing more. The number of Parliamentary Committees increased to undreamed-of proportions, but the results were largely nugatory. It was not a question of money but of will. For an almost infinitesimal sum of money the House of Commons could have been transformed into something resembling a modern, properly equipped, legislature. It did not happen. It did not happen principally because those who in Opposition had cried out for a drastic improvement in the accountability of public departments to Parliament cried out no longer when they were transported into Whitehall. Why should the Opposition be given the raw materials for attacking the Government? Why should hard-worked officials be obliged to explain to back-bench MPs the operations of their Ministers? Labour had promised the creation of a Parliamentary Commissioner, the Ombudsman, to protect the individual citizen from injustice from the State. But the Commissioner, when unwrapped, turned out to be carefully trussed from head to toe.

Labour's experience was to discover what their predecessors had known only too well, that the problems of government had changed very remarkably since the 1940s. Departments had grown to such size, and had such powers and responsibilities, that no single Minister could hope to control them Too often the Minister had become the servant of his Ministry, utterly dependent upon it for everything. Too often, the Department made the decisions; the Minister explained them to the House of Commons. A Minister who attempted to break this system found that he had to embroil himself in profound details, to the severe detriment of his time, energy, and capacity for original thought. He usually ended up even more a servant of his officials than he was before, having become in effect another official. Thus, good ideas and novel thoughts often became diluted and compromised, until by the end they were merely a reflection of the Departmental view.

Here, Labour's admiration for the Civil Service was not an asset. There were some Ministers in the 1964–70 Government who were sceptical of official advice, and tested it carefully; but, in the main, the majority was very willing to conform to what was expected of them. Again, the observer was struck by the desire of the Labour Government to achieve respectability, and to prove that Labour Ministers could be as competent as Conservatives. But the Conservatives tend to have an innate mistrust of civil servants and are possessed in general of greater scepticism of official advice; they accordingly make less comfortable and agreeable Ministers, but often much more effective ones. It is a cardinal tenet of public life that Ministers must not degenerate into civil servants; unhappily, and for a variety of reasons, too many Labour Ministers did so degenerate. It is only fair to emphasize that, as a result of their limited powers and the changed nature of government, their impact could not have been much greater even if they had been more effective Ministers. But the result was that the helter-skelter roared along; much money was spent; many eloquent speeches were made; and the net result was negligible in virtually every major area of public activity.

A particularly melancholy example of how a basically reasonable idea can turn into a political, legal, and administrative nightmare if there is not adequate advance planning may be found in the tragi-comic story of the Land Commission, which was established in 1967 for the purposes of acquiring land for development and collecting the Betterment Levy.

The origin of the Commission was the conviction in the Labour Party that one of the principal obstacles to the development of low-cost housing was the exorbitant price of land charged by individuals whom the Party depicted as 'property sharks'. This was a task that was formidable enough in all conscience, but the Commission had been burdened with the additional charge of a tax-collector when the 40 per cent Betterment Levy was introduced. The philosophy of the Levy was itself dubious, and was described by the second (and last) Chairman of the Commission, Mr George Chetwynd:

If decisions are made by the community such as the granting of planning permission, the installation of essential services and so on, increase the value of a piece of land, the community is entitled to take at least a share of that development land.[1]

But the fact that undermined this justification for the Commission was the introduction of the Capital Gains tax after the establishment of the Commission, and the question of why the tax should not have been framed to cover increases in land and property values was never satisfactorily answered.

At the beginning, there was much talk of the vast income to be reaped from property profiteers, at one point estimated at some £80 million a year. In the event, the Commission averaged less than £20 million annually in its three years of life. There was also talk of acquiring land up to 50,000 acres a year. By May 1970 the Commission owned 2,237 acres, with negotiations in train for a further 9,744 acres. It had aroused the deep resentment not only of everyone involved in the sale and purchase of land, but also of local authorities, who became increasingly unhappy at the Commission intruding upon their planning and development functions from afar. The principal purpose of the Commission had been to ensure that land was available at the right time for the implementation of national, regional, and local plans, and to reduce the cost of land for such purposes. On not a single count did the Commission succeed. The Conservatives had much political mileage out of the inevitable hard cases that flowed from a hopelessly complicated Act and a failure to estimate what could, and should, be done to provide the necessary land and income for housing development. The Commission died unmourned in June 1970. Its birth and brief life may be profitably studied as a *locus classicus* of its kind.

It was not until July 1968, when the Government secured a sterling standby credit of $2,000 million through the Bank of International Settlements, that the dangers of a second forced devaluation really receded. The psychological shock of the devaluation had been severe, but the practical price was also heavy.

One of the first consequences of devaluation was the final

[1] Speech to the Northumberland and Durham branch of the Incorporated Society of Valuers and Auctioneers in Newcastle, 6 April 1970.

decision to abandon any British quasi-military presence East of Suez in total defiance of the previous declared positions of Wilson himself and Healey. (This switch in policy resulted in an incident of high comedy. A representative of the Foreign Office had been despatched to the Persian Gulf in order to deliver copious and firm undertakings to all and sundry that the British were going to stay. On his return, when he arrived at London Airport, he was met by a government official who informed him that his new task was to return forthwith to the Governments he had just quit, to inform them that the policy had been totally reversed.) But the other consequences were of more immediate impact including the restoration of prescription charges, the deferment of extending the school-leaving age (on which issue Lord Longford resigned), the cutting of the housing programme, and the virtual scrapping of the Territorial Army and the Civil Defence Corps; the Budget of 1968 brought a massive increase in taxation, and a special surcharge on large investment incomes which amounted to a Capital Levy.

By this stage the Parliamentary Labour Party was in a condition of deep shock. It veered from horror to euphoria, cheering in ecstasy the faintest gleam of hope, and watching all the while the piecemeal slaughter of almost every one of its most sacred cows. In March 1968 George Brown resigned, stating that he did not like 'the way this Government is run', and in June the Minister of Power, Ray Gunter, went, his letter of resignation also containing phrases uncomplimentary to the Prime Minister and his method of conducting business. Neither of these losses was in itself disastrous. Brown's defects as a Foreign Secretary were only too apparent; the virtues were better concealed.[1] Brown's instincts and judgements were usually very sound, but his cardinal deficiency was his impatience with – and lack of real knowledge of – the necessary cautions and devices of diplomacy. His enthusiasms and his exuberance, although personally highly attractive and professionally valuable, were also a disadvantage. He was, by all accounts, a very difficult colleague; he was certainly a very difficult Secretary of State;

---

[1] Brown resigned as a result of the hurried Privy Council meeting late in the evening of 14 March to proclaim a Bank Holiday, about which he had not been informed. Brown subsequently claimed that this represented a 'presidential method of conducting Government business', and that the episode, although small in itself, was indicative of a deeper malaise, the 'making of tough decisions'.

his tragedy was that the negative aspects of his character gradually outweighed the positive, to the point when he became eminently dispensable. 'He was a man of first-rate ability, a forceful and indeed imaginative administrator, respected by his Parliamentary colleagues and commanding more affection in the wider labour movement than any of us. His strengths far exceeded his weaknesses, but it was his weaknessess which ended his ministerial career.'[1] The actual cause of his departure was not significant; the deeper causes of his disillusionment were. It is sad, but necessary, to record that his departure from the Government strengthened it. His successor was Michael Stewart, a man of lesser personality but greater wisdom.

Gunter had been a good Minister of Labour, and had brought a considerably more interventionist spirit to its work. The virtual emasculation of the Ministry when the new Department of Employment and Productivity had been established was perhaps the final blow to Gunter. Nonetheless, the falling away of senior Ministers was an ominous sign.

In a speech at Newtown, Montgomery, on 6 July Wilson drew attention to the claim by M. Marc Ullman in *L'Express* that 'Britain is on the way to an economic miracle'. He subsequently pointed out that this was a statement that referred not to the immediate future but to the early 1970s: he was certainly justified in feeling indignant that this remark was deliberately quoted out of context by the Conservative Party and Press. Nonetheless, by this time Wilson's optimistic predictions in the past were catching up with him; it appeared, within eight months of devaluation and three months of a very severe Budget, that he was again making grotesque claims. The significance of the episode lay less in the fact that the passage was misquoted than in the fact it was now generally accepted as the sort of thing Wilson was always saying.

It was fortunate for the Government that at this time the Opposition began to have its own troubles, initiated by the speech of Enoch Powell in April in Birmingham, described in Part Three. This furore for some time obscured the fact that the Government's by-election record was moving from the merely awful to the cataclysmic, and that hardly any city of note remained in Labour hands after the 1968 local government elections. This disaster tended to be viewed with equanimity by most

[1] Wilson: *op. cit.*, p. 512.

Ministers. But in fact it dealt a very severe blow to the national position of the Party, and severely damaged morale in the constituencies. The fact that the Government now had to deal with mainly hostile local authorities was in itself a setback; the effect on loyal Party workers was an additional, and in the long run even more significant, factor. In November there came severe imposts on the taxpayer, and another abortive attempt – this time on HMS *Fearless* – to propel Ian Smith towards another victory.

This particular episode had a rather wider significance than the Rhodesia problem. Virtually since the inception of the Labour Party there has been a great but vague yearning for 'a Labour foreign policy', particularly since 1945, and a persistent disappointment that the post-war Labour Governments failed to furnish a satisfying response to the desire. The problem is compounded by the fact that many of the most fervent advocates of 'a Labour foreign policy' are themselves not really interested in foreign affairs, and share the opinion of Miss Nancy Mitford's celebrated father who thought Foreigners and Abroad equally bloody. Matters were further complicated by the fact that the few Labour Members of Parliament who specialized seriously in foreign and defence matters rapidly came to the conclusion that many of the panaceas so beloved of the Party faithful – total disarmament, world government, the United Nations, the abandonment of NATO, etc. – lacked a certain reality in current conditions. The arguments put forward by Richard Crossman, Michael Foot, and Ian Mikardo in *Keep Left* in 1947 for European aloofness from the United States and Russia and the establishment of a purely European security arrangement had withered in face of the events of 1947 and 1948. Since then, no really well-argued case for a Labour foreign policy that was noticeably different from that of the Conservatives came forward apart from that of the advocates of unilateralism. 'An understanding of the power element in politics is the first necessity for a sound foreign policy,' Denis Healey wrote in 1952.[1] Thus, although the record of Britain since 1945 in foreign

[1] D. Healey: 'Power Politics and the Labour Party', *New Fabian Essays* (London, 1952).

affairs may not be a particularly impressive one, it takes a formidable imagination to detect any real difference in *substance* between the two major parties, with the exception of certain episodes, of which Suez is the most conspicuous example.[1]

One of the most interesting features of Labour's foreign attitudes is its chronic obsession with Britain's rôle as a Great Power. The Cabinet Minister who actually banged the table during the NATO meeting and issued fierce 'demands' from his astonished allies was, no doubt, an extreme example of this strange affliction of grandeur, but by no means wholly untypical. Until forced to change course as a result of economic factors, the Labour Government was enthusiastic for a British military presence East of Suez, and firmly retained the nuclear deterrent. At the United Nations, the appearance of Great Power status was vigorously maintained, and in all his forays abroad Wilson bestrode the stage with Churchillian authority. One was reminded of Philip Snowden's fierce pride at driving in a foreign country in a large car with the Union Jack fluttering proudly on the bonnet. For all the talk of realism, the Labour Government abroad was most eagerly nationalistic.

All this, although somewhat comical on occasions, was harmless enough. What was much more serious was its indication of a lack of awareness of Britain's ever-decreasing significance in world politics. Apart from the application to join the EEC, no initiative of any real significance was made in foreign affairs between 1964 and 1970. The dream of Great Power status remained; the confrontation with cold reality was postponed.

Wilson's skill in the 1964–70 Government was to give the appearance of great changes without in fact making any of substance. The nuclear deterrent was preserved, despite the scorn that had been poured on the concept in the 1964 Labour Manifesto ('It will not be independent and it will not be British and it will not deter'); the much trumpeted appointment of a Minister of Disarmament did not lead to any significant shift in policy, and was somewhat compromised by the appointment of an Arms Salesman shortly afterwards; it is doubtful whether the appointment of a Minister of State (Lord Caradon) as

[1] But even on this issue the support given by Labour to the Eden Government in calling up the Reserves and making military preparations following the nationalization of the Suez Canal in July 1956 should be recalled.

Permanent Representative to the United Nations made more than a marginal difference in practice, despite Caradon's remarkable personal qualities; NATO remained a major cornerstone of British defence policy; until forced to reconsider the matter on economic grounds in 1967, the Government remained staunch for a military presence East of Suez; the formal application to join the European Economic Community was made in 1966; despite the theatrical announcement of the ending of arms supplies to South Africa in 1964, other contacts with the Union were sedulously maintained and strengthened; over Rhodesia, the *Tiger* and *Fearless* proposals were evidence of a desire to conclude a highly embarrassing situation on terms that fell far short of the Five Principles established by the Conservatives; United States policies in South-East Asia were tacitly endorsed, and the American connection consistently emphasized. When one surveys the entire field of foreign affairs throughout this period it is difficult indeed to detect any real differences of substance between the performance of Labour and its predecessor.

This is not to say that Labour's policies were wrong, nor that its Ministers were not competent. There is no doubt that Wilson was sincerely intent on securing negotiations on Vietnam in 1964–6, and worked hard to achieve them; the fact that he failed should not, in itself, be held against him. Nonetheless, the practical possibilities of Britain acting as an effective go-between were not great, and contained initiatives – notably the Gordon Walker mission to South-East Asia, the Harold Davies visit to Hanoi, and the proposed Commonwealth Mission – that appeared somewhat jejune. Despite some exceptions, as the circumstances prior to the intervention in Anguilla vividly demonstrated, the Ministers concerned with defence and foreign affairs in the 1964–70 period were conscientious and serious, and their capacity was impressive. Denis Healey was one of the outstanding successes of the Government, a controversial figure, but probably the best Defence Minister since the War, with the inestimable advantage of an uninterrupted five and a half years at the Ministry. The eventual team of Stewart, Foley, Caradon, Thomson, and Chalfont at the Foreign and Commonwealth Office was a strong one. But the differences between the two parties was almost entirely presentational rather than real.

The tangled story of the Rhodesian affair brings out this

point clearly, and can be briefly summarized.[1] The Government's declared objective after the Unilateral Declaration of Independence of 11 November 1965 was to bring down the Smith regime; the South African Government was committed to the preservation of that regime; the Government was determined not to involve itself in a serious dispute with South Africa. No policy can hope to succeed if it contains such a fundamental contradiction of objectives. At first, the Labour Government argued – as had its predecessor – that Britain was not constitutionally responsible to the UN for Rhodesia's internal affairs. It was only by gradual steps that the responsibility was handed to the UN. What made the situation even more serious was the fact that Wilson himself gave too many hostages to fortune immediately after the declaration of UDI and on the introduction of selective mandatory United Nations sanctions a year later.[2] There would be, in any event, much resentment at the failure of the British to impose terms on Smith on the lines of the Principles from the African members of the Commonwealth; that resentment was greatly increased by the feeling that the British had deliberately misled them, a feeling vehemently expressed at the Commonwealth Prime Ministers' Conference of January 1969. Mandatory sanctions were only imposed on British initiative by the UN in May 1968, two and a half years after UDI.[3] The combination of the expression of high sentiments of morality with a policy of *realpolitik* towards South Africa – which also included the active encouragement of British investment in South-West Africa which was contrary to the spirit, and indeed the letter, of a succession of UN resolutions[4] – provoked charges of hypocrisy which were not wholly unmerited.[5]

The Labour Government had found, as had its predecessors

[1] For full details, see *Rhodesia* (Central Office of Information, April 1970). See also, Colin Legum: *The United Nations and the Southern African Question* (Sussex, 1971).

[2] Security Council Resolution No. 232 (16 December 1966).

[3] Security Council Resolution No. 253 (29 May 1968).

[4] And, in particular, the General Assembly Resolution of 1966 that formally terminated the South African mandate.

[5] This point was made at greater length in the author's *Britain's Role in the United Nations* (United Nations Association, 1970). In 1969, Britain's exports to South-West Africa totalled £2 million; imports amounted to £26.4 million, (excluding diamonds). Early in 1970 the Atomic Energy Authority negotiated a long-term contract for the supply of £45 million-worth of uranium.

in 1945–6, that the room for manoeuvre in foreign affairs was limited indeed. Hopes for a rapprochement with the Soviet Union were dashed after the invasion of Czechoslovakia in August 1968 – and it is arguable that the Government in fact over-reacted to that event; the success of Chancellor Brandt's policy of *ostpolitik* in 1969–70 made the Labour Government's efforts seem, in retrospect, somewhat unimaginative. This was all the more curious in view of Wilson's own cultivation of contacts in Moscow before he became Prime Minister, but which had very few practical results subsequently. The commitment to the United States remained total – perhaps too total – and necessitated public support for US policy in Vietnam; not only Labour supporters considered this to be an excessive abasement. In the 1967 Middle East crisis the British fluttered helplessly, their principal achievement – and it was very much a personal one for Lord Caradon – being the November 1967 resolution of the UN Security Council that established the principles for an eventual settlement. But although it would be unfair to belittle this particular achievement, the practical results were minimal. In the Nigerian Civil War the Government had no real choice but to support the Lagos government with arms and other assistance. This tragic conflict aroused deep emotion in Britain, and the Government came under strong attack; but it is very doubtful whether it could have done other than it did. Thus, over the whole area of Defence and Foreign policy, and despite a great impression of urgency and activity, in essentials the Labour record was strikingly similar to the courses that would have been pursued by the Conservatives.

The exception was Europe. Wilson had become intellectually convinced that entry into the Common Market was essential, but it was not a course on which the Labour Party as a whole embarked with notable zest.[1]

The reasons behind the decision to apply for membership of the EEC were principally economic. British trade with the Commonwealth was remaining virtually static, whereas with the EEC countries – despite the high tariff barrier – it was expanding dramatically, and could expand further. The rate of growth of the EEC countries, in such marked contrast with Britain, could not be ignored, nor could the fact that average

[1] For a narrative and documents, see Uwe Kitzinger: *The Second Try: Labour and the EEC*.

weekly wages were now considerably higher than in Britain. The cost of entry would clearly be high, but the calculation was increasingly that the benefits would be infinitely greater.

But there were also important political factors – national and international. On the national side, the advantages of dishing the Tories were self-evident, particularly as the Common Market was the major issue on which Heath's position was publicly known. Internationally, the active presence of Britain in the EEC as a major member of an enlarged community which would account for 40 per cent of world trade, with a total population greater than that of the United States or the Soviet Union, and which would have an immediate gross national product of over £200 billion, might act as the restorative to Britain's faltering position in the world. With considerable tactical skill the Cabinet was pushed in the direction of accepting the application, which was made in May 1967. Thirty-five Labour MPs voted against the application, and many others – estimated at about fifty by most observers – abstained. The chances of President de Gaulle accepting British entry were always minimal, and the veto came in December 1967, after the devaluation of the pound. Many commentators considered – and still consider – that the application was premature, and was the result of Brown's impatience with the long processes of diplomacy. These criticisms have much evidence to support them, but the important factor was that Labour had declared itself, as a Government, in favour of the principle of entry.

Crossman subsequently claimed that the real initiative came from Brown, and has alleged that, 'a search through the Cabinet papers of this period confirms that no collective decision was made either upon support for the Common Market in principle or upon the modifications and assurances required for British entry ... there is no truth whatsoever in the allegation that the Labour government was ever committed to "support for the Common Market" '.[1] This interpretation has been strongly challenged by some of Crossman's colleagues, and certainly the public commitment appeared complete. A second French veto was probably inevitable, but it is more than probable that a Conservative Government under Heath would have made a more vigorous and decisive attempt. Few Cabinet Ministers – Brown, Jenkins, and Thomson being notable exceptions – were

New Statesman, 12 February 1970.

genuinely enthusiastic Europeans, and the doubts and hesitations of the majority were shared on the back benches. Thus, although on the surface there was, after 1966, no difference of policy towards entry into the EEC, between the two main parties there was a very real difference in emphasis and dedication. There were critics of the British entry into the Common Market in the Conservative Party, but at this time it seemed that the real debate had been settled in 1962. Labour had fought the 1966 General Election with a general stance of opposition to further attempts to enter the EEC and the argument that the Party had been committed by the Cabinet to the application without adequate consultation had its point.

If there is ever to be such a thing as 'a Labour foreign policy' – and assuming that it would not be an extremist one, involving unilateral disarmament, the abandonment of NATO, etc. – considerably more detailed prior preparation would have to be undertaken. But the 1964–70 Government showed little interest, in this field as in others, in attempting any radical novelties. On the issues of the admission of the People's Republic of China to the United Nations, and South-West Africa (Namibia) there was no difference at all between the Conservative and Labour approach. In an area where creative imagination could have been profitably limited with realism to provide more of a constructive approach, the Labour Government contented itself with limping somewhat inadequately along the courses charted by its predecessors.

We may return to the beleaguered Administration at home. By the end of 1968 the fortunes of the Government seemed irredeemably lost. The Commonwealth Immigration Act – described in Part Three – was a measure that had outraged all but the most obsessed by the immigrant threat, and Callaghan's rôle in this measure further increased his reputation in some sections of the Labour Party as being more Tory than the Tories on any issue involving support of liberal principles. SET was further increased in the 1969 Budget in order to bring in over £600 million – on which forty-one Labour Members abstained – and British military intervention in Anguilla had the appropriate element of farce that usually accompanies the decline in an administration's fortunes. A clumsy attempt to introduce House of Lords reform was destroyed by a remarkable combination of Government and Opposition back-benchers, of whom the leading participants were Powell and Michael Foot. What appeared to be a blatantly cynical Government refusal to accept the revision of constituency boundaries by the Boundaries Commission for the simple reason that the new boundaries would be to the advantage of the Conservatives drew upon Callaghan personally a storm of criticism.

The accusations of 'gerrymandering' hurled at the Government do not, on close inspection, appear valid. It is doubtful whether the changes would have benefited the Conservatives greatly – Labour estimates were a net gain for the Conservatives of between six and eight seats, Dr Butler's calculation is eleven – and the Government argument that the proposed Redcliffe-Maud local government changes had to be considered at length looks considerably more sensible and reasonable in retrospect than it did at the time. Nonetheless, in politics appearances and public impressions are crucial at the time. And the Government and the Labour Party did not emerge from the episode with distinction. On top of all this, the ancient, fetid, simmering tensions in Ulster erupted into a major crisis.

But even this catalogue of miseries was eclipsed by the violent divisions created in the Labour Party by the attempt to curb the powers of the Trade Unions.

The struggle that raged between January and June 1969[1] was of particular historical significance, as it represented the first attempt by a Labour Government to deal with the industrial problems which the Trade Union movement was either incapable of handling or was unwilling to try to handle. Since 1964 the number of strikes – the majority of them unofficial – had increased alarmingly, and were having a definite effect on foreign confidence in the British economy. Ministers considered, although the evidence is very doubtful, that the seamen's strike of 1966 had been a major factor in the events leading up to the July measures, and that the dock strike of a year later had

[1] Most ably and entertainingly related in Mr Peter Jenkins' book, *The Battle of Downing Street.*

played a significant part in making devaluation unavoidable. 1968 had seen a number of unofficial stoppages by relatively few workers in key areas which had brought much larger industries to a standstill – notably in the motor industry. The more Ministers – and particularly Wilson – looked at the problem, the more did it seem inevitable that some drastic action was required.

There was an important political implication as well. The Labour Party may well have come, in Bevan's phrase, out of the bowels of the Trade Union movement, but behind the public expressions of trust and affection there had always lain a considerable mutual wariness. In the 1960s the Trade Union sponsored MPs were not, collectively, an impressive contribution to the Parliamentary Party in terms of ability, youth, or originality. They tend to regard themselves as the ballast of the Party; their critics within it regarded them as constituting a massive, unimaginative, reactionary, usually bloody-minded deadweight. Relations between the TUC and the Labour Party have varied very considerably since the War, primarily as a result of personalities, but between Labour's assumption of office in 1964 and the end of 1968 they had reached a significantly low point. The appointment of Frank Cousins as Minister of Technology in 1964 had not been a success, and Cousins' denunciations of his former colleagues for their apostasy in proposing a form of wage control had not been appreciated by Ministers. There were, furthermore, certain Trade Union leaders whom Ministers regarded with an aversion that was very thinly disguised, and which was repaid with a deep mistrust of a Labour Government which, by 1968, had only one genuine Trade Unionist (Mr Roy Mason) in its leading ranks. Ministers had become convinced that the Trade Union leaders had treated them worse than any former administration – Labour or Conservative – had been treated; a substantial number of the Trade Union leaders, of whom Mr Hugh Scanlon and Mr Jack Jones were the dominant figures, were equally convinced that this Government was not a Labour Government as they understood the term. And, behind all the talk of high principles, there lay some long-smouldering personal animosities.

But there were other additional political factors. 1968 had been a year of almost unrelieved disaster for the Government, and had culminated in a crisis of confidence early in December in which both *The Times* and the *Daily Mirror* declared that

Labour was clearly unfitted to govern and had called for a Coalition. These severe comments were confirmed by opinion polls, all of which indicated a further massive slump of public confidence. This struck at the foundation of Wilson's long-term strategy, which was to prove that Labour could govern, was a truly national party, and was not afraid of the responsibilities – however harsh – of office.

There is no reason to question Mr Peter Jenkins' view[1] that the new departure owed everything to Wilson's personal will. The vital preliminary had been to transfer Mrs Barbara Castle from the Ministry of Transport to the new Department of Employment and Productivity, which would have full responsibility for prices and incomes. Mrs Castle's spirit and energy at the Ministry of Transport were exhilarating and had had some impressive results. No one, furthermore, could doubt her political courage. She loathed the Tories, and although the feeling was, in general, reciprocated, the less partisan of the leading Opposition members regarded her with respect. A popular and vehement figure at Labour Conferences, and with an unimpeachable record of devotion to Socialism, she seemed not only the ideal person to undertake the new task but virtually the only possible one.

The Report of the Donovan Commission,[2] which had been set up in 1965 to examine the law affecting the Trade Unions, had been published in June 1968. The majority finding was essentially a blessing on the status quo; as Mr Andrew Shonfield commented in a Note of Reservation, the report limited itself to the immediate situation but 'barely concerns itself with the long-term problem of accommodating bodies with the kind of concentrated power which is possessed by trade unions to the changing future needs of an advanced industrial society'. A swift glance at the composition of the Commission explains why this had happened. Particularly the presence of Mr George Woodcock, the General Secretary of the TUC,[3] combined with

[1] Jenkins: *op. cit.*
[2] *The Report of the Royal Commission on Trade Unions and Employers Associations* (Cmnd 3623), published 13 June 1968.
[3] It is to George Brown that we are indebted for the best succinct observation on Mr Woodcock's contribution to the history of our times : 'George Woodcock ... is a most up-and-down fellow: even in his most enthusiastic moments he sounds rather like an undertaker. One day he would be "for it", but the next day you would find that while he was still "for" it he now saw all the snags and the impossibilities.' (George Brown: *op. cit.*, p. 107).

Lord Donovan's desire for a unanimous report, had constituted in themselves a guarantee that the result would be an endorsement of the principles of voluntary agreement between employer and union. Donovan had concluded by rejecting the practicality and desirability of legal curbs on unofficial strikes and urged local voluntary agreements. It recommended the establishment of an Industrial Relations Commission to investigate labour difficulties; labour tribunals to hear individual complaints of breach of contract; and an independent review body to examine complaints against Trade Unions. These proposals had their point, but hardly met the fundamental one that the Report brought out – that about 95 per cent of industrial disputes were unofficial.

The Conservatives had already produced their own action document, *Fair Deal At Work*, which was a very positive advance on the kind of thinking that any political party had undertaken on this issue since the War, and which bore the firm imprint of Mr Robert Carr's experienced and realistic mind. The Opposition was thus in a good position to condemn Donovan, and did so with gusto. Many Ministers were no less disappointed. Those who were most deeply concerned with the matter had wanted an action programme of such radicalness from Donovan that they could have engineered a compromise with the TUC, whereby the most radical proposals could have been shelved yet the Government given those powers which would enable it to exercise some form of statutory control over the unions.

This was the background to *In Place of Strife – A Policy For Industrial Relations*, which was published in January 1969.[1] It was a delicately balanced programme, in which the Trade Unions would gain much in return for the acceptance of certain binding statutory obligations. The fundamental weakness was that the benefits to be conferred *de jure* were already enjoyed *de facto* by the Unions, whereas the restrictions were entirely new. To the Unions, the most alarming features were the imposition of a procedure whereby the Minister could order a resumption of work for twenty-eight days while negotiations proceeded – a proposal lifted straight from the Conservatives' policy, which in turn had been based on the American practice – and powers conferred on the Minister for settling inter-union disputes; finally, and this was very much a favourite of the Prime

[1] Cmnd 3888.

Minister, a strike ballot could be ordered in certain circumstances. The White Paper was very much a joint production of Wilson and Mrs Castle, and was presented to the Cabinet virtually as a *fait accompli*.

This tactic meant that the programme retained its unity and coherence, and was produced relatively swiftly. But it had the danger that always lies in by-passing the normal processes of Cabinet discussion and preparation. Jenkins had promised his support but the deliberate decision to exclude Callaghan from the preparation of the policy was a costly error. It aroused Callaghan's formidable anger, and made him the focal point for resistance to the policy within the Cabinet. This opposition was not slow to develop, and it swiftly moved outside the Cabinet to the Parliamentary Party and the Trade Union movement. At first, Wilson was confident that he could handle the opposition, but the pressures became inexorably more heavy until, by June 1969, it was evident that his own position was in peril.

A British Prime Minister has at his disposal the two most powerful of political weapons; he can hire and fire Ministers, and he can dissolve Parliament. He can resign, but he can only be dismissed by the Sovereign. In the spring and early summer of 1969 there were serious plots to engineer this situation by means of a Cabinet advice to the Queen. Some members of the Parliamentary Party who were privately sympathetic to the proposed legislation now saw it as their long-awaited opportunity to oust Wilson. The prospect of a Cabinet coup was small, and the emphasis was moved to contrive Wilson's deposition by a specially convened Party meeting. Wilson's determination not to build up any of his colleagues into a major contender for the Premiership now paid considerable dividends. Not the least of the problems facing some of Wilson's most bitter critics on the back benches was that the favourite of many of them, Jenkins, was strongly committed to *In Place of Strife*. Callaghan's position as the first declared opponent of the policy was not matched by support in the Parliamentary Party; indeed, this support began to fade away sharply in May, when it was considered that his opposition was becoming too well-publicized for comfort.

The issue was, however, resolved by the Parliamentary Party, and in particular by its chairman, Douglas Houghton. As Mr

Roy Hattersley subsequently wrote: 'The battle was won and lost because of the revolt of the solid centre – the men for whom nine-tenths of their Parliamentary life see loyalty to the leadership as the indispensable political virtue. It was for them that Douglas Houghton spoke. Torn between conflicting loyalties, they made a slow and sad decision.'[1] Wilson and Mrs Castle fought vigorously, but the forces against them were too strong. All that could remain was a formula that would hopefully conceal the extent of their defeat; it took the form of a 'solemn and binding undertaking' that the TUC would do its best to solve the problems which the Government's policies had attempted to meet. Wilson's normal capacity to represent defeat as victory was not as evident on this occasion as it had been before. Mr Peter Jenkins has rightly written that 'he did not climb down, he was dragged down'.

Wilson and Mrs Castle can be criticized on many counts, mainly tactical. They had also revealed a serious misunderstanding of what was possible by direct frontal assault, and had clearly learned nothing from the Clause Four battles of 1960, when Hugh Gaitskell had made essentially the same mistakes. They tried to do too much too quickly, and without sufficient allowances for the depth of the reactions they would arouse. But they had attempted something of very considerable long-term importance. If they had succeeded, they would have removed one of the Conservatives' most substantial planks, and would have established the fact that Labour really was a National Party and was unafraid of restraining the Trade Union movement if the national interest demanded. Although it is arguable whether, on the merits of the case, they were right, it is difficult to deny that they were right on the long-term political implications. The relief of the Conservatives when Wilson had to bow before the pressures was understandable. Every indication at the disposal of the Party leaders was to the effect that there was a mass of opinion in the electorate that the situation was intolerable, and should be resolved. These indications also showed that a very substantial proportion of Trade Unionists were exasperated with their nominal leaders and with a situation of near-anarchy in certain industries. In a situation of rising unemployment, it should also be noted, young workers do not regard the Trade Union movement, with its fixed 'last in,

[1] 'Could Barbara Have Won?', *New Statesman*, 4 September 1970.

first out' policy, as the best protector of their interests. To the dedicated life-long Trade Unionist any infringement of the hard-won freedom of the Unions is sacrilege, but by taking the action it did, the Labour Party had publicly confirmed the Conservatives' jibe that it was not a free Party, and that it was – to adapt Joseph Chamberlain's celebrated charge against the Liberals in the Irish Home Rule controversies – 'a *kept* Party'.

Wilson and Mrs Castle alone emerged from this complex and bitter struggle with some distinction, despite their numerous errors of timing, tactics, and strategy. Although Wilson's principal political defect was his obsession with the short-term and the immediate, on this issue he had shown himself somewhat more far-sighted politically than his opponents. By grasping the nettle of Trade Union reform he had endangered his own position, flung the Labour Party into chaos and staked the existence of the Government. These were high risks, but the stakes were equally high.

Nonetheless, the point must be made again that the necessity of abandoning prices and wages control, as a vital preliminary to the struggle over *In Place of Strife*, demonstrated a fundamental misunderstanding of what was in the long-term national interest. For, as events turned out, both the modest control on prices and wages and the attempt to control the Unions had to be abandoned; by June 1969, accordingly the Government had surrendered much of what power it had slowly built up over this section of the economy. The abrupt and dramatic breaking of the 'wages' dam' was the first consequence, and the subsequent violent increase in the rate of inflation was the second.

But from the political point of view the battle over *In Place of Strife* had not been all loss for Wilson. Indeed, one of the most interesting aspects of the situation was that, in its own strange way, the electorate grasped what Wilson was trying to do; his defeat was much less of a personal humiliation than many political commentators at the time assumed. Mr Peter Jenkins believes that, 'in the course of losing the great battle of Downing Street he perhaps was the victor of some private battle with himself'.[1] It is this commentator's belief that he was also the victor of a more profound battle still. The Conservatives continued to label him as an unprincipled cheater, twister, and

[1] Jenkins: *op. cit.*, p. 167.

charlatan. But, for the first time since 1966, there was a marked lack of public response to these allegations.

This crisis was the last dark shadow before the dawn. The handling of the complex Ulster crisis by the Government in general, and Callaghan in particular, was impressive. The Catholic Civil Rights movement in Ulster, founded in February 1967, clearly had justice on its side, but its emergence, and the violent reaction of the more extreme Protestant elements, created a crisis which the government of Captain Terence O'Neill could not manage. The Ulster crisis was not simply a matter of civil rights for the Catholic minority. Behind it lay generations of animosity, a tradition of hatred, acute social problems, and that irrational urge towards destruction in the Irish character which has baffled the British for more than three centuries. Captain O'Neill was charged by the extreme Ulster Unionists as being too progressive, and by the Catholics as being too dilatory. He was forced to dissolve the Ulster Parliament in February 1969, but, although narrowly victorious, his authority had been fatally damaged. In April 1969 he resigned, to be succeeded as Prime Minister by Major Chichester-Clark, who was eventually to suffer the same fate.

By this stage the fires of religious, social and political bitterness were smouldering ominously in Ulster. Across the border, in Eire, the never-dormant forces for United Ireland seized their opportunity. After a summer of ugly incidents fighting broke out in Londonderry in August which the police were unable to control, and the battle swiftly spread to Belfast and ten other towns. On 14 August the Ulster Government appealed for British military assistance, and British troops were in the Catholic area of Belfast on the following day, hailed joyously by the beleagured Catholics. The British Government insisted that the hated Protestant auxiliary police force, the 'B Specials', be disbanded, and that the civil rights programme be accelerated. On 27 August Callaghan toured the most dangerous areas and was warmly received in the Catholic sectors. His determination and understanding made a considerable impression on all who met him, and it seemed that the crisis could be contained and eventually solved.

Unhappily, too much had happened too swiftly. Ancient memories, fears, and hatreds had been revived. The Reverend Ian Paisley, on the extreme Protestant side, and the diminutive 21-year-old Miss Bernadette Devlin on the Catholic, burst suddenly upon the startled British public. In April 1969 Miss Devlin had won a by-election to the Westminster Parliament, while Mr Paisley – after winning nearly 40 per cent of the vote against Captain O'Neill in the Stormont general election in February – soon found himself another Ulster seat, which he won easily. After August 1969 the tensions in Ulster remorselessly rose again. The British troops were as helpless in this situation as the Chichester-Clark government. The original saviours became regarded by the Catholics as foreign oppressors, and Belfast earned its grim reputation of being, in the words of John Morley, 'the most bigoted city in Europe'.

Given the situation as it was, it is difficult to see how the Labour Government could have done other than it did. The extreme measures of internment without trial and the suspension of the 1920 Constitution seemed likely to lead to even worse trouble. It is possible that the fundamental nature of the Ulster problem was inadequately appreciated in Westminster, and there were certainly few officials who anticipated the subsequent violent deterioration of 1971. But, at the time, and given the situation as it appeared to be in August 1969, the actions of the British Government were sensible. They were the inheritors of a crisis which had deep roots and whose solution was infinitely more complex than the granting of civil rights to the Catholic minority. As the extreme elements on both sides grew in public authority, the stature of the Stormont government withered, and the position of the British Army grew more perilous.

But, at the time, Callaghan's personal performance won golden tributes at a critical moment in his own career. His admitted failure at the Treasury had been followed by the legislation against the Kenyan Asians and the struggle over *In Place of Strife*. Callaghan, no less than the Labour Government, urgently wanted a success and it seemed that he and they had achieved one. And then, at long last, the long-heralded improvement in the economic situation seemed a genuine reality. The trade figures improved and the scrapping in January 1970 of the travel restrictions was the first of what was expected to be a number of measures to relax pressure. The

Budget of April 1970 was cautiously reflationary, and the immediate reactions of Labour MPs was a gloomy one; but the new voice of guarded, well-documented optimism which Jenkins struck impressed other observers. *The Economist* described it as an 'inactively irresponsible' Budget, and pointed out that it had done nothing to curb the now rampant wage inflation. The criticism was a sound one economically, but less so politically. The Budget offended few, and pleased some; and it conspicuously avoided dealing with the one new feature in the economy that was generally popular – the galloping rise in wages. By March 1970 the official reserves had risen to £1,101 million after repayments of more than £94 million; private bank loans had slightly increased; car production was the highest since January 1969; weekly wage rates had risen by 3.6 per cent between October 1969 and January 1970, and were 5.9 per cent up on January 1969. But there was another, and much gloomier side to the picture. Industrial production in December 1969 was only up a fraction on that of December 1968; unemployment had risen by 5.1 per cent between February 1969 and February 1970; retail prices had risen by 5 per cent between January 1969 and January 1970. Exports were up by 11 per cent, but the steep rise in export prices of British goods was an ominous portent. But, politically, the key point seemed to be that the rise in wages now outstripped that of retail prices. Thus, although it was evident to close observers that the chronic malaise in the British economy was far from solved, the surface manifestations seemed hopeful enough for the Labour Party to look forward to an Election with considerably less apprehension that at any time since 1966.

It could hardly be denied that the Labour record since 1966 had been profoundly disappointing. But the fact that the Parliamentary Labour Party and the Government had managed to survive at all was remarkable; it can be partly explained by the creation of that political solidarity which occurs when matters are most desperate, the unity of despair. But more solid factors were Jenkins' competence at the Treasury in 1968-9, and Wilson's personality. The Prime Minister had retained his resilience, optimism, and balance in circumstances that might well have destroyed them in other leaders. His capacity to counter-attack when things were at their worst always encouraged his supporters to believe that, when it came to the final battle, he would destroy Heath as he had done before. We may recall the remark of Harry St John: 'Men grow, like hounds, fond of the man who shows them game and by whose halloo they are used to be encouraged.' Opinion polls demonstrated that his own popularity in the country, except at the time of devaluation, had remained surprisingly steady. His ability to fight himself out of what had appeared to be impossible situations constantly astonished the Conservatives, enchanted Labour, and drew genuine – if often grudging – respect outside Westminster. He had nerve, spirit, and skill. It has been said of Caesar that through great folly and recklessness he frequently endangered himself unnecessarily, and that his talents were not fully demonstrated unless he had to extricate himself from a hopeless situation. The same characteristics had been very evident in Wilson's case. His opponents found it impossible to comprehend why, after such a record, his national position remained so high, and it is in fact a perplexing question only if the quite false portrait of Wilson is accepted.

Throughout the 1966–70 Parliament the Parliamentary Labour Party had shown itself to be highly volatile even by its own standards, sweeping from utter gloom to euphoric ecstasy with unpredictable speed. This volatility, although it had posed its problems, was itself a resilient quality. The very real Ministerial successes of the Government had given the Party confidence that it *could* govern, and that its leaders *could* out-gun the Conservatives.

It was evident that newcomers such as Mr Harold Lever, Mrs Shirley Williams, Mr Ivor Richard, Mr Evan Luard, and Mr Roy Hattersley were of real Ministerial quality, and there had been other successes – notably Mr Stephen Swingler at Transport – which had been quite unexpected. The marked inferiority complex of the 1950s and early 1960s, and the seeping defeatism that had permeated the whole Parliamentary Labour Party during that long period of defeat and humiliation, had been exorcized. Many of the young Labour MPs elected for the first time in 1966 had proved very able, and the Parliamentary Party could see future Ministers sitting amongst it. Even though it could be argued with justice that Labour was a long way from having proved itself a competent governing party, it now at least thought of itself in such terms. Labour had first formed a Government in 1924 and, yet, even after the great victory of 1945, it was difficult to detect in the Party anything equivalent to that *assumption* of being a party of Government before 1964 that has been one of the greatest strengths of the Conservatives. For this, Wilson deserves much of the credit. And Labour accordingly did not face the forthcoming Election, whenever it came, in a mood of defeatism or inferiority.

For this achievement a price had had to be paid. No political party can afford to be the servant of its most devoted supporters, who tend to come from the more extremely committed elements in the electorate; but also, no party can afford to shock and alienate those supporters to the extent that Labour had done since 1966. The argument was that, when the Tory enemy was once again abroad in the land, the faithful would return. But the evidence was that this was a very doubtful assumption. For a party which relies almost wholly on the enthusiasm of a small number of active local workers to compensate for the organization of the Conservatives, this marked alienation was an ominous sign. Here, again, it is necessary to emphasize the devastating effects on the national Party of the wholesale slaughter of Labour candidates in local elections since 1966. These victims came to believe, moreover, that the Party leadership was not greatly concerned about their misfortunes, and was obsessed by the Parliamentary situation. The shrugging-off of local election disasters as mere trivialities unquestionably embittered many devoted party workers.

Wilson may have made the Parliamentary Party think of itself as a Government party; outside, there were many Party members and former activists who considered that a Labour Government operating on the terms that the Wilson Government had operated on was not what they had joined the Labour Party for. The *In Place of Strife* battle had been, for many, the last of a long line of disillusionments.

This factor of the disenchantment of the loyal was seriously underestimated by the Party leadership. One of the major changes in the electorate since 1966 had been the enfranchisement of voters between 18 and 21, and there was a general assumption – not confined to Labour – that this would substantially support Labour. In fact, it was estimated that at least three in ten of the voters were not registered, and that a significant proportion of those who had been registered by their parents were unaware of the fact. Evidence also pointed to the fact that young Conservatives were much more likely to be registered than young Labour or Liberals, and much more likely to vote.[1]

Thus, there was in Labour's mounting confidence early in 1970, a strong element of unrealism. The high claims of 1964 and 1966 now looked decidedly embarrassing in view of the actual achievements and particularly on the economic front. Wilson believed – and with solid justification – that British politics are essentially about the economy. Yet this was in fact Labour's weakest card. Labour had come into office in 1964 with the general view that the solution to the national economic malaise lay in faster economic growth and in the modernization of methods of management of the economy. The average growth rate in the last five years of the Conservative Government had been 2.9 per cent and the forecast of a 3.8 per cent rate in the 1965 National Plan represented a sincere belief that such a rate could be achieved and that its achievement would, by itself, completely transform the situation.

The weakness had lain in the haphazard, unplanned approach to the securing of this goal. The concept of the new Department of Economic Affairs may have been sound, but very little practical work had been done before the 1964 Election to establish its rôle and, most important of all, its relationship with the Treasury. Matters were further complicated by the personalities of Brown and Callaghan, and by Wilson's obsession with keeping the pound sterling at the rate he had inherited. The Government had also inherited a substantial deficit on balance of payments, a fact that was in itself a severely limiting element, but whose seriousness Wilson over-emphasized. The depiction of 'the Tory mess' had very considerable immediate political dividends in Britain, and the half-hearted counter-attack of Maudling seemed to admit guilt. But the manner in which the new Government had laid excessive and dramatic stress on the gravity of the situation had not inspired confidence abroad, and it had, accordingly, not been long before the Government had found itself in a crisis

[1] Professor Richard Rose, *The Times*, 26 May 1970. But see page 278 below.

of confidence which required a series of *ad hoc* measures which had culminated in the forced devaluation of November 1967. Beyond the obsession with the balance of payments and the parity of the pound sterling at $2.80 there had been virtually no Labour economic policy at all until Jenkins managed to inject some measure of common sense and medium-term thinking.

The Labour strategy for 1970 was to emphasize that 'the Tory mess' had indeed been cleaned up at last, that the economy was now strong, and that the foundations had been laid for a great forward advance. The problem with this scenario was that it was a difficult one to sustain. The devices introduced by Labour for the streamlining and modernization of methods of controlling the economy had had their points, but the results, regarded collectively, were hardly impressive. The OECD forecast for the British average growth rate to 1975, published in May 1970, was 2.8 per cent, which was the lowest for any OECD member except Luxembourg; the fact that it was undoubtedly an improvement on the miserably low 1964–70 average of 2.2 per cent was of small comfort. Closer examination of the substantial balance of payments surplus achieved by 1970 revealed, furthermore, that it was based less on the volume of increased exports than on the imposition of higher costs to customers, a fact which produced a quick surplus but which undermined long-term competitiveness.

The full impact of SET is difficult to calculate, and is a matter of some controversy among economists. It was certainly developed into a formidable revenue-raiser; in 1969–70 it yielded a net £600 million, or some $4\frac{1}{2}$ per cent of total tax revenue. Whether it has forced the service industries into becoming more efficient[1] by itself is questionable; there is no conclusive evidence of its effects upon patterns of employment. SET was replete with anomalies; it taxed the retailing of food, and also industries – of which insurance is the prime example – which have export business. Furthermore, the manufacturing industries themselves are very dependent upon the service

[1] The only detailed analysis available is by Professor Brian Reddaway, on the distributive trades, published in March 1970 (*Effects of the Selective Employment Tax, First Report*, HMSO). Professor Reddaway's conclusions have been questioned; a particularly good analysis is to be found in *The Economist*, 7 March 1970, pp. 57–58. The report of the Industrial Policy Group (*The Case Against the Selective Employment Tax*, April 1970) makes the case against differentiating between manufacturing and service industries, but notably fails to put forward valid alternatives.

industries, just as the front-line soldier is dependent upon the munitions worker, with the result that an additional tax burden on the latter affects the former. Much of this could, and should, have been foreseen, and the same general objectives – revenue and increased efficiency in labour utilization – achieved by a flat payroll tax; the additional burden on export prices could have been met by other alternatives. SET was a clever tax; perhaps it was too clever by half.

The real failure had been an inability to produce effective machinery for tackling the two key elements – the low growth rate and the remorseless rise in prices. Curbing the power of the Trade Unions, although attractive, was not central. Up to November 1967 there had been some success in keeping price increases below wage rises, but the subsequent story was very different.

Furthermore, the much-trumpeted surplus in the balance of payments had been purchased at a very heavy price. Between 1964 and 1969 total personal income rose from £27,670 million to £38,571 million, an increase of just under 40 per cent; but in the same period income tax and national insurance contributions rose from £4,245 million to £7,449 million, an increase of just under 80 per cent. Personal income tax as a percentage of the gross national product rose from 9.25 per cent to 13.4 per cent in 1970, a fact which in itself, and without taking into account the rise in prices, greatly reduced the value of wage and salary increases. Furthermore, the series of restrictions imposed by the Government after 1966 were of a nature that no advanced country had experienced since the early 1950s. Prices had risen by an average of 3.8 per cent and in 1969 and the first months of 1970 at an even greater rate. Between 1966 and 1970 the increase in prices was between 25 and 30 per cent. The massive burden of international debts that had been incurred in the vain attempt to save the pound may not have been widely understood, but the effects of the Government's failure could be clearly seen in rising prices, high personal income tax, restrictions on foreign travel, and high interest rates. Small businesses had been particularly hard hit by SET and the extreme difficulty of raising capital.

Another conspicuous failure had been an incapacity to reform the taxation and welfare systems. The British tax structure before 1964 had become an appalling maze which only professionals could hope to penetrate; between 1964 and 1970 it had achieved the seemingly impossible by becoming even more complex. What was much more serious was the fact that, despite Government claims to the contrary, the tax structure was even more inequitable, and its impact upon the moderately well-off – those with an income of £1,000 or so – was in fact greater than it was upon the over-£3,000 group. These facts looked somewhat bleak in the face of the 1966 Labour claim that the standard of living would rise by 25 per cent between 1966 and 1971.

So far as welfare benefits were concerned, the Labour obsession against selective welfare benefits meant that although there had been substantial additional expenditure there was only a minimal impact on the really needy. The figures produced by the Child Poverty Action Group early in 1970 demonstrated this fact with particular vividness. And there is solid foundation for the charge that 'the failure to advance, or even maintain, the differential between the low-paid and pensioners on the one hand and the average wage earners on the other is a real increase in inequality which becomes more apparent as wages spiral, and a serious indictment of the Government'.[1] By 1970 some five million people were living below the supplementary benefits level; in other words they met the Government's own definition of poverty. Given the choice between helping the poor and maintaining the existing social order a book published just before the Election commented, 'the Labour Party in office has chosen, at every turn of policy, those measures which upheld the received status quo.'[2]

This very valid judgement could be applied across the board of Labour Government activity. It was, to the end, a cautious, conservative, tentative Government, deeply suspicious of truly radical departures.

The other glaring failure was in housing. The bold objective of 500,000 houses a year looked somewhat grandiose in comparison with the actual record; the most new houses built in one year was 413,715 in 1968, and in all other years – with the exception of 1967 – the total was well below 400,000. The death-bed repentance during the 1970 Election campaign, when the new Minister (Mr Robert Mellish) promised to 'turn the

[1] *The Economist*, 30 May 1970.
[2] K. Coates and R. Silburn: *Poverty: the Forgotten Englishman* (London, 1970).

whole housing policy of this country right on its head', to 'lead a campaign for a genuine property-owning democracy', and to enable council house tenants to buy their own houses (a promise which had to be quickly toned down) emphasized the failure of the housing drive under Labour. The comment of Des Wilson, the courageous and persistent advocate of the poor and the homeless, may be recalled: 'If words were houses, every Englishman would be living in a castle'.

Unemployment, which by 1970 had reached the highest level since 1940, told its own story, and in its desperate attempts to reduce it the Government abandoned the original purpose of the Industrial Reorganization Corporation, which inexorably became, in the words of one commentator, 'an almoner for the halt and the lame'.[1] The surge towards technological leadership and the elimination of what Wilson had repeatedly derided as obsolete 'candy-floss' or 'soft centre' industries thus culminated in a series of lavish propping-up operations for manifestly decaying and inefficient industries. And, all the time, the unemployment figures rose. This was the real price paid for the economic improvisations of 1965–8. It was described by Wilson as 'redeployment', and was an admitted consequence of the Government's measures.

But the full impact on the electorate of this record was greatly reduced towards the end of 1969 by what was in effect the total abandonment of attempts to keep wage increases under control. The comment of the *Guardian* (28 May 1970) that 'the minimal rise in the standard of living under Labour since 1964 is probably the most formidable obstacle in the way of their re-election' was to the point, but the breaking of the wages 'dam' at the end of 1969 seemed to have greatly reduced this factor. In five years there had been a general increase in prices of nearly 30 per cent, without comparable corresponding rises in wages; the rectification of that situation, whatever the long-term consequences, combined with the handsome balance of payments surplus, cast a screen over what had happened before. Or, at least, that was what the Government hoped.

Labour was quite justified in pointing to its record on the social services. The proportion of GNP spent on education, to take a particularly impressive example, rose from 4 per cent

---

[1] Peter Wilsher, the *Sunday Times*, 24 May 1970.

in 1964 to 6 per cent in 1969; old age pensions for a married couple rose from £5. 9s. 0d. to £8. 2s. 0d. per week, and the restrictions previously imposed on earnings were removed, a fact which in itself made increases in real income considerably more substantial in many cases; family allowances for a family with three children rose from 18 shillings to 38 shillings a week; supplementary benefits (the new version of National Assistance) rose very considerably (for a man with a wife and two children between five and ten years it went up from £7. 10s. 6d. to £11. 3s. 0d. per week, with a further increase of 19 shillings due in November 1970).

But, as has already been emphasized, the trouble was that the dramatic increases in prices and wages, particularly in 1969-70, very considerably covered these increases and in reality put the poor back where they had been in 1964. People living on low fixed incomes were particularly hard hit by the inflationary process. The Government, in short, was in a classic cyclical process. Increase in benefits meant increases in taxation, which had their own inflationary effect which in turn necessitated further increases in benefits. So far as the social services was concerned it was a question of running hard in order to maintain even existing standards.

Labour had come into office in 1964 with a determination to extricate the country from the 'stop-go-stop' lurches of the post-war economy. It was immediately faced with a serious crisis for which it had a partial responsibility and from which it never really recovered. The fundamental Labour obsession with the distribution of wealth rather than its acquisition played its part, but the real deficiency had been one of prior planning. 'Pragmatism' degenerated into a series of expedients which, by the summer of 1966, emphasized the total lack of a real strategy to meet the fundamental problems of the British economy. Wilson's own invincible optimism was a source of much strength, but it was often held in the face of facts that gave no cause for optimism whatever. It can be argued that the inherent defects in the British economy of obsolete techniques, inefficient management, Trade Unions, and low productivity were insoluble by one government, and that a price would eventually have had to be paid for these weaknesses. But it is difficult to absolve the Labour Government from its responsibility.

The Election, therefore, would be fought by Labour on two fronts. In the first place, it would vigorously allege that, despite massive difficulties, it had solved the economic crisis, that the way was now open for the fulfilment of the 1966 promises which had hitherto not been possible. In the second, it would charge that the Conservatives would imperil the future of social reform by using this financial advantage selfishly and narrowly. And, if Heath chose to make the Election a personal contest between himself and Wilson, Labour had no objection.

Part Two

THE CONSERVATIVES – THE LEADER AND HIS TASK

THE Conservative Party in Opposition resembles some unhappy creature of the deep that has been suddenly and
tragically removed from its natural environment and is thrashing around desperately in its bewildered anguish. The observer
of this confusing spectacle has considerable difficulty in his
attempt to chronicle and analyse it with reasonable precision.
Even at the best of times the Conservative Party is not a simple
confederation to portray with accuracy and fairness, and the
period of 1964–70 was not the best of times.

The 1950s had been for the Conservatives a decade of success
and ever-increasing confidence – a confidence which had survived Suez and the gradual recognition of the changed position
of Britain in the world. The Party had recovered completely
from the defeat of 1945, and forced their opponents back to the
position that the future of the Labour and Liberal Parties was,
by 1960, a matter of serious conjecture.[1] But by 1966 this serene
and contentful situation had been shattered, and the Conservative Party was once again presented with the task of
beginning yet another revival.

A modern British political party is a perplexing, complex
human federation. It is concerned with its own identity and
history, claims and distinguished lineage, and believes that
history has a satisfying completeness, and an ordered, honourable development; this is a claim which less committed
observers may view with scepticism, yet is central to that
feeling of family which binds the Party together. It is not
possible to categorize precisely why most people join one party
or another, why some change their allegiances, or why others
drift away. 'Few of us,' as Nigel Nicolson has written, 'could
say that we joined our party after prolonged self-examination.

[1] As one indication of this changed mood, it is significant to compare Lord
Hailsham's *The Conservative Case*, published in 1959, with his pamphlet *The Case
for Conservatism*, which had been published in the dark days of 1947.

We usually joined because our friends joined, or because there was a long family tradition, or because social circumstances steered us naturally in that direction. Having joined, we are reluctant to change, and we spend the rest of our lives explaining to ourselves and each other why we could never have done anything else.'[1]

The modern Conservative Party is a national coalition party, and contains numerous and substantial diversities created by geography, tradition, and local circumstances. But although it is perilous to regard 'the Conservative Party' as a single entity the cohesion of this remarkable national coalition over the past century emphasizes that it possesses and retains its basic unities. The Conservatives have held together firmly and successfully for so long, and in social circumstances which would appear to have moved so firmly against them, that it stands on its own record as the most durable, formidable, and resilient political confederation in British political history. The obsequies of the Conservative Party have been delivered on many occasions, only to be rudely confounded by its vigorous refusal to die. For the Conservatives, like Mr Gladstone, are terrible on the rebound.

It can be argued that Peel was the originator of the modern Conservative coalition in the 1830s, but the case for Disraeli seems somewhat stronger. In particular, the struggle within the Conservative Party over the passage of the 1867 Reform Act was a key incident. The Conservatives do not exist for obscure or ideological reasons. They accept that change is inevitable, and believe that it should be done by themselves, on their own terms, and in their own good time, and based upon the improvement of existing institutions rather than by the creation of new ones. They are suspicious of doctrines, of excessive enthusiasms, of intellectual cleverness, and disturbing innovations; they have survived because these views are not confined to any single section of the British people, nor to any single geographical area.

The fundamental fact of political life for the Conservatives is that they depend for their survival upon the establishment and retention of this national appeal. In 1965, over 70 per cent of family incomes in England and Wales were under £1,000 per annum, and the Conservatives of necessity have to secure

[1] Nigel Nicolson: *People and Parliament* (London, 1958), pp. 29–30.

substantial support from such households. It is an all-class national party because there is no alternative. This was the message taught by Disraeli, Lord Randolph Churchill, Baldwin, Butler, and Macmillan. If the Conservatives forfeited this national appeal and national support they would be finished. Conversely, if Labour established itself firmly in the working-class and lower middle-class vote it would be in office for ever. Thus Labour can afford to be a sectional party, and there are those members of the Party who would wish it to be nothing more than that; the Conservatives cannot be. Thus, the portrayal of the Conservative Party as an upper middle-class grouping, dependent for its support and votes from that grouping, is false. A glance, however cursory, at the results of British General Elections in the twentieth century makes the point at once.

The Conservative Party is a very English party, with a sense of national continuity and purpose and with the Englishman's scepticism of panaceas, millennia, and ideology. It is significant that it has rarely made any serious permanent inroads into Scotland and Wales, and that the Irish vote in Britain is overwhelmingly Labour. In some industrial areas in England, where the Conservatives are historically identified with harsh employers, narrow-minded local authorities, and rack-rent property profiteers, they are deeply hated. But the 'Tory working man' is not a mythical creature. He constitutes – if only numerically – a major part of the Conservative national coalition which, despite the need for regular re-establishment and reform, has successfully survived a vast social revolution and two World Wars. As Dr Butler and Dr Stokes have noted: 'The attention paid to the working class Conservative is largely due to one grand historical paradox; the first major nation of the world to become industrialized, a nation in which 70 per cent of the people regard themselves as working class, has regularly returned Conservative Governments to power.'[1] This phenomenon would indeed be remarkable were it not for the fact that the Conservatives have actively realized since the 1860s that their expectations of power have relied very heavily upon winning and keeping working-class votes. Baldwin's emphatic dictum that 'the Conservative Party must recruit from the

[1] Butler and Stokes: *Political Change in Britain*, p. 105.

Left' has not always been agreeable to the Conservatives, but it has been accepted – if reluctantly by many – as a fundamental truism. In the post-war years this was principally achieved by the Conservatives presenting themselves as the party that actually achieved positive results, and in this connection the attention to housing in the 1951–9 period was a major factor.

One of the dilemmas facing the Conservatives in the 1960s was whether this widespread support was not beginning to crumble. Dr Butler and Dr Stokes have emphasized one feature of Labour's position which merits attention. This may be described as the 'cohort' interpretation of political loyalties, whereby the development of attachment to a party is carried on to children, with the consequence that its base of popular support steadily widens. 'Given the extent to which party loyalties are transmitted in the childhood home,' they write, 'time was needed for historic attachment to the "bourgeois" parties to weaken and for "secondary" processes to complete the realignment by class.'[1]

At first glance this interpretation is logical, and is strongly backed by the statistical evidence produced by the authors in their researches. The weakness lies in the fundamental hypothesis, which over-rates the importance of class in party identification and assumes a high degree of political commitment in the home which is communicated to children and fashions their political behaviour. The 1959 General Election in particular stands in opposition to the 'cohort' theory; indeed, the overwhelming conclusion from 1959 was that there had been a very substantial and deliberate movement to the Conservatives by working-class people who considered that they had risen in the world and no longer had an identification with Labour. Furthermore the very volatility of the British electorate in the 1960s, which all studies emphasize, also argues against the 'cohort' theory as a major factor in practical politics. The conclusion to the 'cohort' theory is a remorseless reduction in the numbers of working-class Conservatives and the establishment of a permanent Labour-orientated working-class vote. The revival of Labour after 1959 necessarily aroused concern in the Conservative Party that there might be something in

[1] Butler and Stokes: *op. cit.*, p. 107.

90

this. If there was, the prospects for the Party were bleak indeed.

The question of why this had not happened before the 1960s is a complex one. Some observers have concluded that an important element in the Conservative survival has been 'deferentialism', a reminder of a fundamental respect for a ruling – or at least an officer – class. In some areas, particularly in some English counties, this is probably very true, and there are certainly villages and towns in the north known to this commentator where the Conservative faith is so profound that it is accepted almost without question as an unchangeable, and unchanging, fact. Although deferentialism may not be a factor of any real magnitude in other areas, and particularly among voters under thirty, one occasionally does wonder about even those areas – those, that is, that have not intense and bitter memories of industrial cruelty which are laid at the door of the Conservative Party. Without exaggerating the importance of this element in the Conservative survival, it would be unwise to dismiss the factor of deferentialism too lightly. But was it now in decline?

It could be argued though, that a more powerful element lies in the ambivalence in the Labour Party about office, and a continuing public suspicion of Labour as a governing party. As has been emphasized in the preceding chapter, the elimination of this suspicion was Wilson's principal task in 1964–6. His success was ominous for the Conservative appeal, but the events of 1966–70 inevitably revived doubts which were not confined to any class or sector of the community.

Elaborate studies have been made of the kind of people who vote Conservative, who work for the Conservative Party, and who are active Conservative politicians. No study, however elaborate, can hope to be comprehensive, and none so far has provided the clue to the question of why the Conservatives have survived, and in such strength, and particularly in the turbulent and difficult post-war situation. The argument that the Party represents a comforting refuge from uncomfortable radical alternatives is hardly sufficient. The claim that it survives as a consequence of the ineptitude of its opponents is difficult to sustain as a single factor when the calibre and achievements of the Liberal Government of 1906–14 or the Labour Government of 1945–51 are examined. Its efficient organization should be seen as a result, rather than as a cause, of its basic strength. And its much-vaunted wealth becomes, on close examination, considerably less impressive and significant.[1]

The answer to the question lies in a multitude of factors, but of which the most significant is the thrust towards power that runs throughout the Party, and – which is inseparably linked with the first factor – a readiness to change course. The Conservative Party survives, in essence, because it is a remarkably flexible and sensitive federation. Its opponents may deride its structures as undemocratic, but in essence the Conservatives are very democratic in the crucial sense that they are keenly aware of popular trends, desires, and movements, knowing that if they were to stand still they would perish.

In short, the modern Conservative Party is dedicated to the proposition that, as change is inevitable, that change should be undertaken by itself. Although this coalition has changed a great deal over the past century, it remains in essentials remarkably close to that which was created by Disraeli in the 1860s, and which was consolidated over the last thirty years of the nineteenth century. 'The Tory Party, unless it is a national party, is nothing,' Disraeli had declared. 'It is not a confederacy of nobles, it is not a democratic multitude; it is a party formed from all the numerous classes in the realm – classes alike and equal before the law, but whose different conditions and different aims give vigour and variety to our national life.' Accordingly, the *raison d'être* of the Conservative Party must be office, for as Disraeli emphasized in his duels with the fiery Lord Cranborne in the 1860s, abstract principles are all very well, but power is vital.

The Conservative coalition has faltered only when the Conservatives became obsessed by points of ideology – as, for example, over Tariff Reform in 1903–11 – or when they were

---

[1] This was particularly the case in 1964–66, when expenditure was exceeding income at a rate of about £300,000 per annum, with reserves of less than £1 million. The immediate crisis was solved by drastic economies and by the appeal launched by Lord Carrington. It is doubtful whether the requirements – introduced by the Labour Government – for firms publicly to disclose contributions to Party funds had any substantial impact on this aspect of Conservative resources, but it certainly forced the Party towards a more positive and widespread drive for funds. The Labour Party, with its Union resources and the Political Levy, was in fact in a much better overall situation in this period. Its failure to make use of that position in the form of more efficient organization was another factor, not directly related to the overall financial situation of the two parties.

dominated by men whose interests were sectional and whose outlook was narrow. Principally as a consequence of Joseph Chamberlain, the coalition disintegrated between 1903 and 1914, and had to be laboriously revived by Baldwin in the 1920s. It collapsed in the Second World War, and had subsequently to be revived by the strange but powerful combination of Lord Woolton and R. A. Butler – two men whose outlooks were wholly different on most matters, and whose personal relationships fell something short of amicable, but whose collective contribution was invaluable. It was one of the supreme ironies of Churchill's remarkable, uneven, and many-faceted career that, over the last ten years, he perforce presided over the careful re-creation of the pre-war Baldwinite coalition. The task was, in Butler's words, 'to convince a broad spectrum of the electorate, whose minds were scarred by inter-war memories and myths, that we had an alternative policy to Socialism which was viable, efficient and humane, which would release and reward enterprise and initiative but without abandoning social justice or reverting to mass unemployment'.[1]

By 1950 the essential work had been done, and the coalition triumphed throughout the 1950s. By the early 1960s, however, it came under pressure once again from its revivified opponents and from within the Conservative Party. In particular, many Conservatives began to wonder where the differences between Labour and themselves lay, and in the euphoria after the overwhelming 1959 victory there was a general assumption that the Party could afford itself the luxury of ideological introspection. Reaction against what was depicted as 'Butskellism' grew; the creation of the Monday Club in 1961 was a significant portent;[2] the phrase 'consensus politics' began to fall into disrepute. A new obsession with ideology arose, and the party's sympathy with the heros of the 1950s – Macmillan, Butler, Maudling, and Macleod – faded. This new temper in the constituencies was reflected in the men and women being selected as Parliamentary candidates, particularly in safe seats. There was therefore a real danger by the 1960s that, in this new obsession with ideology and a demand for a clear-cut exposition of Conservative principles, the importance of the preservation of the all-class national coalition might take a secondary place.

[1] Lord Butler: *The Art of the Possible* (1971), p. 132.
[2] See pp. 199–208 below.

The factor that gave this movement such force was the fact that the policies and philosophy which had been so attractive and successful in the early 1950s were proving much less satisfactory in the context of the early 1960s. The leadership was itself looking tired, and the intellectual momentum was evidently faltering. Labour, prematurely written off by many Conservatives in 1959, was reviving itself vigorously, and, first under Gaitskell and then under Wilson, was attempting to create an equivalent of the national coalition that the Conservatives had built, but which was now eroding.

In part, this decline was caused by factors beyond the Conservative Government's control. It is now somewhat difficult to recall the confidence and optimism with which the British faced the 1960s. After the strains of war, and the frustrations and privations of the immediate post-war period, the 1950s had been a decade of remarkable economic improvement, bringing with it the impression of an arrival into the sunlight after a long, dark journey. On virtually every count, Britain was a happier, richer, more efficient and contented nation in 1960 than she had been for more than twenty years. The Conservatives, not altogether unfairly, were the political beneficiaries of this restored confidence and prosperity. But it was their inability to maintain the advance of the 1950s that created the initial check to their public support in 1961, and not only provided Labour with its opportunity for repairing its ravaged reputation but also for the Government's critics within the Conservative Party.

This sudden slump in the national self-confidence was a startling phenomenon, and it is difficult to determine whether it was not at least in part induced by a series of books and articles which emphasized the deficiencies of British society. As Professor Medlicott has commented, 'The "state of England" question was discussed more generally with remarkable thoroughness and gloom by a wide range of writers at this time.'[1] It could be argued that this emphasis on failure, error, and misfortune was a very necessary antidote to the excessive self-satisfaction of the late 1950s; what is less controversial is the fact that the Conservatives were, politically, damaged by this movement, and that their own self-confidence was affected. At a critical moment it appeared that the party leadership had

[1] W. N. Medlicott: *Contemporary England, 1914-64* (London, 1967), p. 582.

itself lost its nerve. Macmillan's abrupt dismissal of seven Cabinet Ministers in July 1962 hardly improved matters, and the handling of certain episodes – notably the Vassall and Profumo cases in 1962 and 1963 – were significant less in themselves than as being symptomatic of this new unsureness. The fact that Macmillan was succeeded by Sir Alec Douglas-Home in October 1963 was indicative less of an Establishment conspiracy than of the changed mood of the Conservative Party as a whole. Home was a popular choice in the Parliamentary Party and outside. No single event could have demonstrated more forcefully what had happened to the Conservatives since 1959.

The real problem was that the Conservatives' strongest appeal – their superior capacities as a governing party – was fading. If the Conservative Party has regarded itself since the 1860s as the natural governing party of Britain, a quick examination of its record emphasizes why this is so. In the period 1868–1964 the Conservative Party was in office (including the wartime coalition) for sixty-two years. In the present century, up to 1964, it had been in office for forty-six years. Until 1964, furthermore, it had not lost in this century a General Election in what might be described as reasonably normal peacetime conditions since June 1929 – and even in 1929 it secured a substantially larger proportion of the national vote than the victorious Labour Party. And in 1964 it was to lose only by a fraction.

Nonetheless, by the early 1960s the Conservatives were becoming acutely aware of the uneasiness of their position. Here, the 'steering' of the economy was the critical element, and it is clear that the Conservative superiority first began to falter in 1961 with heavy criticism of the manner in which the Government in general, and Mr Selwyn Lloyd in particular, were undertaking this task. As soon as doubts about the Conservatives' basic competence as a governing party were established – and exploited by their opponents – the principal ingredient in the cement of the national all-class coalition was compromised.

It can be argued that this mounting criticism and disillusionment was excessive and unfair. But it undoubtedly existed. Partly, the long years of power had created a situation in which rising national expectations exceeded their possible provision; but there was also a more difficult, and more general, disquiet at the spectacle of political and social issues being interpreted solely in economic and materialist terms. Macmillan had been aware of this feeling, and his attempt to join the European Economic Community in 1961 had been considerably motivated by his conviction that the nation urgently needed new challenges and frontiers, and to adopt a new outlook. He was also convinced that these should be provided by the Conservative Party. When the attempt failed the Conservatives found themselves, as one observer has remarked, 'crusaders without a cause'.[1] Their subsequent disarray emphasized the extent to which they had lost their way. In essence, the Conservatives' task was now to provide an amended philosophy of government that was not wholly preoccupied with material benefits and which was in contrast with its own performance and priorities in the 1950s and what Labour had to offer. This was never achieved. In a letter to his constituents in June 1962, Reginald Maudling posed the problem, albeit somewhat opaquely:

The Conservative Party will regain its supremacy if, and only if, it can find the answer to the real needs of the 1960s. They are not the needs of a country haunted by Jarrow and the Rhondda, nor any longer the needs solely of a country breaking away from the austerity of war and the meshes of socialism. They are the needs of a people conscious of the greatness of their past, enjoying the affluence and freedom of the present, but feeling in their hearts the lack of a sense of the purpose of this freedom and affluence.

This did not, however, really meet the point of what 'the needs of the 1960s' really were. This criticism applied to the purely economic issues. There might be a high general level of prosperity, but it was far from universal, and although there were unquestionably problems stemming from rising and unfulfilled expectations in some areas, in others they emanated from the absence of all real expectations. The real point of Maudling's letter was to reflect concern at a general feeling of lack of purpose in the nation, which seemed to be passing through a

---

[1] Pierre Uri (ed.): *From Commonwealth to Common Market*, p. 52.

period of loss of confidence and sense of identity, a feeling that was to prompt Mr Quintin Hogg[1] to declare: 'Can anyone doubt . . . that we are a people that has lost its way?' Perhaps it is not to be wondered at, given the traumas that Britain had passed through since 1939, and whose psychological consequences were difficult to identify, but which were clearly profound. Britain seemed to be in a phase of nervous introspection, and the overwhelmingly practical theme of the Conservatives' 1966 Manifesto ('Our first aim is this: to run this country's affairs efficiently and realistically so that we achieve steadier prices in the shops, high wages, and a really decent standard of social security') did not seem to offer much in the form of imaginative leadership. The tone of the Labour Manifesto was more vigorous: 'The motive and inspiration of Labour remain, and always will remain, to secure the prosperity and welfare of all the people – the workers by hand and by brain who must be the backbone of our economic recovery, the old, the sick and the children.' And there was considerably more excitement in the Labour claim that, 'Since we took office we have started on the long process of modernizing obsolete procedures and institutions, ending the dominance of vested interests, liberating the forces of youth, and building a New Britain.' Building a New Britain! In contrast, the Conservatives solemnly promised 'to break away from the growing constraint of Socialism and the dreariness which stems from it: from the pattern of inflation and stagnant production which has been created'. Maudling had been right in his general diagnosis, even if he had produced no answer. By the early 1960s the era of austerity had passed, but it had not been replaced by a mood of grateful complacency. The erosion of confidence in the Conservatives' competence at government, the seizure by Labour of the most powerful of the Party's appeals, and the failure of the Conservatives to match the attractiveness of

---

[1] Mr Hogg succeeded his father as Viscount Hailsham in 1950, having previously been Conservative MP for Oxford since 1938. In November 1963 he disclaimed his peerage under the provisions of the recently enacted Peerage Act (under which the Earl of Home also disclaimed). Lord Hailsham, who had been a member of the Government since 1956, accordingly became Mr Hogg again; he was elected for St Marylebone in December 1963. In June 1970 Mr Hogg became Lord Chancellor, received a Life Peerage, and became Lord Hailsham once again. It is to be hoped that future historians will be able to differentiate between Mr Quintin Hogg (1907–50), Lord Hailsham (1950–63), Mr Quintin Hogg (1963–70), and Lord Hailsham (1970–).

Labour's new appearance presented new and complex challenges to the Conservative Party.

Remarkably, the Conservatives had emerged from the defeat of 1966 in considerably better heart than might have been expected of a party that is so dedicated to office and which feels such a gloomy deprivation in Opposition. But there was in the Party a general recognition of the fact that the electorate had taken Labour's achievements since 1964 at their face value and had resolved to give the Government a more substantial majority. Very few Conservatives had seriously believed that they would win in 1966, and most accepted that they were waging a containing battle against a strong tide. To go into an Election in such a mood might be described as defeatist; in fact, it was cool realism. The Party leadership realized that its principal task was to build the foundations for next time, to use the publicity of the Election to establish the new message and the new leader, and to fight hard to keep the Labour majority down to a reasonable size. In the main, they succeeded in these objectives.

It has been stated that 'one of the supreme ironies of the 1966 election was the final emphasis of the Conservative leader on the need for radical change and of the leader of the Labour party on the need for patriotism and stability'.[1] The 'irony' lay only in a somewhat traditionalist concept of the two parties, and certainly did not take into account the personality of Edward Heath. It was true that there were Conservatives who considered that it had been unwise to seek a radical and progressive image but this emotion was very much a minority one. There was a general feeling abroad in the Party in 1966 that it had fought a good fight and knew where it was going in the future, whereas Labour, although victorious, had given no real thought for the morrow. 'No-one likes to lose,' Sir Michael Fraser subsequently remarked. 'But at least, in losing, we said the right things, we forced Labour on to a number of hooks which were to prove extremely embarrassing to them in the years ahead, and we went a long way towards establishing our

[1] Butler and King: *The British General Election of 1966*, p. 124.

credibility for the next battle.'[1] It was, therefore, with an intense and mordant satisfaction that the Conservatives beheld the triumphant Labour Government so swiftly in the toils.

The Conservative task in 1964–6 had been to establish a programme of priorities. Heath had taken charge of policy preparation after the 1964 defeat, and the results of his establishment of a number of specialist bodies – which included some industrialists, businessmen, and academics, who were permitted to remain anonymous – were seen in *Putting Britain Right Ahead*, published in 1965. The significance of this document is discussed later in this chapter, but the problem of the Party was two-fold. In the first place, it had to operate against a record in office that was under sharp attack, and against a Government that was apparently disproving the classic Conservative thesis that it alone possessed the secret of the art of government. Then, it had very little time at its disposal. The 1964–5 exercise was, accordingly, a very rushed operation, and the change of the Party leadership in July 1965 was an additional complication.

In the immediate aftermath of the 1966 Election there was only limited discernible criticism of Heath personally. He had campaigned with spirit, and his final television broadcast and his press conference after the result were particularly praised. There was a general recognition that circumstances had been thoroughly against him, as they had been against Attlee in 1955 and Hugh Gaitskell in 1959, and that he had done well enough. But although the criticisms were muted, they were there. In part, they were the result of the bitterness still felt in some quarters about the treatment of Sir Alec Douglas-Home only a few months before, and of the fact that Heath's Parliamentary disappointment as a challenger to Wilson was now matched by a failure in a larger arena. The failure was, of course, not personal but collective, but already there were those Conservatives who were not indisposed to place a disproportionate amount of the blame on their new leader. These criticisms, to use a celebrated phrase of J. L. Garvin's in a very different context, 'aroused fungoid growths in the shade'. Nonetheless, the Party was not afflicted with the same sense of shock that it had experienced in 1945. Heath himself, although regretful at the size of the

[1] Speech to the International Association of Political Consultants, London, 15 December 1970.

Labour majority, determined to lose no time in laments or recriminations. A detailed study of the lessons of the Election was ordered and put in hand, but the real lesson was already evident to the leader. Despite the shortage of time available, the Party had been set on the right course, and the major work had been done. As Fraser has said: 'Much of what we did in the following four years was really no more than a continuation and development of what was done then [in 1965].' The policy groups set up by Heath were expanded, until nearly 400 individuals were involved in their work, of whom about half were MPs. It was now necessary to keep on that course and to work to ensure that the electorate would gradually appreciate its virtues. In addition, Heath fully shared his Party's confidence that the fundamental shallowness of Labour's philosophy and the lack of competence of most of its leaders would be swiftly revealed. In assessing the cause of the remarkable degree of confidence and even cheerfulness felt by the Conservatives in April 1966, the feeling that Nemesis would surely overtake Labour should not be omitted. But what if this assumption proved to be false? Where would the Conservatives be then?

The Conservative leader was himself something of an enigma to his Party. He was the first leader of the Party who had been elected in a ballot by Conservative Members of Parliament, and eventually a man of substantial qualities with an excellent record. Yet, to the Party at large, he still seemed vaguely alien, one of them yet not one of them.

Heath had been a Conservative from a very early age, and none of his contemporaries could surpass his record of devoted service to the Cause, which had made him a familiar figure at local meetings throughout the country. But, although the dignitaries and the rank and file were very grateful, and their gratitude had been one of the major factors in his election to the leadership in 1965, the relationship was not in 1966 altogether a very comfortable one. It was something which the observer could not identify precisely but he could note a certain lack of warmth, of enthusiasm, and of awe which his predecessors had achieved. As has already been mentioned, he was the first leader elected since Bonar Law who was not, or had not been, Prime Minister, and it is not inappropriate to recall an estimate of Law written by one of his colleagues in 1911:

Bonar Law is a curious mixture. Never very gay . . . still he has a great sense of humour – a first-class debater – and a good, though not a rousing, platform speaker – a great master of figures which he can use to great advantage. He has all the qualities of a great leader except one – and that is he has no personal magnetism and can inspire no man to real enthusiasm.[1]

Heath was an unusual Conservative in other ways. He was born at Broadstairs, Kent, on 9 July 1916, the first child of a carpenter, and the grandson of a dairyman, who was subsequently a railway porter. Heath's mother had been a lady's maid. The family background was working-class, and the Heaths were industrious and respected. Heath's education was self-made. He went to Chatham House, a grammar school at Ramsgate, at the age of ten; his academic record was good, without being regarded as outstanding, and his major distinction was in music; but he succeeded in reaching Balliol College, Oxford, where he subsequently won the organ scholarship. His interest in politics now developed, to the point when he described his future career to the admissions tutor as 'professional politician'. He set out to transform the University Conservative Association, and to become President of the Union; in both ambitions he succeeded. He went to Spain in the Civil War on a student deputation, and returned a convinced supporter of the Republican side. He was a vigorous opponent of the Chamberlain Government, and campaigned actively against Quintin Hogg in the post-Munich Oxford by-election. 'Grave, courteous, perfectly agreeable, not sparkling, successful, old for his years,' a Balliol contemporary, Roy Jenkins, has described him.[2] Another contemporary was struck by Heath's sternness of outlook, which he has described to this commentator as 'bordering on priggishness'. His academic record could not be compared to that of a Hogg, a Wilson, or an Enoch Powell, but one has the impression that he got rather more out of Oxford than many considerably more able undergraduates have done.

When war broke out Heath joined the Army, and served with distinction in the Royal Artillery throughout the War; his service included the advance from D-Day into Germany, and he ended a lieutenant-colonel. He determined to enter politics,

[1] Harold Nicholson: *King George V* (London, 1963), p. 165.
[2] George Hutchinson: *Edward Heath: A Personal and Political Biography*, p. 33.

and after a spell as a civil servant in the Ministry of Civil Aviation and a curious interlude working for the *Church Times*, he entered Parliament in the 1950 General Election as Conservative Member for Bexley, having won a difficult marginal seat by a majority of 133.

These are, of course, only the outlines. Heath had risen so far and so quickly principally as a result of a calm determination and self-control, coupled with a meticulous attention to detail. He was a thoroughly nice man, with no apparent social or class preoccupations, somewhat solitary but with good friends, keen to learn but already with a mind of his own. His love of music, and his enjoyment in making others love it also, was a warming characteristic. Although manifestly ambitious and serious, Heath does not appear to have given any of his contemporaries an impression of coldness or calculation. He was a Conservative from an early age, a fact which is remarkable only to those who are obsessed by class as the only factor in the development of political affiliations. But Heath did not drift into Conservatism; it was a positive decision, and the result of an ever-growing conviction in the virtues of an ordered society with opportunity for those who are prepared, like him, to work and rise. He was a Conservative as a schoolboy, and was confirmed in his political faith at Oxford. He was a devout admirer of Churchill in the late 1930s at a time when such were few indeed. Although able, he was modest, and in human relationships affectionate. Some of his contemporaries have subsequently claimed that they detected in him great qualities as a young man; most have admitted that they saw him as an agreeable man of above-average ability, but without any special features. 'He seemed to me,' one Oxford contemporary has remarked to this commentator, 'the sort of man who would disappear from one's life, to reappear many years later as managing director of a large firm, or bank, or head of a civil service department. I knew of his keen interest in politics, but I confess that it never occurred to me that I would awake one morning to learn that he was Leader of the Conservative Party.'

The fact that Heath was a puzzle to the Conservative Party was not wholly surprising. He is not a man who seeks public affection or popularity, and he is often notoriously deficient in the minor charlatanries. It is not surprising to find that his former headmaster commented on him that 'he was anything but popular. He never tried for popularity. He wasn't actively liked or actively disliked. He was respected and accepted.'[1] In public he often epitomized the highly descriptive American adjective 'uptight', approaching his audiences with a wariness and tenseness which sometimes communicated itself tangibly, and which can create an uncomfortable atmosphere of shared unease. In private, in a small and congenial company, he was warm, confident, and civilized. He was also genuinely kind and considerate. It is, unhappily, the case that relatively few politicians improve on closer acquaintance. In this respect, as in so many others, Heath was an exception to the general rule.

It would be easy to depict Heath's rise as though there were something incredible in the fact that a man of such genuinely humble origins should become Leader of the Conservative Party. It is, of course, remarkable, but what is much more interesting is the *manner* in which he rose.

Perhaps the two greatest disasters that can befall an able new Member of Parliament are to join the Whips' Office or to become a Parliamentary Private Secretary. There are many compensations, but the long-term disadvantages far outweigh them. The most serious is that the young politician escapes the frustrating but essential period of apprenticeship, when he is endeavouring to discover how to interest and impress the House of Commons, and thereby to establish himself as an identifiable individual among six hundred and thirty. It is not a particularly enjoyable period of a political career, but it is an essential one; the relatively late rise of Baldwin and Macmillan — to take two conspicuous examples — owed a great deal to their long periods of learning what Sir Alan Herbert has happily described as 'the black arts of debate'.

After a maiden speech in which he urged British entry into the Schumann Plan, Heath disappeared almost immediately into the Whips' Office for seven years. When he answered his first Parliamentary question as Minister of Labour in 1959 he broke a House of Commons silence that had been interrupted only by the formal moving of Parliamentary writs, motions for the adjournment, and the closure. The spoken word is the politician's most crucial weapon. Heath's eight years' silence in the Commons played a significant part in his failure to develop his own style.

[1] Hutchinson: *op. cit.*, p. 14.

The immediate advantages of his rapid elevation were, of course, very considerable. With the exception of Macleod, promoted straight from the back benches to the Ministry of Health, Heath quickly outstripped his contemporaries who had entered the House of Commons in 1950, and the perception of Mr Patrick Buchan-Hepburn (now Lord Hailes) was spectacularly demonstrated when Heath succeeded him as Chief Whip in 1955 and, almost at once, had to face the trauma of the Suez Crisis.

One of his former colleagues does not exaggerate when he says that 'the Party would almost certainly have fallen apart without him' during Suez. His most remarkable achievement was to gain and retain the admiration and respect of those Conservatives who were most distressed by the Government's actions. He himself had strong doubts about the policy, but he saw it as his duty to hold the Party together. To achieve this demanded very considerable qualities of insight and timing. He demonstrated that he was not only tough, clear-headed, and well-informed – by then, none doubted that he possessed these qualities – but that he had a sensitiveness and a comprehension that had not been so widely appreciated. It was characteristic of Heath that he went to very considerable trouble to help those Conservatives who found themselves in serious trouble with their local associations, because of their opposition to, or lack of enthusiasm for, the Suez policy. Much of this work was done in private; some actions – as his support of Nigel Nicolson in Bournemouth – are known. Most were successful. It is difficult to think of any Chief Whip of modern times acting in this manner towards rebelling MPs. But it was significant that those Conservatives who were hostile to the Government for not pressing on were less sympathetically viewed. What became known as 'the Suez Group' constituted the first organized element in the Conservative Party that viewed Heath with hostility.

Suez did not, by itself, definitely establish Heath's reputation. This was achieved in the aftermath, and in the long, difficult, climb back to the Conservative victory of 1959. Heath was a very professional organizer of the business of the House. He was always approachable; and his understanding of the House and of the Parliamentary Party was acute. He had his personal antipathies, and although he respected sincere divergences from the Party line, he could be harsh on those whose motives did not impress him. His information organization was a very comprehensive exercise in itself, and a vast advance on anything that any Whip's Office had had before. Some Conservatives felt, uncomfortably – and probably with good cause – that he knew rather too much about them. But he was, during this period, a very relaxed and cheerful man, with whom it was a genuine pleasure to do business, and who acquired a reputation for ability, knowledge, and courtesy in his dealings with officials, and particularly with junior officials. These qualities are not as common as they should be in politicians. He was virtually unknown outside Westminster,[1] but in Parliament and Whitehall it was already clear that he was a coming man.

But Heath was always something more than an organizer, and his influence on policy matters during this period was very significant. The crucial importance of his contribution to the Conservative revival of 1957–9 was even more clearly seen when he was succeeded as Chief Whip by a man of many excellent qualities but not of comparable calibre. In particular, the breakdown in communications between the Treasury Bench and the Parliamentary Party between 1960 and 1963, which was one of the principal contributory factors in the destruction of the Macmillan Government, would have been inconceivable with Heath as Chief Whip.

In January 1957, on the evening of Macmillan's accession to the Premiership, Heath had had a celebrated dinner of oysters and champagne with the new Prime Minister – an event that led some commentators to deduce a direct connection between Heath's rôle and Macmillan's (to some) unexpected preference over Butler. There was, in fact, *some* significance. Heath was spiritually and intellectually on the Left of the Conservative Party from the outset of his career, and his connection with Macmillan – which began in the Oxford by-election of 1938, when they campaigned together against Quintin Hogg – was based on personal admiration, an instinctive sympathy for Macmillan's romanticism and courage, and a shared conviction that the Conservative Party must never, ever, return to its lamentable pre-1939 condition. Both saw the Conservative

---

[1] In 1961, when addressing a meeting in the north of England, this commentator picked out Heath as a future Prime Minister. It was evident that the majority of the audience had never heard of him.

Party as the party of ordered change, the party that learned from its mistakes, the party that could only survive politically and morally if it was a truly national party. Macmillan's origins were far from humble, but he had worked for many years for a wretchedly poor constituency, he had seen much that revolted him, and his book, *The Middle Way*, published in 1938, stands as one of the most humane and advanced political documents of its time. Macmillan retained a profound contempt for what he derided as 'the industrials', those 'casino capitalist' Conservatives who sat for comfortable seats in prosperous areas, who lived well, and who constantly lamented the laziness and obscurantism of the working classes – the kind of man who Baldwin once dismissed as he who, after an evening killing the greenfly on his roses with his cigar-end, considered he had done a day's work.

It is now somewhat fashionable to depict Macmillan as a superb but unprincipled actor whose performance eventually collapsed disastrously. There is no need to have illusions about Macmillan to emphasize that this portrait is a grotesque travesty. He was, without doubt, a very shrewd and sharp operator; but even the most cursory glance at this career reveals the courage and sensitivity that lay behind the deliberate façade. He was, furthermore, the best post-war debater in the House of Commons, at his best more than a match for Bevan – his opponent when he was Minister of Housing in 1951–5 – outstandingly better than Butler, Eden, or Gaitskell, and far superior, in this commentator's judgement, to Wilson. It was this combination of sincerity and charlatanry, genuineness and posing, sensitivity and ruthlessness, that makes Macmillan so fascinating a man and made him so formidable a politician.

His extraordinary achievement in the years 1951–6 was to convince the Conservative Right that he was their man, whilst at the same time persuading the newcomers that he was, in fact, more progressive than Butler. It was this devastating combination that left Butler so pitifully isolated in January 1957. Suez was not the cause of Butler's disaster; it was the *coup de grâce*. The charge that Heath somehow engineered Macmillan's succession in January 1957 totally ignores the realities of the then situation in the Conservative Party. No one who was in the House of Commons at that time, or had beheld the Suez debates, could seriously doubt who was the first choice of the Parliamentary Party. How so many observers from the Press Gallery missed all this remains a major mystery. Heath believed that Macmillan would be a better leader of the Party than Butler; it was significant that the Cabinet agreed, with only one exception.

This personal relationship with Macmillan had given Heath a quite exceptional position as Chief Whip, and, after a relatively brief period at the Ministry of Labour, it was logical that Heath should have been Macmillan's choice as the chief negotiator for entry into the Common Market. In this complex episode Heath was in his element – a cause in which he deeply believed, a mass of intricate detail to be mastered, and a highly talented team of colleagues and officials to work with. Europe, and Britain's place in it, has been among the most powerful of the strands running through Heath's career, and his reputation among European politicians, businessmen, and officials was high before the Common Market negotiations. His conduct of those negotiations raised it even higher. This commentator recalls one speech by Heath to the Assembly of Western European Union in Paris in the early 1960s which was ecstatically received. In the House of Commons his self-confidence steadily increased. One private speech, to a sceptical Party audience, was described by a former Cabinet Minister – not over-disposed to bestow praise on others – as the most brilliant and convincing performance he had ever heard in public life. Nonetheless, an ominous note of thinly-veiled intellectual contempt for those in his Party who opposed the application was sometimes clearly apparent in Heath's speeches. He routed them totally in debate, but perhaps too totally for his own good. Many of his critics were, no doubt, ill-informed and obtuse, but they were voicing a sincerely held, if muddled, apprehension that was seeping through the Party at this unexpected and alarming development. For the first time, one was conscious of a substantial hostility developing towards Heath in some quarters of the Conservative Party, based less on the policies he was advocating than on the manner in which he dealt with his critics. Many of them were easy targets for a man of his capacity and application; but there are times in politics when it is wise to deny oneself the gratifications of flattening easy targets, and it was a temptation to which Heath succumbed too often for his own good.

The disappointment to Heath of the de Gaulle veto on British entry into the EEC was severe, and this check was quickly followed by another. The abolition of Resale Price Maintenance, was, no doubt, highly desirable. What was unfortunate and damaging was for Heath to adopt a truculent, and at times abusive, attitude towards those Conservatives who opposed his proposals. It was an internecine battle that was fought with great bitterness, and, although it is generally forgotten today, it left its mark. The feature of Resale Price Maintenance that Heath regarded as particularly odious was the practice of collective enforcement by manufacturers, who would combine to boycott a retailer and refuse him supplies if he sold goods under the retail price established by the manufacturer. Once Heath had become convinced that this must go, he was adamant. A majority in the Cabinet, and a substantial element in the Party, were vehemently opposed to Heath's Bill, and the Chairman and Deputy Chairman of the Party – Lord Blakenham and Lord Poole – shared this hostility. Mr George Hutchinson – then responsible for Party publicity – has related that, 'I have never myself heard a Cabinet Minister so much abused by his colleagues, so badly spoken of and so widely condemned in the party, as Heath was then.'[1] But he secured the crucial support of the Prime Minister; he stood his ground; and he won – if at a heavy cost.

On the face of it, it could be seen as a further development in the process of 'setting the people free'; in fact, it dealt a deadly blow at the small shopkeeper, kept in business by the fact that his wealthier competitors were obligated by law to charge the same prices as he for the same goods. The small shopkeeper occupies a very special place in the Conservative heart. For one thing, he is a staunch Conservative, which is a fact not to be lightly disregarded, particularly when a General Election is imminent. For another, his presence in a town is a comfort in itself, a pleasant reminder that England has not declined to the situation when the giant impersonal conglomerations totally dominate. The small shopkeeper represents Choice and Competition, both basic tenets of the Conservative faith. Thus, it was argued, to threaten his existence was not only politically lamentable, but also carried profound moral and social overtones. The arguments that Heath brought forward

[1] Hutchinson: *op. cit.*, p. 129.

were indeed powerful; why should a handful of great combines dictate to the people what their goods were to cost in the shops? But, to the defenders of the already heavily pressed small shopkeeper, such arguments burked the main question. Heath and his critics never really spoke the same language throughout the dispute, and they increasingly developed a strong mutual antagonism. It was indeed difficult at the time to decide whether to applaud Heath's determination or to lament his obstinacy.

This episode revived, and indeed accentuated, the emotions against Heath in the Conservative Party that had arisen in the Common Market disputes; and in the turmoil that surrounded the sudden resignation of Macmillan and the subesquent accession to the Premiership of Sir Alec Douglas-Home in October 1963 his name was never seriously mentioned. Indeed, so deep had been the wounds inflicted by the Resale Price Maintenance dispute that it was very fortunate for Heath that, by June 1965, his principal rivals for the leadership had effectively eliminated themselves from serious consideration. By this stage, Macleod and Butler were out of the running – the latter having retired to Trinity College, Cambridge – and the choice was reduced to Maudling or Heath. Maudling had formidable support, but some of it had faded in the previous year, and not least because of what was regarded in the Party as his inadequate response to Wilson's charges of the handling of the economy in 1963–4. And there were also some Conservatives who privately shared Wilson's view. Maudling's thrust for the leadership was respectable rather than dynamic, and had an amateurish and half-hearted air, in marked contrast with the approach of Heath's followers.

The full story of Heath's elevation to the Party leadership has not yet been told, and it must remain for a future historian to relate. Briefly, the situation was that a strong and well-organized campaign to oust Home was launched soon after the narrow General Election defeat of October 1964; to quote a sad but valid phrase of the time, 'Alec did not fall, he was *putzsched.*' His critics in the Party had been greatly assisted in their task by the fact that Home had proved an inadequate Leader of the Opposition, his inexperience of the House of Commons now proving a much more serious liability than when he had been Prime Minister. Home had not made matters easier for himself by constantly asking his colleagues and friends for their advice as to whether he ought to resign. It was at this point that Heath startled even his admirers by a sustained performance of outstanding ability in the debates on the Finance Bill, and the pressure on Home was deliberately and systematically increased, until Home had had enough. Heath has always vehemently denied – and Home has always fully accepted his denial – that he was a party to these manoeuvres, which were conducted with considerable skill and ruthlessness. But the fact was that the principal architects of Sir Alec's removal were also those of Heath's subsequent campaign for the leadership left an aftertaste of bitterness in some parts of the Party which took some time to fade, and which took the form of denigration of Heath's capacity and background. This caught Heath on a vulnerable point, and for a time had a real effect on his self-confidence.

In the period when he was aspiring to the leadership Heath had assumed an aggressive personality, even in private, which was new, and which was ascribed by some observers to his advisers, who were busily building up an 'image' of a leader who could take on Wilson at his own game. By this stage it was evident that the Conservatives were looking for a leader who would stand in marked contrast not only to Labour but to the 'consensus' hierachy of the 1950s. Although Home was essentially a stop-gap leader, there was a majority in the Party that was determined not to return to the character of the leadership of the 1950s. This mood was particularly evident among the new men elected in 1959 and in the constituency associations. Maudling epitomized the previous period of Conservative leadership, and it was accordingly necessary for Heath to separate himself sharply from it. Whatever the cause, it was out of character and not attractive. The easy, amusing, and relaxed Chief Whip of the 1950s had been replaced by a taut, nervous, and unnatural creation that was entirely alien to the real man.

It is a contentious point as to whether the personalities of individuals actually alter as a result of circumstances or whether circumstances merely illuminate hitherto unseen qualities or defects. It can certainly be said of Heath that, as soon as he had the Party leadership in his sights, the outward manifestations of his character changed sharply. The subsequent adjectives bestowed upon him – 'abrasive', 'cold', 'calculating', 'ruthless', 'insensitive', 'technocratic', 'harsh', and so on – would have occurred to very few who had known the earlier Heath. His reputation in a limited but influential circle was in fact based upon very difficult evaluations. He was attractive and impressive principally because he was competent and relaxed, efficient and humorous, hard-working, but always with time for his friends and new acquaintances. He was, in every sense of the much-abused adjective, a civilized man whose company was always agreeable and worthwhile. The 'new' Heath was a very different creature, and it is impossible to assess whether he had changed, or whether he had perforce to wear a new mask, or whether the first presentiment had been an imposture. Of all these possibilities, the last seems the least probable.

He quickly showed that he was certainly not another Wilson in terms of Parliamentary quickness and political initiative, and the Conservatives watched in dismay as the Prime Minister dealt with their new leader even more effectively than he had Home. It is appropriate to emphasize at this point that, as a Parliamentarian, Home has tended to be under-valued, particularly when he was Prime Minister. He had a real capacity, when nettled, to disturb Wilson and if he had followed his own inclination of aloof disdain and had not been urged to challenge Wilson at every point and if he had not been severely limited in his knowledge of the House of Commons, it is possible that in time he would have mastered his mercurial opponent. Heath could not bring to his aid the skills and assumptions of superiority and experience which Home had effortlessly possessed, and he was emphatically worsted in debate. It was now that he had to pay the price for the years of enforced silence, and the absence of apprenticeship in public debate. What was even more serious was the fact that Heath's alleged support in the constituencies – which his supporters had used so effectively in the campaign for the leadership election – was proving to be brittle.

The first – and this, politically, the most important – point to grasp about Heath is that he is a particularly and very unusual type of Conservative leader – the *idéologue*. This had been very evident in the concept of the abolition of Resale Price Maintenance. He came to the Conservative Party through thought and conscious decision, not as a consequence of birth, heredity, or early circumstances. When one contemplates his passion for logical, clear, and well-ordered policies and programmes, carefully prepared and then vehemently adhered to, one is reminded more of Joseph Chamberlain than of any other modern major Conservative figure. The Disraelian and Baldwinite concept of the Conservative Party as a complex national coalition, bound with ties that they could feel and understand yet which were very difficult to categorize, is wholly alien to Heath's approach. The contrast between his attitude towards policy formulation after 1964 and that of the formidable Woolton–Butler combination after 1945 was striking and, although the circumstances were very different, this contrast is significant. In 1945 there had been a real need to return to first principles; but in 1964 Heath considered that it was not necessary – and, indeed, not possible in the circumstances – to review the Party's general objectives and philosophy; what was necessary, in his view, was the urgent preparation of new programmes to meet specific problems, and not the establishment of general policies on the 1945–50 pattern – which were, as Butler himself said, 'impressionistic'. Heath's new policy study groups involved MPs, party officials, and some businessmen and university teachers. The work was put in hand with some urgency until some thirty-six advisory groups – each with between eight and twelve members – were active. The results were seen in *Putting Britain Right Ahead* – published within a year of the 1964 defeat – when it appeared that all this energy had produced the discovery that heavy direct taxation acted as a disincentive, that Britain should join the Common Market, that some modest Trade Union reform – to take the form of new types of industrial courts – was required, and that welfare benefits should be concentrated on those most in need. But the really significant feature of *Putting Britain Right Ahead* was what was left out. There was a very marked absence of reference to any incomes policy – which had been part of the 1964 Election Manifesto – and to national economic planning. The other feature of *Putting Britain Right Ahead* was the firm commitment to EEC entry, which had not received prominence in the 1964 programme. The document bore Heath's personal stamp, and established the principles on which he operated for the next five years. At first glance they appeared unexceptionable; it was only gradually that it became apparent that they represented, collectively, a radical departure. This was a marked and significant movement away from 'Butskellism'.

Heath's principal objective when he had assumed the responsibility for the reassessment of Conservative policies in 1964 had been to devise a new approach. After thirteen years of office, the Party was exhausted, and the bulk of the original programmes laid down in the immediate post-war years had been fulfilled. Heath had come to believe that the nation, no less than the Conservative Party, needed jolting out of an out-of-date cast of mind and lethargic acquiescence in the status quo. The immediate results, in the shape of *Putting Britain Right Ahead*, were hardly dramatic, but the establishment of priorities and the method of business – for that is what it was – were highly significant. They help to explain why Heath's approach attracted such support in the Parliamentary Party and in the constituencies in the vital months before the leadership crisis – support which made the difference between victory and defeat. But although this approach was popular in the new Conservative Party, its relevance outside it was more controversial, and gave rise to doubts as to the depth of Heath's political comprehension. Modern British society is a very complex organism, which requires keen and sensitive understanding. It can be argued that Heath's approach dangerously under-estimated these complexities, and that he devised a blue-print for national resurrection that was heavily based on his own preconceptions of what kind of country he would like to live in. This approach aroused suspicions that Heath's fundamental deficiency was his imaginative remoteness from what was really happening in Britain. He travelled around the country a great deal; he saw many people; he studied papers with care and thoroughness. But the total of this activity, it was claimed, was strangely unsatisfactory. His facts were unassailable, and his logic inexorable; yet it all added up to something that did not strike responsive chords. It seemed that, although he possessed many political qualities he lacked one; the quality of imaginative vision. 'He is,' as one of his colleagues remarked, 'a politician's politician.' The British may appear cynical, prosaic, and cautious, but in fact they respond with much fervour to dreams, and visions, and goals. And at this time Heath gave them solemn lectures – and dull lectures at that. 'The trouble with the Tories is Ted,' Mr Robert Carvel commented with sharpness, 'and the trouble with Ted is that he does not seem real.' His election to the Party leadership was in fact a reflection of the face that the

Conservatives in their desperation were seeking a man who was real to them, and who would regard himself as ideologically alien from the Labour Party.

In the Conservative Party the principal charge against Heath in 1965–6, and repeated thereafter, was that he failed to excite his followers. The charge was similar to that levelled against the unsuccessful Stafford Northcote:

> Where he failed was in manner. His voice, his diction, his delivery, were all inadequate. With real ability, great knowledge, genial kindness, and a sympathetic nature – all the qualities, indeed, which evoke regard and esteem – he had not the spice of the devil which is necessary to rouse an Opposition to zeal and elation.[1]

The comparison is, of course, far from a close one. As a debater in the 1966–70 Parliament Heath was by no means as inferior to Wilson as some commentators have alleged, and he was often very formidable when on the attack. But his skills are essentially expository, and are seen to better advantage when he is in a position of authority. An Opposition leader should be always on the pounce, with an eye for the Ministerial slip that can be converted into a Government embarrassment, and ever alert for the chance of exploiting the inevitable weak links in the Administration's chain. Then, although he must be careful not to expose himself to charges of lacking patriotism and rejoicing in natural misfortunes, he must make Ministers feel uneasy when they behold him advancing to the Dispatch Box. At the same time, he must stir his own supporters, and not merely lead but inspire. It is, of course, an impossible combination of requirements for any individual to fulfil, and the celebrated passage in Disraeli's *Life of Lord George Bentinck* is apposite:

> But he who in the Parliamentary field watches over the fortunes of routed troops must be prepared to sit often alone ... Adversity is necessarily not a sanguine season, and in this respect a politician is no exception to all other human combinations. Indoors and out of doors a disheartened opposition will be querulous and captious. A discouraged multitude have no future. Too depressed to indulge in a large and often hopeful horizon of contemplation, they busy themselves in peevish detail, and by a natural train of sentiment associate their own conviction of ill-luck, incapacity, and failure, with the most responsible member of their confederation.

[1] Rosebery: *Lord Randolph Churchill* (London, 1906).

The story of the Conservative Opposition between 1966 and 1970 is very closely linked with Heath's personality, methods, and approach, because there was a deliberate and determined attempt to apply his own sense of priorities and methods of work on the Conservative Party. A Conservative leader is, to a far greater extent than his counterpart in the Labour Party, *the* Leader, with a power over his choice of colleagues in the Shadow Cabinet and Party machine that is very considerable. 'The Conservative leader,' as Dr McKenzie has written, 'whether in power or in opposition, has the sole ultimate responsibility for the formulation of the policy and the electoral programme of his party.'[1] But this position of authority must be handled with care, and it has its dangers, for failure can be taken directly to the door of one man, and the Conservatives have a record of considerable decisiveness in disposing of leaders who have been deemed to have failed. Heath himself knew well enough that he was on trial, and that if the Party failed he could expect to receive no forgiveness. He had sought the Party leadership not just for the thing itself, but because he wanted to do something with it. He believed that Britain was drifting limply into a secondary status, and urgently required the test of challenge and new attitudes to reverse this dismal trend. He was convinced that Britain required leadership – industrial and commercial, no less than political – of higher quality and higher ability. He believed that government should be seen in terms not of political tactics but of competent and enlightened management. He knew that if he failed to convince the country of this his political career would be virtually ended. Unquestionably, he would have resigned the leadership if he had lost a second General Election, in preference to lingering on and becoming 'another Balfour'.

Heath shares with Wilson a considerable vulnerability to criticism, and he is acutely sensitive. He has a high sense of probity and loyalty, and his tension when in the presence of persons for whom he does not have respect is very evident. Dr David Butler,[2] has claimed that 'as a former Chief Whip

[1] Robert McKenzie: *British Political Parties* (paperback ed., 1970), p. 21. It should be emphasized that the practice in the modern Conservative Party is much less authoritarian than this statement implies. 'In practice,' as a senior Conservative has commented, 'we start with an authoritarian constitution, and lean over backwards to make our actual processes democratic.'

[2] David Butler and Michael Pinto-Duschinsky: *The General Election of 1970*, p. 76.

[Heath] was almost obsessively concerned with internal unity'. This connection between Heath's period as Chief Whip and his conduct of the Party leadership has frequently been made, but it is not really valid. Party unity has been an obsession of all modern Conservative leaders (and not only Conservative leaders), and it is based on the firm conviction that nothing harms a party's public support – to say nothing of its political effectiveness – more than disunity. Heath was not, however, a 'unity at any price' man, as his firm support for Boyle against persistent Party criticism and his dismissal of Powell from the Shadow Cabinet in April 1968 demonstrated. There is a difference between a profound concern to maintain a genuine Party unity and an artificial unity of the kind that Balfour attempted in 1902–6. Heath's approach was the former one, and the fact that he had been a Chief Whip was not, in this context at least, really relevant.

As a Party leader, Heath did not, initially, appear to possess all the requisite qualities. His manner was too direct, and his language often too blunt. He did not appreciate criticism and opposition. He often unnecessarily distressed individuals who were genuinely endeavouring to assist him. He certainly often alienated individuals outside politics who were sympathetic to the Conservative Party. The qualities of warmth and consideration, which had won him so many adherents in the 1950s, seemed to have been relegated to the past. Thus the impression which many observers received was of a leader who inspired respect rather than admiration, apprehension rather than devotion.

But these surface manifestations, although politically significant, were evidence of the difficulties of Heath's position. They were in reaction against a feeling of personal and political insecurity. The burdens of political leadership are always heavy; to a sensitive, solitary, sincere, single man they can at times be almost intolerable, and there were occasions on which Heath's personal resources to combat these tensions appeared to be inadequate. Only those who were close to him knew how difficult this initial period was, and how deep was Heath's depression and unhappiness on occasion.

But we must return to the public man. Heath is not invariably tactful, and he can be brutal when in the mood. He has a reputation as a man who is authoritarian and who dislikes the long processes of collective decision-making. There is something in this, but it should not be exaggerated; Heath's method is essentially to force people to argue their case; some politicians and officials found this stimulating, but others did not. Those who had something of value to say and had the evidence to support their argument, and were in fundamentals *bien vus*, did not find Heath obstinate or unsympathetic. Others, who had some vague complaint or suggestion to make, resented what they regarded as Heath's aggressive and hectoring manner. And there is no doubt that his coldness can be disconcerting, even for those who like and trust him best. But he also has a quick temper, which is not a political quality. One of his closest associates has emphasized to this commentator that, in his experience, this feature of Heath's character was seen most on relatively minor issues, and that he remained cool on the big ones. Certainly Heath, when angry, is formidable and alarming, and it is curious that despite considerable self-control in other matters, he has often failed in this one.

But if certain aspects of Heath's personality concerned some Conservatives, the real worry lay in his public manner. His shyness and reserve, and his managerial concept of politics, make the publicity aspects of modern politics and all the impostures implicit in them repugnant to him. He has no taste for large London meetings and becomes noticeably happier when in the constituencies and, for preference, with some heckling to stimulate him. He is no phrase-maker, and has what is almost a civil servant's dislike for anything glib or meretricious which might, however, attract public attention. Heath's stiffness in political speaking is not seen in other contexts. George Hutchinson has commented on the quality of Heath's memorial address on his friend Sir Timothy Bligh, in March 1969, which made a deep impression on all who heard it. This commentator has also heard Heath speak with eloquence, warmth, and sensitivity – and without any notes – in an informal and non-political atmosphere. His many friends outside politics – and they are a diverse group, reflecting not only the width but the depth of Heath's interests – are astonished to read of his alleged coldness, abrasiveness, and unsympathetic public personality. Many of them assume that a hostile Press, resenting Heath's general contempt for journalists, is determined to show him in the worst possible light.

But the fact is that this is the true impression of Heath's political oratory. He is, as George Hutchinson has rightly written, 'addicted, perhaps by now, incurably, to the factual statement, the plain exposition, marshalling and enumerating his facts and policies like a laundry list'.[1] It is this commentator's view that the eloquent, warm, and sensitive man is the real man, but the public impression is what matters politically. Yet all attempts by his colleagues and advisers to persuade him to change his public style were curtly rejected. 'It is not my style', or 'I do not say that kind of thing', has frequently killed a phrase thought up by an associate. Yet whenever he has allowed himself to speak with warmth on matters on which he feels deeply the results are extremely effective. The relative rarity of these public glimpses of the real man undoubtedly affected his political position, and gave Wilson the opportunity – eagerly and skilfully taken – of presenting himself in sharp contrast. There is some truth in the comment of an unfriendly observer that 'Mr Heath radiates a kind of seriousness which is almost insupportable. He is a walking, talking Blue Book, chattering out statistics and minatory sub-clauses; lecturing the viewer, and making him feel guilty of neglecting his political homework.'[2]

Most of these characteristics could be held to be to the credit of the man, and up to a point, they are. But they also pointed to something else that was less estimable, and which reduced his effectiveness as a party leader. A political party and a mass electorate require some wooing and persuasion; for the politician to appear to consider such practices as being beneath contempt implies a certain degree of contempt for the audience itself. Modern techniques of mass communication may be objectionable, but they have their purpose. Heath's most serious deficiency as a party leader was an inability to communicate effectively beyond the Party to the larger national audience. One speaker in the 1966 Conservative conference read out a letter from the Leader's Office which stated bluntly that if people did not know what Conservative policy was they had not troubled to make the effort to find out. The speaker had a real point, as did another, who attacked 'the abject failure in communications' and 'lack of aggressive presentation to the

[1] Hutchinson: *op. cit.*, p. 186.
[2] *New Statesman*, 29 May 1970.

public'. 'Whatever one may think about democratic government,' Churchill has written, 'it is just as well to have practical experience of its rough and slatternly foundations . . . Dignity may suffer, the superfine gloss is soon worn away; nice particularisms and special private policies are scraped off; much has to be accepted with a shrug, a sigh or a smile; but at any rate in the end one knows a good deal about what happens and why.' Heath's dislike for most journalists was perhaps understandable, but it might have been less apparent than it was, and his detestation for what he regards as the trivial gimmickry of political television did not help to make him an effective exploiter of the medium. In order to be a good Prime Minister – which was the centre of Heath's ambition – it is first necessary to reach the position. Heath's emphasis between 1966 and 1970 seemed to be to prepare himself and the Conservative Party for the heavy responsibilities of office, and it appeared that the initial obstacle of winning the Election took a much lower priority. The impression grew that the Conservative leadership waited for the people to come back to them in despair at the performance of Labour.

Furthermore, Heath's authoritarian approach, and his insistence upon being, and being seen to be, the leader, appeared to give few people a real share in the Party's councils. He had devised the strategy; the Party must follow it. That was what leadership was about. The trouble about politics is that it is not as simple as military command or business administration. Heath's approach was simple and direct. The Conservative national coalition is not, however, a simple element, and there was, at least initially in his leadership, a certain gulf between the leader and his followers.

But there are serious dangers in over-simplification of what Heath was actually doing. The damaged reputation of the Conservatives as a governing party had to be restored, and this could only be done by persuading the electorate that they had recovered their competence. In his own words: 'People today are so cynical and sceptical about the whole machinery of government that detail is needed to convince them that you really intend to carry out your promises.'[1] The creation of the Public Sector Research Centre and the specialization of Shadow Ministers were two major indications of this conviction. The

[1] Butler and Pinto-Duschinsky; *op. cit.*, p. 66.

philosophy was well expressed by Mr David Howell in his pamphlet *A New Style of Government*, published by the Conservative Political Centre in May 1970:

> To change the direction of government policy, in some cases to establish any direction at all, will require not only just statements of intent but thorough and detailed preparation for carrying aims into practice.

But this was not all. Heath belongs to the most interesting type of politician – those in whom there is a complicated mixture of strong personal ambition and genuine public ideals. The late Robert Kennedy provided such a mixture, as did Harold Macmillan. But Heath, without Celtic blood or the Celtic approach to life, was inadequate at conveying in public the inner faiths and beliefs that make him something considerably more impressive and infinitely more interesting than the abrasive self-made politician that he is usually depicted.

Although most politicans are sensitive, they are usually predominantly sensitive to their own problems, hopes, opinions, and ambitions. Heath is also sensitive in an entirely non-political way. He has always found deep solace in music, and, although not a scholar, he is considerably better read than most politicians. These resources give him a self-sufficiency which few men possess, and certainly few in public life. It is not just the fact that these are civilized pursuits which is significant, but that they are essentially private and solitary. Most politicians are only too eager to talk of such matters; Heath's dislike of intrusion into his private life is formidable, and his coldness towards several journalists stems not only from an intellectual contempt for their capacities and integrity, but also from his view of their relentless fascination with what he regards as trivia.

It would be difficult for any thoughtful man to describe what are precisely his most personal beliefs. Heath's faith in the value of personal initiative is fundamental to his political philosophy. 'It was in freedom, not in reliance upon the State, that Britain achieved greatness,' he has said. 'It was the acceptance of personal responsibility, not dependence upon the central government, that made this small island so dominant in this world.' Heath is a Conservative because he believes that the Conservative philosophy is liberating to the individual whereas the Socialist philosophy is essentially restrictive, narrow, and limiting. The difference was, accordingly, an ideological one.

His dislike of Wilson – and 'dislike' is too gentle a description – was based on his judgement that Wilson himself has no philosophy at all, and feels obliged politically to make concessions to his party whose total effect is restrictive to the freedom of the individual. It was, therefore, a curious experience to see these two men in vehement opposition; the pragmatic, easy-going, opportunistic Labour leader, and the severe, doctrinaire, taut Conservative!

Heath's view of the country he wants to live in, despite the strong emphasis on practical matters, is partly nostalgic and even sentimental. He believes intensely in individuality and self-help, but the gulf that separates his views from those of Enoch Powell on such matters is large. He does not believe in an all-out capitalist society; he does not believe in *laissez-faire*; he does not believe that the rôle of the State should be dormant or passive. He is deeply concerned by what is, after all, one of the major problems of the second half of the twentieth century – the determination of the point at which the intervention of the State in a free society becomes destructive of enterprise and individuality, and the point at which the absence of State intervention exposes the weak, the poor, and the ill-favoured to cruel hardship and deprivation. He has thought a great deal about this problem and, if he has not reached any definitive solution, he is not alone in this, and it is, at least, something that one contemporary Party leader is seized of the problem. But his attitudes are also characterized by that certain element, which is so difficult to define or describe, that betrays a certain emotional and intellectual rootlessness. He seems to lack a basic confidence in certain verities. His intolerance of contrary opinions and challenges to his arguments is one clear sign of this. Certainly in 1966 his political character lacked the gentleness and compassion which warms and impresses opponents and which exercises a wider appeal and confidence.

Another key facet of Heath's personality is his vehement patriotism. His contempt for bogus patriotism is the contempt of a true patriot for the prostitution of something of deep importance to himself. At least part of Heath's detestation for Wilson was based on his conviction that Wilson only banged the patriotic drum when he thought that there were votes in doing so, a belief that was unfair to Wilson. But Heath's brand of patriotism has its dangers, as was well seen in his emotional opposition to devaluation, which he regarded as a national humiliation, a British defeat, an insult to the British genius, rather than as a long-overdue recognition of international facts. His espousal of a British presence East of Suez and the thinly-veiled anti-Americanism of his European commitment were also significant indications. His consistent advocacy of active British involvement in Europe was the result less of any feeling for vague internationalism, or even of a vision of a cohesive Western Europe, than of a cool appreciation of British interests. The root of Heath's Europeanism is that British involvement in Europe would be to *Britain's* advantage.

Heath's patriotism is based on a feeling for his country that is profound and passionate. Unhappily he has rarely been able to give memorable public expression to his love of England and its institutions. At the conclusion of his speech to the 1968 Conservative Conference he embarked upon a lengthy peroration on Britain's place in the world, in which he took the peculiarly unhappy simile of a lighthouse on a rock. It would be unkind to quote the passage in full, but its significance lay in Heath's inability to articulate something that he felt very deeply. Heath believes, quite simply, that the story of England is one of gradual movement towards a society that represents the ideal. It is a country where tolerance and a sense of fair play is deeply inbred, a country where every man and woman is born free, lives and works without fear of intimidation or discrimination, and is protected by the State from the worst consequences of misfortune. 'The Tory Party,' he has said, 'has never been the Party of *laissez-faire*; it has always been the Party of order which enables people to live fruitfully in freedom.' He believes in Britain as a nation which reveres its history, yet is unafraid of the future – a nation that has given much to mankind, but which has much more yet to give. 'What we have to do now,' he has said, in one of his rare public references to his philosophy, 'is to carve out a new place for Britain – to carve it out without nostalgia, without bitterness, and without regret; but with imagination, skill, and determination.'

Thus, to regard Heath, as he has so often been depicted, as 'a creepy technocrat with too much zeal and not enough ballast',[1] is as inaccurate as the depiction of Wilson as a shallow

---

[1] Anthony Sampson: *Anatomy of Britain Today* (London, 1969), p. 78.

opportunist. But Heath shares with Wilson an insecurity which has at least part of its origins in his background. In his advance to the Party leadership he had made many enemies, and the personal denigration to which he was subjected, and to which reference has already been made, forced him into an inflexible position. In a sense, he overreacted, for, like the central figure in Kipling's 'If', he always heard suppressed laughter around corners. Inexorably, everything became a test of his personal authority, his leadership, and his Tory *bona fides*. The strain made him a distinctly more nervous and tense man, quick to notice deviations from the chosen course, and eager to take opportunities for assuring the Party that he stood firmly in the traditional line. And, as this process developed, his public attraction suffered.

But Heath's qualities gradually became increasingly apparent to the Conservative Party. He was evidently a man of strong personal convictions and integrity, and his persistence and determination won him an ever-increasing circle of genuine admirers in the Party. Thus, although there were few indications that Heath was arousing any substantial national audience, in the Conservative Party he was quietly but emphatically establishing his personal authority. Indeed, one of the most important developments in the Conservative Party between 1966 and 1970 was the gradual elimination of the leadership issue as a major factor. It can be argued that this was partly due to the realization that Heath was not going to be unresistant to any move to replace him, and it was also very substantially the result of any alternative candidate – other than Powell in 1968 – propelling himself forward. But the real cause was Heath's patient touring of the country, his meetings with local party officials and supporters, and his careful expounding of the Conservative case. These unpublicized, and sometimes quite private, visits and meetings not only flattered and pleased Party workers, but enabled them to see Heath in a new light. As has already been emphasized, Heath is at his best in a small group, and gradually the Party at large became impressed by him. This change in mood was gradual, but by the time of the 1969 Party conference his closest associates had no doubt that, so far as the Party was concerned, Heath had established himself completely.

Looking back, it is possible to see that the Conservatives' recovery began immediately after the 1964 defeat, and has been described as 'one of the most ambitious efforts at internal reform ever undertaken by a British party and deserves to rank with the modernizing era of the Conservative party after 1945'.[1] The 1966 Election came too soon for the changes to have had sufficient impact, but the foundations had already been laid for the subsequent recovery.

Organization does not, by itself, restore the fortunes of a political party, but it is difficult to see how the Conservatives would have made their remarkable recovery without these changes.

The new emphasis was on making the central organization much more political and policy-orientated, and less obsessed by administrative issues than it had been in the late 1950s and early 1960s; at the same time, the administration itself was examined to ensure that its renowned efficiency – which had shown distinct signs of decline – was maintained and improved. Two committees, chaired by Lord Chelmer and Iain Macleod, reported in favour of substantial improvement for the status and salaries of constituency agents and the reorganization of the Young Conservatives, respectively.

Publicity was, and remained for some time, the most serious difficulty. It was generally recognized that the Party's publicity could have been much better than it had been, but there were substantial differences in assessing the most suitable answer. In particular, there was for a time a fundamental disagreement about the value of professional advertising and public relations firms. Some argued that public relations was a highly professional business, like personnel management and could no longer be left to amateurs; others argued, with equal vehemence, that there was a very considerable difference between selling consumer goods and a political party. These debates took place a long time before the full extent of the employment of Madison Avenue advertising agencies in American politics was appreciated – and, indeed, at that stage the degree of that employment was very limited in comparison with what was done in the 1968 Presidential Election. The solution to the publicity problem was crucial if the Conservatives were to make

---

[1] David Butler and Anthony King: *The General Election of 1966*, p. 53.

a substantial impact. Perhaps the most difficult part was to secure the willing participation of several Conservative leaders – including Heath – who tended to regard several aspects of political publicity and propaganda, and particularly television, as a necessary evil. The key figures in this process were Mr Geoffrey Tucker, appointed Director of Publicity in 1968, and Mr James Garrett. 'I think, in retrospect,' one who was closely associated with this process has written, 'that the really important achievement was that Mr Heath was persuaded that this kind of operation was not only necessary but rather fun, provided it was done in congenial circumstances. I would rate this as Geoffrey Tucker's main achievement before the election.'

Until 1968, when Tucker based the programme on careful market research, the Conservative publicity suffered from an unsureness about what it ought to be doing and how it ought to be doing it, and it was not surprising that the Conservative publicity was something less than inspired and was largely ineffective. There were severe financial restraints, but money is not the principal factor in effective publicity. This was one area in which the Conservatives had lagged badly behind their opponents.

One of the first major organization changes in 1964 had been to make Sir Michael Fraser, the director of the Research Department since 1951, Deputy Chairman of the Party and secretary to the Shadow Cabinet. The change was not made entirely for organizational reasons. The position of Chairman of the Research Department provided a power base within the Party hierarchy which could provide a challenge to the authority not only of the Chairman of the Party but to the Leader. Lord Poole had given consideration to this centralization in the 1950s, but the idea had had to be shelved because – amongst other reasons – it would have been unacceptable to Butler, who had been Chairman of the Research Department since 1945. But by October 1964 Butler's position in the Party had been severely eroded, and his widely-reported observations to a journalist in the course of the 1964 Election, in which he had made comments on his colleagues which were regarded by them as unhelpful, had not disposed the then leadership of the Party to continue the arrangement. Butler, whose zest for politics was by then in marked decline, took the matter well, and retired gracefully. Not long afterwards he accepted Wilson's offer to become Master of Trinity College Cambridge. His departure took from the Party, and from public life, one of the most baffling and enigmatic participants in, and one of the best minds devoted to, modern British politics; it also opened the way for new developments and new men. For the new arrangements made Fraser the Party's Permanent Secretary, to use the Whitehall analogy. Fraser was, in Butler's words, 'the best adjutant the party has ever had', and the new arrangement would have been impossible without Fraser's unique experience and the complete trust and respect which he evoked. He continued, as Deputy Chairman of the Party, to have a special responsibility for the Research Department and one of his major functions was the co-ordination of the work of the Research Department and Central Office. Unquestionably, this centralization was long overdue. Another major innovation was the establishment of machinery to co-ordinate the work of Central Office and the Parliamentary Party, and, in particular, to bring the Shadow Cabinet and the organization much closer together. These changes produced, not without some difficulties and offended susceptibilities, a new cohesiveness in the Party machinery that had been lacking since the palmy days of Lord Woolton, and which was infinitely superior to the Labour organization.

But the really significant advance lay in the use to which this new machinery was to be put. Elections are not won by single events, and the fortunes of political parties are not restored by one initiative, but there is a certain justification for the case that the 1970 General Election was won in the summer of 1965.

After the narrow defeat of 1964, many Conservatives were dominated by the feeling that British politics had entered a period when the old guidelines were becoming irrelevant. It was plain that the Labour leadership, under both Gaitskell and Wilson, had abandoned even the mild post-war Socialism which the Conservatives had successfully built up into a monstrous, unfeeling, and un-British ogre. What was there to attack, apart from Labour's competence as a governing party? What had happened between 1959 and 1964? Why had Labour so unexpectedly 'come back'? What was the new political environment in which they had to operate?

For some time both political parties had employed polling organizations for specific and limited purposes. Some politicians viewed these with considerable reservations, comparable to canvass returns, which can be notoriously inaccurate, but by the mid-1960s the reputation of the polls was such that only the most sceptical politicians were not impressed. The problem was however, that while these could give some answer to the question of what was happening, they could not and did not give any real guide to the deeper causes. To use a simile of a senior Conservative official, the polls revealed the ripples of public feeling but not the tides. Thus, while the usual sample polling arrangements were retained and developed, it was decided to undertake a much more lengthy and deeper analysis than had been attempted before, by the use of a large and carefully selected panel of voters.

The first report from this exercise was received in 1965. An exceptionally large sample of the population, which included teenagers not yet entitled to vote, had been selected, covering a wide spectrum of social positions, professions, and education. Of the sample, 49 per cent had voted Labour in 1964, 40 per cent had voted Conservative, 8 per cent Liberal or other parties, and 3 per cent were 'not stated'; these percentages compared with national ones of 44 per cent, 43 per cent and 13 per cent respectively in the 1964 Election. This sample was re-interviewed several times between 1965 and 1970.

The exercise also concerned itself very seriously with what Dr Abrams had depicted in 1960 as the 'target voter', a group of electors under 45 years of age who identified themselves 'weakly' or not at all with any particular party; this group has been estimated at 14 per cent of the total electorate, or just over 5 million voters. It was estimated that, in this group, 1.4 million were 'weak' Conservatives, 2.4 million were 'weak' Labour, 0.5 million 'weak' Liberals, and 0.8 million had no party identification at all. Analysis of the 1964 Election led to the conclusion that whereas some 15 per cent of 'target voters' had voted Conservative, 34 per cent had voted Labour, and 7 per cent Liberal; allowing for 10 per cent who were too young to vote in 1964, but who would soon be eligible – and 2 per cent whose voting could not be established, this left a massive 32 per cent – or 1.6 million – who had not voted at all. It was also estimated that whereas some 80 per cent of 'weak' Conservatives in fact voted Conservative, 95 per cent of 'weak' Labour voted Labour, and over two-thirds of the 'non-identifiers' voted Labour. The target group, it was concluded, had certain significant characteristics. The target voter was more likely to be a woman (56 per cent of the group, it was estimated); he or she was likely to be younger than the average elector; was more likely to be a member of the skilled working class (47 per cent); more likely to have a full-time job; was basically unpolitical; was slightly more likely to vote for a political team than for a set of policies; was more interested in housing than the condition of old age pensioners; tended to regard Labour as being more capable than the Conservatives of understanding his problems; was less likely to watch party political broadcasts; and was much more likely (44 per cent) to read the *Daily Mirror* than the *Daily Express* (23 per cent).

After the 1966 Election the same sample was re-interviewed and other analyses were made of what had happened. The most startling discovery was the extent of the new volatility of the electorate, which was emphasized by the remarkable conclusion that some 33 per cent of the electorate (some 11 million electors) had changed their voting behaviour between 1964 and 1966. The Conservatives calculated that whereas they had lost some two million votes in 1966 from those who had voted for them in 1964, they had picked up 1.4 million 'new' votes. These analyses confirmed what many politicians and political observers had felt in their bones for some time – and which the work of political scientists had also demonstrated – that the days of the large 'bloc' vote, with the small floating element that decided elections, were definitely over. The argument that elections were won by the party that captured 'the middle ground' also began to look very suspect indeed. The key, the Conservatives now believed, lay with the target voter, the young-ish, uncommitted but Labour-inclined, principally skilled working-class voter. His significance was emphasized further, when the detailed analysis of the 1966 results led to a breakdown of the electorate, that pointed to the fact that the 'very strong' Conservative element in the electorate amounted to 12 per cent (4.9 million), the 'fairly strong' element was some 19 per cent (7.4 million), and 'not very strong' at 8 per cent (3.2 million);

the Labour figures were 14 per cent (5.4 million), 18 per cent (7.2 million) and 11 per cent (4.4 million) respectively. Liberals – 'weak' and 'strong' – were estimated at over 3 million, and indeterminates at about the same total. If these figures were correct, at first glance it seemed that the claim that Labour was in fact the natural governing party was very well founded. Thus, if both parties polled their full strengths and shared the 'indeterminate' vote, this gave Labour something in the region of a built-in 6 per cent superiority. But the gleam of hope in this situation for the Conservatives – and in the circumstances it was a powerful one – was the volatility of the electorate that the studies had disclosed. If it were true that eleven million voters had changed between 1964 and 1966, could they not do it again?

These analyses gave the Conservative leadership a clearer indication of what the new political environment was. They could expect violent shifts in voting behaviour, and need not be excessively elated or dispirited by their results. But they also knew that the crucial factor would be the reaction of the target voter to their attitudes and policies.

Over the following four years the Conservatives gained significant information from what they received from their heavy sample, which showed them 'the tides', while also receiving information from other sources – notably Opinion Research Centre – on 'the ripples'. The sample demonstrated a solid swing toward the Conservatives thoughout the period, based primarily on concern for domestic issues – principally housing, immigration, and the economy – on which it was felt that Labour was proving inadequate. This movement also demonstrated the invalidity of the later 'cohort' theory, and provided confirmation that the announcement of the demise of the Conservative working man had been premature. But this movement did not confirm the enormous leads in the opinion polls which the Conservatives were given in 1967–9, nor by their by-election victories. 'From an early date,' Fraser has said, 'we assumed that the most likely result of a General Election would be a small or medium Conservative majority.' The research showed that the Conservatives were slowly winning, and were retaining the target voter by their emphasis on these particular areas of domestic policy. Only one in six of the sample mentioned international affairs as a major item, as opposed to immigration (one in three) and economic affairs (principally costs and prices), which one in four stated as a major concern. The final analysis, reported in April 1970, was that there was a 10 per cent Conservative lead in voting intention, but, after allowance for other factors – principally abstention – the real Conservative lead was only 4 per cent. As this was almost exactly the margin of the Conservative victory in the 1970 Election, the value of the new techniques hardly needs emphasis. It also goes some way towards explaining why Fraser and other Conservative leaders – although not all – never lost confidence throughout the 1970 campaign.

Opinion Research Centre, whose prediction of the Election result made it suddenly celebrated in June 1970, participated in the long-term panel working on the consistent sample, but its work was primarily on conventional quota sampling techniques. These, also, demonstrated the new volatility in the electorate and, until the spring of 1970, were very much in line with the reports of the panel. At that point, new trends of a Labour recovery could be discerned, and Mr Humphrey Taylor of ORC warned Central Office that any complacency was misplaced, and that the evidence of his polls gave no cause for such confidence, thus bringing up the very alarming possibility that in elections, the ripples were of greater importance than the tides, after all.

The point was, of course, that this double approach covered a much wider area of the electorate and its voting behaviour than had ever been available before to a political party in Britain. If their results confirmed certain facts which had been apparent to more casual observers beforehand – as, for example, that the average Conservative worker is socially very untypical of the electorate, whereas the Labour worker is socially more typical but is politically untypical in his party dedication – this statistical confirmation was, in itself, of value. And the identification of the target voter and the deliberate shift in the presentation[1] of Conservative policies to appeal to him must be regarded as a development of major importance in the revival of the Conservative Party.

[1] It should be emphasized that the Conservative strategy was laid in 1964–5, before the sample investigation had been initiated. The exercise did not *affect* Party policies, but it gave important indications of how they could be *presented* most effectively.

The Conservative Party possesses several outstanding advantages over its opponents. The Conservatives *believe* in organization and in a professional approach, do not consider money spent on organization as money ill-spent, as the Labour Party tends to do, and have an abhorrence of the 'it'll be all right on the night' approach of the Labour organization. The recruitment, training, remuneration and utilization of agents are matters of high priority in the Conservative Party, and are grievously neglected by Labour. It is something of a mystery to many Conservatives how the Labour Party survives at all, and, if efficient organization – central and local – were the criterion it is very doubtful whether it would. In 1967 the Conservatives decided to concentrate their principal efforts on seventy Labour-held marginal seats, and to ignore their own marginals – even to the point of leaving Sir Harmar Nicholls, who had held Peterborough by three votes in 1966, to fend for himself. This concentration involved all aspects of central and local organization, and was a very thoroughly conducted exercise.

It was, significantly, an aggressive decision, and was designed to ensure that in the Labour-held marginals the Party machine would be as well prepared and supported as was possible. This was another crucial decision in the Conservative revival, for no less than sixty-four of the seventy seats were won in 1970.

The prime asset of the Conservative machine is the fact that it is the servant of the Party leader. The Central Office is, by its constitution, the political office of the Party leader, whose principal officers are appointed by him personally. It is, in a sense, all very undemocratic, but the system gives to the Party leader a control that is entirely absent in the Labour Party, which, with its selected National Executive – which apart from its manifest other defects, is perhaps the most 'leaky' political group in modern politics – and the hopelessly complex myriad of committees and groups with no direct chain of responsibility, has no such advantage. In the 1966–70 Government the gulf between Transport House and the Government became an enormous chasm, and even if Wilson had wanted to improve the situation substantially he would have found it difficult to achieve much. The Conservative leader, however, has very substantial powers, of which the most substantial of all is the right to hire and fire the Party Chairman.

Heath had inherited Mr Edward du Cann – the youngest Party Chairman since J. C. C. Davidson's appointment in 1926 – from Home. On the surface, it seemed that they had much in common, but this was quickly seen not to be the case. It is vital to the effective working of the Conservative machine that there is a close personal and political harmony between the Leader and the Chairman of the Party. With the wisdom of hindsight it is clear that, given the clear and evident personal incompatibility between Heath and du Cann, the new leader should have taken the initiative, either by inviting du Cann to resign, or by establishing a clear *modus vivendi* which could have worked satisfactorily for at least a time. In the event, Heath took neither course, relations between the two men deteriorated, and du Cann eventually resigned in September 1967 under circumstances that could not be described as amicable.

Du Cann had been a very conscientious and hard-working Chairman, who had given up a great deal of time and energy – and had incurred personal financial sacrifice – to the task. In particular, his imaginative and thorough reorganization of the Party's system of financial control must be emphasized. His successor, Anthony Barber, concentrated his efforts on certain definite areas, of which the critical constituencies and the link between the Parliamentary Party and the Party in the Country were the most important. His principal interest lay in matters which directly involved votes. Viewed in retrospect, it is fair to remark that each man was, in his own way and at his particular time, a very competent Chairman. But, given the problem of clashing personalities, du Cann's departure from Smith Square was essential to the harmonious management of the Party organization. Barber was – and is – an underestimated man. He applied himself assiduously to the problems of the Party, and acted as the direct link between it and the Shadow Cabinet. His contribution was not dramatic, but was of immense importance in improving the cohesion of the Conservative national coalition between 1966 and 1970. He was a good listener, and did not hesitate to report the fact when comments on the constituencies were critical of the Party leadership.

Despite the power exercised by a Conservative leader, he is not in reality master of his house.

It is not advisable – although quite possible – for him to dump, with scant ceremony, men and women who have served the Party for many years, nor to bring forward in their places newcomers whose experience is limited but whose promise is claimed to be great. It is therefore necessary to bring about changes slowly and tactfully. These are the rules, and they have their value. Heath's approach appeared to be, initially, rather reckless. In particular, the abrupt manner in which the candidates' list was re-drawn by du Cann caused offence.

Part of this resentment lay in the collective character of the new men who reached prominence under Heath. The jibe of a Labour wit that 'they all look as though they have done uncommonly well out of the Affluent Society' was harsh, but there was a certain collective unattractiveness that was not merely apparent to those who had been so suddenly usurped. That most of them were young was not the point. To political observers they seemed a new species of Conservative altogether, somewhat cold and aloof, with upper-class accents which seemed to have been attached by plastic surgery, grey in their dress, demeanour, and imagery. Older Conservatives viewed them with the warm enthusiasm of a company that is suddenly invaded by icy Time-and-Motion experts. There had already been growls of complaint at Heath's use of outside experts in his policy groups; now there was an additional cause of protest. Their emergence was interpreted as an indication of Heath's 'managerial' concept of government, and his determination to ensure that the Conservatives were well supplied with men who shared this approach. But in fact Heath's critics were ascribing to him personally a change in the composition of the Parliamentary Party that had been evident since the early 1950s. The leader has no more control over the selection of Parliamentary candidates than has Central Office, but the emphasis had consistently been to urge constituencies to select younger candidates, and to bear in mind the importance of attracting men and women of all social backgrounds. The constituencies had responded to this advice and the selection of men like Heath himself, Powell, du Cann, Robert Carr, and Peter Walker was the result. There was, accordingly, a new generation of Conservatives rising in the Parliamentary Party through the 1950s, and the fact that they reached senior positions under Heath was natural, and was not the consequence of Heath's personal preferences. Nonetheless, the suspicion that he was rebuilding the Party in his own image existed, and was a source of potential trouble. The hostility to the new men was not merely one of personality; there were Conservatives who considered that politics – and particularly Conservative politics – were much more complex than management techniques could fathom, and that modern society demanded a greater degree of sympathetic understanding than men of such limited experience and approaches could supply. It was this feeling that must have principally prompted an article in January 1966 by Mr Angus Maude in the *Spectator* which stated that, 'For Tories simply to talk like technocrats will get them nowhere.' Maude, a front-bench spokesman on colonial affairs, was promptly asked by Heath to resign, and did. But the doubts which he had expressed about the fundamental approach were far from assuaged.

But in reality the introduction of the new men emphasized Heath's respect for professionals, for people who worked hard at their job, who did not regard politics as an agreeable pastime, and who valued the political profession with great care. Perhaps he over-valued the capacity of some of them and undoubtedly there was little in them to excite the imagination or fire the blood. Meanwhile, summarily relegated to the back benches, the displaced eyed their successors without charity. In the brief period between Heath's election in July 1965 and the General Election of March 1966 these disharmonies were sedulously muffled, but their presence was known to most of those who kept a close eye on the political situation.

This was a major source of criticism against Heath within the Party, but in fact it was not justified. What Heath did was gradually to build up a team which was based essentially on his judgement of its members individual merits, and those who still believe that he was obsessed by re-creating the Party in his own image should examine his close relationship with William Whitelaw, Home, Lord Carrington, and Lord Jellicoe. Some of his choices for Shadow responsibilities did not make the grade and they were accordingly omitted from the Government which was formed in June 1970; others were relegated to a lower place than their Shadow ranking. But, in the main, Heath's selections for Shadow responsibilities were successful. Some others, with relatively minor rôles in Opposition, were brought into the Government in 1970, not because they provided a balance between one element or another, but because they had caught Heath's eye and won his respect. There was also the point – which is not without significance – that as a former Chief Whip Heath knew a great deal about his colleagues, more, perhaps, than any previous Party leader. Several Conservatives who had flaunted themselves flamboyantly in Opposition but who were indolent or too relaxed in their approach to the responsibilities of public life, were passed over when victory came. As has been stated, Heath's judgement on men is far from infallible, but it was a heartening factor for Conservative MPs to realize that the way to success consisted of application, seriousness, and professionalism, and that the classical route of cleverness, fawning loyalty, social connections, and self-advertisement was firmly closed. One Shadow Minister made the fundamental error of making elaborate consultations before he made any public observation. While Heath believed in collective consultation, in loyalty, and teamwork, he could have no confidence in a man who was so manifestly dependent on his superiors.

Far from having a group of close cronies, Heath deliberately did not create a special group of favourites. There were some – Barber, Mr James Prior, Mr Anthony Kershaw, Fraser, and Whitelaw come at once to mind – but these were colleagues and friends rather than cronies. As Heath's biographer has commented, 'His relations with most members of the Shadow Cabinet tend to focus on particular spheres of work and policy.'[1] Heath's approach to political work is brisk and businesslike, with a well-prepared agenda and a firm allocation of functions in the Shadow Cabinet. In this he followed the example of Hugh Gaitskell and not of Churchill in the 1945–51 period of Opposition, and there were Conservatives who disliked the limitations this system imposed. But it reflected not only Heath's passion for order and system but a conviction that future Ministers must specialize long before they come to office. He thus built up a team of specialized individuals rather than a team of generalists. The very beneficient results of this approach were seen in the first weeks of the new Administration in June–July 1970, when officials were startled to discover how thoroughly prepared the new Ministers were. But one of its disadvantages was also seen when Iain Macleod died, and imperilled the entire carefully-created structure.

Party leadership is essentially a collective process – collective

[1] Hutchinson: *op. cit.*, p. 172.

not only with the Shadow Cabinet but with the Parliamentary Party, the central organization, and the Party outside Westminster. Despite the power that he wields, the Party leader cannot act in a quasi-dictatorial manner. Heath did not fall into this error, but his vigorous personality, determination, and dedication to his task made him something considerably more of a leader than a *primus inter pares*. In particular, the Conservatives' economic policies, which developed between 1965 and 1968, bore the strong imprint of Heath's own attitudes and philosophy. His fundamental assumption was that the nation was slithering inexorably downhill, and that if this slide were not reversed the chronic current economic ailments – an almost stagnant rate of growth, rising unemployment, and remorseless inflation – would become permanent. He also believed that recovery could only come from the public will. Government could guide, assist, and manage its own area of competence. Elsewhere, it should encourage those who had initiative and skill to exploit them, and refuse to prop up – or 'bail out', as the new phrase went – those who were manifestly lacking in such qualities.

The main lines for achieving these strategical ends were as follows. The burden of direct taxation – personal and corporate-tax must be reduced; the tax structure must be radically reformed; the impact of governmental interference in industry must be sharply cut – with the Industrial Reorganisation Corporation and SET high on the list of doomed machinery and organizations; there would be no statutory wages and incomes policy, but the establishment of firm guidelines, backed by firm action in those areas directly under governmental influence and control; social benefits must be established and distributed more equitably for those in most need. It was, collectively a much more elaborate and sophisticated policy of 'setting the people free'. It had, however, several weaknesses. It did not in reality deal with the problems of 'steering' the economy, and the emphasis on the rewards to be obtained from structural reforms was excessive. Heath was personally committed to increased growth, but the Party's economic policy gave no clear indication of how this was to be achieved without relapsing into the familiar 'stop-go' cycle. The commitment to an East of Suez military position was at variance with the need to maintain sterling and the balance of payments.

The programme, while it contained many sensible features, was strategically simplistic. One was reminded of the fact that neither Heath nor Macleod had been at the Treasury in their ministerial careers, and that the reputations of the two Conservative ex-Chancellors – Lloyd and Maudling – were not high. One was also reminded that Heath's experience (like that of Wilson) had been at the Board of Trade. It is important to emphasize the closeness of the working relationship that gradually developed between Heath and Iain Macleod, a relationship which was all the more notable in view of Macleod's own past ambitions for the Party leadership and the differences in personality and temperament between the two. Heath's decision to give Macleod the shadow Chancellorship had been regarded with certain misgivings in some quarters. Macleod had once written that 'the Treasury was the only one of the many offices that Churchill held that he did not adorn',[1] and there were apprehensions that a similar epitaph might have to be written of Macleod himself in due course. He was a man of warmth, imagination, daring, and ambition, who loved to roam in exciting and political realms, dealing in the great human themes of the age. Although he worked hard at everything he undertook, his evident preference was for colour and drama, and his sense of theatre and occasion was substantial. Certainly, he was no civil servant manqué. A skilful Parliamentarian, he was also one of the best platform speakers in British politics. In the Conservative Party he had secured a devoted group of adherents and admirers who saw in him a humanity, a size, and an extent of vision which they found wanting in other notables of the Party. But the task of shadow Chancellor seemed temperamentally and intellectually unsuitable to his talents, interests and experience.

It must be frankly conceded that these apprehensions proved to be not wholly ill-founded. The fact that he had not hitherto taken much serious interest in economic affairs was particularly apparent in small well-informed groups. But Macleod's outstanding political quality was his capacity to undertake new tasks with thoroughness and application and, in the main, Heath's decision was justified. Macleod was particularly adept at organizing the Opposition's tactics in the Commons, and in ensuring that his selected team – of which Mr Patrick

[1] Iain Macleod: *Neville Chamberlain* (London, 1961), p. 125.

Jenkin and Mr Terence Higgins, both elected in 1964, were
particularly successful – was thoroughly equipped on technical
points. 'It was this quality of critical opposition on complex
technical points which was really outstanding,' one who was
closely involved with Macleod has commented; 'if the Opposition really does its homework all kinds of technical points emerge
which otherwise go through on the nod.'

Macleod's tactical leadership of the Opposition team was
undoubtedly a considerable success, but the long-term strategical task was a more severe challenge. The gradual establishment of the Party's new economic strategy was an arduous,
lengthy, and complex process, and involved the participation
of a considerable number of people. It had to be undertaken,
furthermore, within the framework laid down in 1965. The
final 'package' necessarily reflected political and other com-
promises, and did not impress all observers; in particular, the
rash commitment to the immediate abolition of SET[1] was
increasingly regretted in private, and involved a greater reliance
on a Value-Added Tax and economies in public expenditure.
VAT has much to commend it as an alternative to purchase
tax for, although it is the consumer who pays in the end under
both systems, VAT is considerably more difficult to evade and
contains important encouragements to export. But, by itself,
it has limitations as a revenue earner. The basic Conservative
dilemma was that undertakings to reduce the burden of taxation were remorselessly eroded by rises in costs and by other
Party commitments – not least on Defence. The search for
economies was still continuing when the 1970 General Election
was announced.

Although this was a serious and detailed exercise, which was
much more thorough and professional than any hitherto
undertaken by an Opposition, the public presentation was not
convincing. This was in part the result of an understandable
caution about prior commitments before taking office – an
eventuality which was, until the late spring of 1970, taken for
granted – but which gave an impression of irresolution.[2] There is,

[1] See Macleod's speech to the Conservative Party Conference, Blackpool, 1968.
[2] See, for example, Heath's speech to the Confederation of British Industry on
21 May 1969 when he said that it would be 'a grave mistake to announce firm
solutions to a lot of hypothetical problems in a situation which cannot yet be
clearly foreseen'.

therefore, real validity in the criticism made by Dr Butler and Mr Pinto-Duschinsky that the combination of detailed proposals and general statements caused a situation where 'the former [were] too intricate to be fully comprehensible to the electorate, [while] the latter [were] too general to be convincing'.[1] This was to become particularly serious when it appeared that Labour had in fact found a solution to the economic malaise in the spring of 1970.

The difficulties facing the Conservatives should not be under-estimated, and the attempt to establish a definite and different economic strategy was a courageous one. But the final result was unsatisfactory because it relied too heavily upon the value of structural changes and was obsessed by the task of reducing direct taxation. Each was, perhaps, desirable, but collectively they did not form an economic strategy. When the uncomfortable matter of economic growth arose, the response was 'we have done it before and we can do it again', which was not invariably a comforting reflection. Increasingly it was argued that growth would stem naturally – indeed, virtually assuredly – from a reduction in Government expenditure, Trade Union reform, a reduction in direct taxation, and an increase in savings. It was not altogether surprising that many observers could not accept this as a realistic economic strategy by itself.

The Conservative economic policy very clearly reflected Heath's own sense of priorities, but this was the result of the close relationship between himself and Macleod rather than any domination of the shadow Chancellor. Nonetheless, while it must be emphasized that this was a partnership, the imprint of Heath's personality and convictions is clear.

Macleod's sudden death shortly after he took office as Chancellor in June 1970 will leave unanswered the question as to how he would have fared in that office. Far from being a cool and calculating man, he was a romantic, and his personal calculations were often woefully wrong. His refusal to serve in the Home Government in October 1963 was an honourable decision, but it further damaged a career that had already been checked by his surprisingly ineffective leadership of the Com-

[1] Butler and Pinto-Duschinsky: *op. cit.*, pp. 91–2. For a good example of the 'too general' approach, see Macleod's speech to the Party conference in 1968, and particularly the closing passage.

mons and Chairmanship of the Party from 1961 to 1963. At one stage, in the late 1950s, it had seemed that he was almost bound to become leader of the Party, but he lost ground severely between 1961 and 1965, and never really recovered it. Personal factors must not be ignored in any evaluation of this political decline. The burdens of public life were grievously accentuated by a progressively more painful and debilitating disease, which he bore with marvellous courage and determination, but which exacted its toll; and there were other private worries. In these sad circumstances his qualities and achievements were all the more remarkable. He was a strong and important link with those elements in the Conservative Party – and particularly the younger members – who felt that the Party was moving too far to the Right for their comfort. But Macleod was something more than a Conservative politician with strong liberal feelings. He had a style, a warmth, a humanity, and a zest for combat that won him a respect that went far beyond his Party. He was, intellectually, a limited man; he was certainly not 'too clever by half', as a former colleague once described him. But in politics personality is more important than intellect, and it was Macleod's personality which was the element that made him the most attractive politician of this period. But, whatever the causes, his was a muted voice in the years 1966 to 1970, and this commentator regretted that his abilities had not been directed into other channels. His death was a far greater tragedy than the loss of a man who had trained himself to be a capable Chancellor of the Exchequer.

The most persistent criticisms of Heath's approach as Leader of the Opposition was that it was a 'Government in exile', and that it lacked flexibility. It is doubtful whether Heath would have particularly resented such criticism. He saw it as his task to build up an alternative government that was a credible alternative and which possessed the necessary expertise to carry out its tasks efficiently. He recognized – perhaps too clearly in some areas – the advantages that the real Government enjoyed in terms of information and official advice, and there were some aspects of Conservative policy – again, notably on economic matters – which were deliberately kept vague until the Conservatives were in office again. The exercise, taken as a whole, can be regarded as a success and certainly the Opposition was technically and organizationally well prepared. But this emphasis on specialization, and Heath's manner of conducting meetings, irritated some of his colleagues, who felt that this arrangement gave Heath himself much greater freedom to roam around the political board while they were trapped. In the view of several observers this was one of the factors that exasperated Enoch Powell to the point that he increasingly spoke out beyond his allotted fields – first transport, then defence – outside Westminster, and created a tension which, in April 1968, became a matter of major public importance.

By this stage, the position of the Conservatives was a curious one. Disillusionment with the Labour Government was intense, and the Opposition was winning seats almost at will. In 1967 the Conservatives had captured Glasgow Pollok, Walthamstow East, Cambridge, and South-West Leicester, had narrowly failed to win Manchester Gorton, and had gleefully seen a 1966 Labour majority of 16,576 at Hamilton converted into a Scottish Nationalist Party victory of 1,799 in a higher poll (73.7 per cent) than at the 1966 General Election. In March 1968 the Opposition captured Acton, Meriden and Dudley. On every possible count – by-elections, local government elections, and public polls – the Conservatives were riding high. The local government elections had been a particularly valuable tonic to the rank and file, and had given it a taste of power in areas where Labour had enjoyed a long period of control. Some politicians are uninterested in local government; others tend to over-estimate its significance. But for a national party, the winning of power in local government elections is a very significant element in its general self-confidence and morale.

Nonetheless, there were many Conservatives who did not share the euphoria that was sweeping over the Party. The hard evidence was that although there *was* a movement towards the Conservatives, it was nothing like the scale of magnitude that was indicated by the polls and by-elections. The very volatility of the electorate indicated that, unless the Party was making really solid gains in the target voters, there could be an equally rapid and violent movement back towards the Government. There was doubt about whether Wilson's credibility had been destroyed, uneasiness about the superiority in the House of Commons of several Ministers over their 'shadows' and concern over the inability of Heath to make any apparent noticeable public impact. The Conservatives might have a vast lead over Labour in the polls, but Heath's personal rating remained obstinately low.

It is not strictly accurate to state that 'Mr Heath . . . did not inspire confidence among the electorate or the Party faithful'.[1] The former statement is difficult to prove or disprove; even if true, for the reasons already given, it is doubtful whether the political effectiveness of the Conservative Party was seriously impaired. The second statement, although also very general, can be tested in certain terms. It was certainly the case that the decisive factor in Heath's election in 1965 was the very positive reaction to his candidature by the constituency associations. Unquestionably, his conduct of the leadership aroused misgivings in 1966 and early 1967; but the fact that he successfully rode the Powell storm in April 1968, and the support given to him by area chairmen and associations was highly significant. It could be claimed that the Party felt that it had no choice, and could not change its leader again so soon after Home's departure. But there was something more positive than this. So far as the Conservative Party was concerned, while admitting that critics existed, confidence in Heath personally steadily increased between 1966 and 1970, and was demonstrated with particular vividness at the Party conferences.

But the Conservatives' concern went rather deeper than this. Had they in fact found the answer to 'the real needs of the 1960s'? In the course of the 1970 Election campaign Quintin Hogg demanded: 'Do we really have to go on like this, mouthing statistics, when for want of vision the people perish?' It was this feeling that acted as a nagging worry, and made several Conservatives alarmed at the consequences when, as it must do, the tide would begin to turn.

The Conservatives' determination after 1964 to create an identifiable and clear alternative to Labour was the result of a deliberate attempt to emphasize the fact that, despite many areas of 'overlap' between the parties, a genuine gulf of attitude separated them. Put at its most simple, the Labour Party believed that the collective success of the society could be

[1] Butler and Pinto-Duschinsky: *op. cit.*, p. 63.

planned and directed; in this situation, individual selfish achievement was anti-social and destructive. The Conservative philosophy – to which Heath gave considerable emphasis – is that the collective success of the community is built up on the successes and achievements of the individual. The State may guide and help those who are prepared to help themselves and support those in need, but the basis of national success is individual success. There was here a real and genuine difference of outlook, a fact that had become blurred in the late 1950s and early 1960s and which Heath was determined to sharpen.

The most serious danger confronting the Conservatives in 1964–70 was that of cultivating difference for the sake of difference. The danger was increased by the antipathy not only of the leadership but most of the Party towards Wilson personally. It must be conceded that this antipathy was understandable. It was less the major acts of unpleasantness towards the Opposition that rankled so much as what were regarded as the minor, and often rather cheap, thrusts. Wilson, for so long the outsider, was enjoying his power, and he often used it in a manner that provoked his opponents to a degree of bitterness that was without parallel in modern British politics since the death of Gladstone. Nonetheless, for all his provocation, it can be argued that in some areas the Conservatives over-reacted.

Heath himself was increasingly influenced negatively by Wilson, to the point where he went to considerable lengths to be as different from Wilson as possible. This was not a calculated movement, but was a profound reaction against Wilson's style and methods. Heath's estimate of Wilson became much sharper and harsher than has been customary between political leaders in recent British politics – even in the Macmillan–Gaitskell relationship – and had the result of making Heath intolerant of any proposal that had even a quasi-Wilsonian flavour. Dr Butler said of Heath that 'He used language which exaggerated his ideological differences with Labour.'[1] Yet in fact the differences – personal and ideological – were substantial even in 1966, and became more substantial thereafter. And one of the more significant contributory factors in this process was Heath's estimate of Wilson's overall approach to government. His introduction to the Conservative Manifesto in 1970 was personally written and was deeply felt. Wilson's

[1] Butler and Pinto-Duschinsky: *op. cit.*, p. 68.

influence on the Opposition was, accordingly, a very considerable one.

It so happened that on a number of matters the Government
was clearly right; there were others on which the Conservatives'
political interests – to say nothing of the national interest – lay
in cautious support. Machinery for the control of prices and
incomes was a significant example. It can be argued that
a more subtle and farsighted Conservative leadership would
have encouraged Labour on its course, while publicly reserving
its position. If the policy had been successful, the Opposition
could have claimed part of the credit; if it became the Government, it could gratefully inherit the machinery created by
its opponents. If the policy failed, the Conservatives could have
pointed out that such a melancholy situation would never have
arisen had the Government harkened to the informed and
experienced warnings of the Opposition.

This was, above all, one area in which the much-condemned
consensus politics could have contributed something of great
value to the national interest. If the two major parties, by the
close of the 1960s, had hammered out a machinery for limited
control of prices and wages which was an advance on that
attempted by Selwyn Lloyd a decade before, the nation would
have benefited substantially. But, because of the breakdown in
Government–Opposition relations, this did not happen.
Labour was forced to abandon this control in April 1969 in
deference to the more obtuse elements of the Labour Party, and
in face of vehement hostility from the Conservatives.

Political wisdom and an understanding of the national
interest are not the prerogatives of one political confederation,
and one of the most hopeful signs of British politics between
1954 and 1960 had been the process of mutual education
between the two major parties. Gradually, after 1966, and
particularly after devaluation, the possibility of learning from
Labour was anathema to the Conservatives; after 1966,
Wilson did not accept that he had anything of value to learn
from the Conservatives. Thus, there was a distinct movement
away from consensus politics. Had the debates been on
matters of profound principle, this division might have been
acceptable, but to the electorate it increasingly seemed to be
predominantly based upon personal and often artificial
ideological differences that had no relevance to the true prob-

lems of the late 1960s. Bevan had described the Labour policies in 1959 as 'pre-war Liberalism brought up to date', and the comment had an even greater validity in 1964 and 1966. Socialism had become almost a banned word, and Heath's problem was to emphasize that there *was* a difference between the two parties. By the beginning of 1968, and despite the decline in the Government's national position, it seemed doubtful that he had succeeded. Indeed, the impression had been created that the nation's political leaders were dominated by small issues, while the great ones slipped noiselessly by.

By the beginning of 1968 the Conservative Party was in a condition of unease, and it was not possible to claim, with any real certainty, that the Heath approach was going to be success-ful. It was in this context that in April 1968 Enoch Powell made his startling intervention.

Part Three

THE CONSERVATIVES – THE CHALLENGE OF POWELLISM

I^T is not necessary to accept Baldwin's dictum that the man who says that he can see far ahead is a charlatan to concede the point that the cultivation of the art of what is now termed 'futurology' is somewhat perilous in politics. Who, in 1965, would have anticipated the eruption of radical violence in American universities (or who, in 1968, could have anticipated its subsequent decline)? Who could have foreseen, in the last weeks of 1967, the long consequences that would flow from the deposition of Novotny and his succession by an unknown Slovak, Mr Dubček, to the leadership of Czechoslovakia? Politics is a frustrating and tantalizing pursuit. As soon as it appears that a pattern is developing, it is disturbed by some entirely unexpected event or a combination of circumstances whose significance is only suddenly and belatedly appreciated. The politician may appear to be the master of events, but in reality he is usually their helpless and baffled victim, swept along on violent tides, pushed first one way, then another, on occasion hurled on to rocks, on another left inert in a backwater. He may subsequently rationalize this tumultuous experience, or have it done for him by his biographer or the historian. But the fascination – and the peril – of politics lies in the fact that so little is predictable, and that what is predicted usually turns out quite differently.

It is as well to recall this fundamental fact when the history of race relations and politics in Britain in the 1960s is examined. For it would have seemed quite inconceivable in the 1950s that one of the most volatile political and social domestic issues of the following decade would be that of race relations.[1]

[1] This section is substantially based on the very extensive and thorough work that has been undertaken by the Institute of Race Relations, and in particular the indispensable report, *Colour and Citizenship*, published in 1969, of which a shorter version was published in 1970 under the title of *Colour, Citizenship and British Society*, and for which my colleague Nicholas Deakin was substantially responsible. The literature on this subject is large, and of high quality.

In 1950 the total coloured population of Britain was approximately 100,000 and coloured immigration into Britain was very much a phenomenon of the late 1950s and early 1960s. West Indian migration to Britain only began to assume mildly significant proportions in 1954, after the passage of the 1952 McCarran–Walter Act had effectively closed the United States to West Indians. Until 1961 this migration was highly responsive to labour demands in Britain, and its benefits to the British economy were not inconsiderable. The total of net inward migration from the West Indies, India, and Pakistan between 1955 and the end of 1960 was 211,640. In 1959 the net flow inward from India and Pakistan was 3,800, and by no stretch of the imagination could this be regarded as seriously significant. The 1961 Census revealed a total of all Commonwealth immigrants in the United Kingdom – including whites – of 596,755.

It was only slowly that the potential significance of this development was generally appreciated, and then only in those specific areas where it was physically obvious. The fact that any Commonwealth citizen could of right settle in Britain was generally established and accepted, and the presence of considerably less than half a million coloured immigrants in 1961 was not regarded as a matter for great concern. Thus the announcement, in the autumn of 1961, of the intention of the Conservative Government to make provision for controlling immigration of Commonwealth citizens aroused great dismay in the Labour and Liberal Parties, and in some sections of the Conservative Party. This hostility was based on the belief that the Government was destroying an outstanding feature of the Commonwealth system in order to meet what was hardly a serious problem. The fact that Mr (later Sir) Cyril Osborne, the Conservative Member for Louth, had been vigilantly campaigning for some time to curb coloured immigration did not make many thoughtful people elated by the Government's decision. Yet it was not necessary to like Osborne to recognize his pertinacity. Furthermore, he was not hypocritical, for he did not trouble to conceal the fact that his hostility to immigration was hostility to *coloured* immigration; 'This is a white man's country, and I want it to remain so,' was Osborne's *credo*.[1] It

[1] *Daily Mail*, 7 February 1961 (quoted in Paul Foot: *Immigration and Race in British Politics*, p. 129).

was only some time later, and with deep and reluctant repugnance, that it was recognized that Osborne may have had a point when the race problem, seemingly so small and irrelevant in the 1950s, quickly developed into something that threatened much more than the comfort of political parties.

But the tragic irony of the 1962 Act was that it helped to create the very menace for which it was allegedly legislating. Confronted by the possibility of a ban on immigration, there was a vast influx of new immigrants particularly from India and Pakistan, where population and economic pressures were mounting sharply. The figure for the net inward migration from the West Indies, India, and Pakistan from the beginning of 1961 to before the end of June 1962 (when the Act came into force) was 191,000. Furthermore, the Act did not limit immigration; all that it did was to limit adult male immigration. The Act permitted dependants and children under 16 to enter, with the consequence that the pattern of Indian and Pakistani immigration was dramatically shifted from one of temporary migrant workers to one of permanent settlement. Three-fifths of the migration from India and over half from Pakistan took place *after* the 1962 Act. Asian immigration until 1961 had been almost imperceptible, and certainly of little account numerically. West Indian immigration had created problems in certain areas, but the many compatibilities between the West Indian outlook and that of the British had softened these to a very manageable level. The Indian and Pakistani immigrants caused no problems primarily because they were virtually entirely single men. But when their families arrived, and the temporary stay became a permanent settlement, the many and profound differences between their civilization, society, attitudes, and experiences became a major problem in themselves. One has only to look for example at the rôle of women in a Moslem community, and compare it with that of women in a British or West Indian community, to make the simple – but essential – point. There was unquestionably the genesis of a major problem before 1961, but the Act of 1962 created a problem – and one that was in fact much more serious and difficult than the one it was designed to solve. The Act introduced a system of vouchers for those with definite jobs in Britain ('A' vouchers), those with particular skills but without fixed jobs ('B' vouchers) and a third category which was

abolished in 1964. In 1962 the total figures (including dependants) fell to 16,453, but in 1963 it had jumped to over 56,000.
Thereafter, although the controls on voucher holders were
progressively tightened, the number of dependants gradually
increased; 8,218 in 1962; 24,459 in 1963; 35,738 in 1964;
39,228 in 1965, and up to a peak of 50,083 in 1967. And this was
not the end. One careful estimate at the end of 1967 calculated
that about 235,000 more dependants were eligible for entry.

Thus, the new situation largely created by the 1962 Act, was
that the coloured immigrants were not transitory beings; they
had come to stay: and they had children, and were producing
more children. Looked at in this light, the 1961 figure of 'less
than half a million' looked considerably less comforting. In
1966 the coloured population of England and Wales was
estimated at 924,000 of whom 213,300 had been born in
Britain.

If even this number of immigrants had been spread over the
country, the impact would still have been relatively small, but it
was not. In London and the Midlands in particular the influx
was very substantial. By 1966 the coloured population in the
West Midlands was 2.8 per cent of the total population; in the
Greater London area it was 3 per cent. But the impact was
seen most substantially in areas within these general areas. In
Wolverhampton it was, even in 1966, approaching 5 per cent
and steadily rising. Most serious of all was the effect on housing.
In area where young couples had to wait for years for a council
house the arrival of a mass of new applicants was not welcome.
'The contrast between the position in 1950 and today is not
only a numerical one,' as Dr Abrams wrote in 1967. 'Today,
Britain's coloured people are no longer isolated in a handful
of dockland areas; they are to be found in almost every large
town in the country and in most industries . . . They no longer
consist overwhelmingly of male adult workers leading more or
less celibate lives in lodgings and hostels; today the majority
are living as families and their basic concerns are, therefore,
precisely the same as those of the rest of the population.'[1]

The great majority of the male immigrants brought a considerable value to the community. In 1969 doctors alone made
up 57 per cent of the 'B voucher' entrants,[2] and the 14,000

---

[1] Introduction to W. W. Daniel: *Racial Discrimination in England*, p. 10.
[2] Cmnd 4327.

overseas doctors in Britain represented 22 per cent of all doctors; coloured nurses and midwives constituted between 25 per cent and 35 per cent of the total in the profession. There was, inevitably, a debit balance as well, and one need not accept the more lurid accounts to accept that some of the newcomers would have been unwelcome whatever their colour or nationality. Problems of language, living standards, and religion were in themselves serious enough; to these were added others produced by methods of exploitation employed by some immigrants. The unfortunate West Indians set upon and beaten up in Nottingham and Notting Hill Gate in 1958, and others elsewhere, were paying the price for being identifiable members of a group that the indigenous population was learning to hate and fear. It would be superficial to allege that these incidents arose from racial factors alone. But, confronted with this situation, many immigrants who had wished to integrate were forced back into what their enemies categorized as ghettoes – and which, in some cases, they did in fact become. A dangerous gulf between the coloured and white populations began to develop in certain areas. There was no single race or colour problem; what developed was a number of different race problems, of varying seriousness from the acute to the minor. But increasingly, in the public consciousness such subtleties were becoming irrelevant. Between 1962 and 1965 the picture of a Black Invasion slowly but remorselessly developed, to the point that even the existing problem was transformed into something infinitely more alarming. Initially this fear was confined to those areas that were directly affected, but eventually it spread outside, until very considerable agitation and alarm was being experienced in areas which had no coloured immigrants whatever.

An additional factor – and one of substantial significance – was the development of mounting scepticism in Britain with the Commonwealth concept itself. This can probably be traced back to the aftermath of Suez, and, in particular, the resentment against what were regarded as double standards by certain Commonwealth members – notably India – as between Suez and the Russian suppression of the Hungarian rising. The burst of African decolonization at the turn of the 1950s and 1960s had been followed by events – particularly at the United Nations – which had increased British reservations about the value of the Commonwealth. The fiasco of Ghana, the horror of the Congo, the contemptuous Chinese incursion into India, the chronic and bitter India–Pakistan disputes, and the manifest gulf between protested objectives and actual performance of many new Commonwealth countries, all played their part in this mounting disillusionment. Powell had been ahead of his time when he had publicly – albeit anonymously – assailed the Commonwealth concept in 1964 as 'a gigantic farce', but by 1968 his views had a very widespread support.

Thus, there developed a situation in which it became a positive disadvantage to be a coloured *Commonwealth* immigrant, and thus, to be regarded as a representative of a backward, ungrateful, incompetent country. This abrupt and profound cynicism was, no doubt, unfair; but it undoubtedly existed. Thus, the Commonwealth itself was being regarded with increasing disfavour at the same time as the influx of Commonwealth immigrants was assuming significant proportions; and it was this combination of circumstances that inflamed what would have been, in any event, a major social problem.

In a situation of this kind it is important to emphasize both that the principal impact was confined to certain areas – a fact which makes the recital of national statistics misleading – and that the very suddenness of the invasion was in itself disturbing. On the second point, the dramatic rise in the immigrant population in the early 1960s speaks for itself. But the first point is perhaps the more significant. By January 1969 coloured pupils amounted only to 3.2 per cent of all children in primary and secondary schools in Britain; yet in one part of London (Hackney) 29.3 per cent of pupils in primary schools were coloured. In Wolverhampton over 15 per cent of children in primary schools were coloured, and the figure for Birmingham was over 10 per cent. In January 1968 there were 18,785 schools in Britain with no immigrant children at all; 4,847 had under 2 per cent; 2,838 had between 2 and 10 per cent; 610 had between 10 and 15 per cent; 392 had between 15 and 20 per cent; 1,036 had over 20 per cent.[1] The national proportion of coloured children is, therefore, relatively statistically insignificant; the *local* population in some areas was, however, very significant indeed. Furthermore, this significance is bound to become greater, as another conspicuous feature of the coloured

[1] Institute of Race Relations: *Facts Paper on the United Kingdom 1970-1.*

immigration has been its low average age. In 1966, 34 per cent of the coloured population was under 15 years of age, and 55 per cent was between 15 and 45; only 11 per cent were over 45. In fact, there has been a very striking decrease in the immigrant birth-rate with the availability of contraceptive facilities,[1] but this was difficult to foresee in the early 1960s. The 'breeding like rabbits' charge was widely believed and, because of the fact that most of the immigrant women were of child-bearing age, it was quite true that the coloured birth rate was relatively high. Thus, to those subjected to the full force of the coloured entry, the future seemed even more dismaying than the present. In these circumstances what amounted to panic in these areas could not be allayed by national statistics or national projections.

The existence of an entirely novel problem of such formidable potential seriousness dawned only slowly upon politicians in the late 1950s. The unexpected arrival of Indian and Pakistani immigrants led to attempts to reach arrangements with those countries whereby their governments agreed to curb the migration. The race troubles in Nottingham and London in the late summer of 1958 were a disturbing portent, as was the decision of Sir Oswald Mosley to contest the North Kensington constituency in the General Election of 1959. But the combination of severe sentences on white youths and the total humiliation of Mosley in the Election seemed to have obviated the need for major government intervention. Another factor that inhibited any desire to attempt to curb coloured Commonwealth immigration was the decision of the newly re-elected Conservative Government drastically to accelerate decolonization in Africa; African policy was heavily based on trust in British intentions among the shortly to be independent black African states.

There is no question that that Government – or, at least, a substantial majority of its members – had no desire to introduce restrictive legislation for Commonwealth immigrants. But the gradual increase in Commonwealth immigration was causing concern and at this stage a definite movement in favour of controls was evident in a small section of the Conservative Party, principally in the Birmingham area. The Birmingham Immigration Control Association had sufficient influential members

[1] Dr R. E. D. Simpson: *Race Today*, May 1970.

to require that it be heeded, and the sudden upswing in immigration from the West Indies in 1959 and 1960 gave it further impetus. The attempts to limit the migration at source failed, and, not without considerable uneasiness the Conservative Government launched the Commonwealth Immigrants Act. Its passage was vigorously opposed by the Opposition, and there were many Conservatives who were clearly unhappy. When it was passed, the Conservative leadership relaxed. The Birmingham Group pressed for stronger measures, but without success. There the matter rested until the success of avowed immigration-control Conservative candidates in the Birmingham constituencies of Smethwick and Perry Bar in the 1964 General Election jolted confidence. For the first time in modern British politics, coloured immigration had become a major political issue. 'The factor of racial prejudice, new in British politics and as yet unmeasured, must now be taken into account as a serious element in political life,' the Nuffield study of the 1964 Election sombrely concluded.[1]

The Labour record on immigration control between 1962 and 1968 closely matched that of the Conservatives.[2] Although Labour vehemently opposed the 1962 Act, even at that stage it was apparent to the close observer that there were significant variations in Labour hostility to the measure. MPs and candidates in areas in which coloured immigration was rising were already aware of the problem, and some were uneasy at the social implications and political liabilities of continuing Gaitskell's extreme view of retaining the free and unfettered right of every Commonwealth citizen to enter Britain as of right. The subsequent compromise was first seen in the debate on the Expiring Laws Continuance Bill in 1963 and took the form of proposals for bilateral controls, an emphasis on the necessity for the banning of racial discrimination, and government aid to areas in which there was a substantial degree of immigration. This could certainly be regarded as considerably more realistic politically in the changed circumstances than the

[1] Butler and King: *The General Election of 1964*, Appendix IV, p. 368.
[2] For a recent critical analysis see 'Labour and the Minorities' by Mervyn Jones, *New Statesman*, 6 August 1971.

former Gaitskell approach. In the 1964 Election the matter was only cursorily referred to in the Party Manifesto, but it was, significantly, a reference to the importance of *limiting* entry, which marked a distinct change from the 1962 Gaitskell line. Wilson's post-election depiction of the Conservative victor at Smethwick as a 'Parliamentary leper' was followed by the August 1965 White Paper,[1] which itself followed the Mountbatten Mission to the Commonwealth, which had been an unsuccessful renewed attempt to secure unilateral controls. The White Paper separated the statistics of immigrants from Canada, Australia, and New Zealand from 'other Commonwealth countries', a fact that in itself led to not unjustified allegation of racial prejudice. Under the new policy, voucher entry from the Commonwealth was reduced from 20,800 a year to 8,500 (of whom 1,000 were to come from Malta) and more stringent deportation procedures were introduced. It has been claimed that this policy 'marked the triumph of popular opinion over the initial opposition of nearly all politicians to the imposition of controls',[2] but a more critical assessment would lead to the conclusion that the dominant feature of the policy lay in its negative approach, particularly in the crucial area of housing. The new organizations created by the Labour Government – the National Committee for Commonwealth Immigrants and the Race Relations Board – were not given adequate powers or support, which further aroused suspicions about the genuineness of the Government's attitude towards the problem. But it could be argued that these attempts were an advance on anything offered by the Conservatives, whose immigration policy contained in the 1966 Manifesto followed the recommendations of the Party's study group. The conspicuous feature of the report of this group – and the resultant section in the Manifesto and the *Campaign Guide* – was its neglect of the positive aspects of racial integration. Here the Conservatives' prior planning was even more inadequate than that of Labour, whose policy had essentially derived from the work of a committee chaired by Anthony Greenwood. Government grants to local authorities which had been identified as having substantial immigrant problems were nearly doubled between 1964 and 1969, and it can be fairly claimed that the Labour

[1] *Immigration from the Commonwealth*, Cmnd 2739.
[2] Butler and King: *op. cit.*, p. 15.

policy did at least contain some positive aspects; that of the Conservatives contained none at all.

What had clearly happened was that the Labour leadership had come to the decision that here was an issue that could cost the Party much support in its traditional areas, and on which it would be fatal to be outflanked by the Conservatives. Many Labour supporters had been very alarmed by the positive stand of Gaitskell in 1961–2, and had been relieved by what they consider to be Wilson's greater political realism. But for those who had believed that the Labour movement stood for something better than opportunism of this kind, the experience was a bitter one.

The more one examines the Labour record on this issue the more do certain features stand out. Here was an area of social policy which had urgently required to be examined long before the 1964 Election, and a coherent stategy planned as a basis for government action. Despite the Greenwood Committee, the really essential work was only belatedly put in train after the 1964 Election and entrusted to the able and sincere Mr Maurice Foley; but the 1965 White Paper was rushed forward before Foley had had time to complete his findings and make his proposals. Throughout the 1960s – or, at least, after Gaitskell's death – the Labour Party was reacting rather than initiating, was reacting politically, and usually reacting in some confusion and incoherence. It is clear enough that the problem was never considered to have been a high-priority of social reform, and what initiative that there was did not come from the top. The 1965 Act made unlawful any discrimination on grounds of colour, race, or ethnic or national origin and penalized incitement to racial hatred. This was an advance, but the enforcement machinery was weak, and such legislation could self-evidently not touch the real problem. 'In the sectors we studied – different aspects of employment, housing, and the provision of services – there is racial discrimination varying in extent from the massive to the substantial,' the authors of a survey reported in 1967. 'It is moreover impossible to escape the conclusion that the more different a person is in his physical characteristics . . . the more discrimination he will face.'[1]

It is difficult to avoid the conclusion that the Labour leader-

[1] Daniel: *op. cit.*, p. 209.

ship was obsessed by the economic situation, and was intellectually preoccupied in many areas with the problems of the
early 1950s. There existed in the Labour Government, without
question, some individuals whose real views on race were not
far removed from those of Cyril Osborne. Then there were
those who, although concerned, failed to grasp the magnitude
and complexity of the problem, and who had a vague notion
that if moderate controls were in force the immigrants would
somehow become integrated without much effort from the
Government. There were those who were simply not interested.
There were some who realized the problem, but whose proposed solutions were equally simplistic. And there were those
who really understood, really cared, and really tried. Unhappily, the last group was a small minority. One need not go as far
as Mr Paul Foot has done[1] to accept that the Labour record
on race relations between 1962 and 1968 was somewhat lacking
in comprehension and imagination.

But there was a general impression by the beginning of 1968
that although race remained a social problem, it had ceased to
be a political issue. It would be quite wrong to allege that there
had been a conspiracy of silence between the parties on the
issue since 1964. What had happened was a deliberate de-fusing
of the dangerous elements in the situation undertaken principally by Roy Jenkins and leading Conservative spokesmen –
notably Hogg, Maudling, and Boyle. The trouble was that this
was a Parliamentary front-bench de-fusing, which hardly
extended to the back-benches, let alone the rank and file, and
particularly the Conservative rank-and-file. It was a good
example of the phenomenon of a Parliamentary consensus
being quite unrepresentative of extra-Westminster feelings. This
is not a condemnation of what happened in Parliament, which
was sane, far-sighted and desirable, nor is it an approval of what
happened elsewhere – which could hardly be described in
similar terms. It is a statement of an evident fact – that there
was a large gulf between Parliamentary agreements and
national feelings.

By this stage, both major parties had been obliged to forget
promises which they had made in the past, and the vigorous
opposition which both had shown to the restriction of coloured
immigration. In December 1958 a junior Conservative Minister

[1] Paul Foot: *The Politics of Harold Wilson* (London, 1968).

had declared that the granting of citizenship, 'is simply a fact which we have taken for granted from the earliest days in which our forebears ventured forth across the sea'; in the same debate the Labour spokesman declared that, 'the central principle on which our status in the Commonwealth is largely dependent is the "open door" to all Commonwealth citizens. If we believe in the importance of our great Commonwealth, we should do nothing in the slightest degree to undermine that principle.'[1]

Ten years later, this principle had been abandoned by both parties, but virtually everyone concerning themselves with race relations took the view that although hostility to the presence of coloured immigrants still persisted, this was gradually diminishing, and was not characteristic of the situation as a whole. Among politicians, there was a general relief that, however undignified the process had been, the major political parties had reached general agreement, that although Commonwealth immigration was to be strictly controlled the principal emphasis was to be on absorbing those who had come, and integrating them into society. It seemed significant that the Smethwick and Perry Bar results in the 1966 Election had reversed those of 1964, and the general concordance between the parties was well expressed by Enoch Powell in a review article in the *Sunday Times* of 14 June 1964, when he had written that, 'the immigrants who have come already, or who are admitted in the future, *are* part of the community. Their most rapid and effective integration is in the interest of all. Anything which tends to create a separate market for the labour and abilities of the immigrants prejudices the general interest as well as that of the immigrants themselves.'[2] In an article in the Wolverhampton *Express and Star* 10 October 1964, Powell emphatically declared that, 'I have set and I always will set my face like flint against making any difference between one citizen and another on the grounds of his origin.'

Such attitudes had been a disappointment to some Midlands Conservatives, who had deliberately made use of the race issue in the 1964 Election. In 1966, however, the emphasis was more muted, and when Mr Peter Griffiths went down to defeat at Smethwick one observer wrote that 'Immigration, as an

[1] Quoted in Paul Foot: *Immigration and Race in British Politics*, p. 125.
[2] A. Roth: *Enoch Powell – Tory Tribune* (1970), p. 313.

election-winning issue, was dead – possibly for all time.'[1] Although profoundly unprophetic, this was certainly a representative view at the time, and one that seemed justified. Most politicians had hated the whole race business, and were deeply relieved that it seemed to have faded away as a political issue. Even those members of the Labour Party who had intensely disliked the 1965 White Paper reluctantly accepted that it had proved a reasonable solution to a potentially dangerous situation. 'In terms of judicial action and electoral behaviour,' Dr Abrams wrote in 1967, 'the British people decisively rejected both physical violence and political extremism as acceptable methods of dealing with the problem.'[2]

Now, with the wisdom of hindsight, we can see that the problems were far from resolved, that the actions of the Government had been inadequate, and the race issue was smouldering grimly. This fact was dramatically revealed on Sunday 21 April 1968, when an astonished public – and several even more astonished politicians – read detailed reports of a speech delivered by Enoch Powell on the previous afternoon to the West Midlands Conservative Political Centre. The speech had, moreover, been televised. Within hours it was evident that a major political event had occurred.

The immediate background to Powell's speech was the Commonwealth Immigrants Act of 1968, which in its turn was the result of legislation enacted by the Kenya Government specifically directed against Asians who had not taken up Kenyan citizenship. The Kenyan Government Immigration Act, which came into effect on 1 December 1967, required these Asians to have entry-work permits, which would be processed by the Kenyanization Bureau of the Ministry of Labour. These measures did not greatly surprise anyone who was aware of the deep-seated antipathy felt in East Africa against Asians, and particularly Indians; indeed, perhaps the only matter for surprise was the fact that this action had not been taken much earlier.

This situation faced the British Government with a difficult predicament. Under the Acts of independence of the former

[1] Butler and King: *op. cit.*, p. 253.
[2] Daniel: *op. cit.*, p. 10.

colonies, residents were given the option of retaining their United Kingdom citizenship; those who did so were not affected by the Acts of 1962 and 1965, and were accordingly entitled to enter Britain without restraint or limitation. Some 230,000 Asians in Kenya, Uganda, and Tanzania had taken up this option,[1] and in Kenya alone there were 120,000 UK passport holders.[2] There was a sharp increase in Asian entrants to Britain from East Africa in December 1967 and January 1968, and in the three-month period November 1967–January 1968 inclusive over 7,000 had arrived, larger than the total for 1966. Roy Jenkins – at that time still Home Secretary – denied in November 1967 that the situation was one of a 'mass exodus', and resisted back-bench Conservative pressures to close what Mr Duncan Sandys described as 'this loophole in our immigration controls'. The figures for the following two months served to give some grounds for the rapidly escalating apprehensions of a swarm of displaced Asians from East Africa descending on Britain, but hardly justified the apocalyptic forecasts which began to be heard in January 1968.

Although it must be accepted that some Government action was required, it must be seriously questioned whether this situation at all justified the precipitate step now taken by the Government. On 22 February, Callaghan announced his intention of introducing immediate legislation to restrict the number of entrants of this category to 1,500 entry-vouchers a year.[3] The Commonwealth Immigrants Bill was published the next day and was rushed through both Houses by 1 March.

It should be emphasized that the measure was a bi-partisan one, and that – with very few exceptions – the Bill was supported in Parliament by the Conservatives. Indeed, the existence of the 'menace' of a massive Kenyan Asian influx had first been raised by Sandys, Enoch Powell, and other Conservatives. This does not absolve the Government from its reaction, but it is fair to point out that this was essentially an agreed measure. On 21 February 1968 the official Conservative Five Point Plan for controlling immigration was published, which stated clearly that, 'There would, obviously . . . be most serious social con-

---

[1] Speech by Callaghan, House of Commons, 15 February 1968.

[2] Statement issued by Kenyan High Commissioner in London 19 February 1968. Lord Gardiner, House of Lords, 29 February, gave the Kenya figure as 167,000.

[3] This limit was extended to 3,000 by the Conservative Government in May 1971.

sequences if large numbers of Kenyan immigrants were to come to Britain at a rate which could not be absorbed.'

In justifying the measure, Callaghan said that, 'I very much regret that it is not possible for this country to absorb these persons, to whom we have the most solemn obligations, all at once. If we did, I fear that it would cause racial disharmony and explosion.' He went on to make the point – made even more dramatically in the Lords by the Lord Chancellor, Lord Gardiner – that the legislation covered all Commonwealth citizens with British passports, amounting to one million persons. This argument could hardly answer the accusation that the legislation was directed specifically against Kenyan Asians, and that it was brought in, moreover, without discussions with those bodies in Britain which had been set up by the Government to advise on community and race questions. In this context, matters were not really assisted by the assurances of Mr David Ennals, a junior Minister at the Home Office, in the Commons debate that:

We are determined to avoid the situation which has developed in the USA, where patterns of prejudice and discrimination have created an under-priviliged indigenous minority, many of them react violently against what they conceive to be second-class citizenship. This must not happen here, and it is part of the responsibility of the Government and the House of Lords to see that it does not.

Giving his support to the Government, Maudling said that, 'I believe that this country has handled the racial problem very well . . . But even here there is bound to be a flashpoint . . . somewhere, and if the flash occurs everyone will be burned, and probably seriously burned.' Hogg also supported the Government: 'We desire no second-class citizens . . . no race discrimination, and no dilapidated areas housing different communities.' It was evident that factors beyond the fate of the unhappy Kenyan Asians were involved.

Not all the Members of Parliament were convinced that this was the case. There was the principle of the abrupt abrogation of a former commitment, entered into freely by the then Conservative Government; not all were convinced that the much-vaunted threat of a vast influx of Asians had any solid justification; others were concerned by the effect the legislation would have on British relations with the Third World; and others were apprehensive of the psychological impact on the immigrant communities actually in Britain. In these circumstances many Ministers and former Ministers found themselves in an acutely difficult personal position. Government absentees in the Second Reading Division included Mrs Castle, Anthony Crosland, Richard Crossman, Ray Gunter, Kenneth Robinson, Miss Jennie Lee, Mrs Shirley Williams, and Goronwy Roberts. Fifteen Conservatives voted against the Bill, including Iain Macleod, Mr Nigel Fisher, and Mr Terence Higgins; absentees from the Division included Sir Alec Douglas-Home, Peter Walker and Sir Keith Joseph.[1] The House of Lords, after a marathon sitting of over nineteen hours, eventually passed the Second Reading by the small majority of 109 to 85. Twenty-one Conservatives voted against the Government.

Two thousand Asians left Kenya on 27 February alone to beat the deadline. Those who could not get out in time became pathetic nomads, shuttled between Africa and London. Organizations to smuggle Asians into Britain illegally sprang up in Europe. There are no reliable estimates of how many entered Britain by this expensive route, but the numbers may be considerable. And these stateless persons were holders of British passports! It was a shameful episode which merited the scathing indictment of providing evidence 'of bungling, cynicism, opportunism and malice'.[2] The passage of the Act, the manner in which it was done, and the emotions which it aroused, provided the perfect background for Enoch Powell's intervention.

It is doubtful whether any British political speech in peacetime had had an immediate effect comparable to that created by Powell's Birmingham speech of 20 April 1968, since Joseph Chamberlain had flung down the gauntlet of Tariff Reform, also at Birmingham, in May 1903. But Chamberlain had been a political figure of the first rank, a Cabinet Minister, the

[1] 372 supported the Second Reading (209 Labour, 163 Conservative); 62 voted against (35 Labour, 15 Conservative, 10 Liberal, 1 Scottish Nationalist, 1 Welsh Nationalist).
[2] Nicholas Deakin: *Socialist Commentary*.

erstwhile 'Radical Joe' of the 1870s and early 1880s, the author of the radical 'unauthorized programme' of 1885, the man who had deserted Gladstone over Irish Home Rule in 1886 and brought the Liberal Party to temporary ruin, the man who had served under Salisbury as Colonial Secretary and had been principally responsible for accelerating the crisis with the Boer Republics which had precipitated the South African War – in Churchill's words, 'a splendid piebald; first black, then white; or, in political terms, first Fiery Red, then True Blue'. Chamberlain's unshakeable political base had been Birmingham, which had loyally – although not without political bloodshed – followed him in his extraordinary career from Left to Right. A major Chamberlain speech, particularly at Birmingham, was, *ipso facto*, an event. This position was very different from that occupied by Enoch Powell when he rose to speak on the afternoon of 20 April.

Powell was without question the most interesting and perplexing personality who was prominent in public life in the 1960s. Wilson, for all his individualities, can be categorized; Heath, although a curiously unusual Conservative leader, can be recognized without difficulty; Powell defies categorization or recognition. For a brief period he exercised an extraordinary public attraction, and the causes of his remarkable public emergence and its equally remarkable brevity merit analysis.

We must begin with the man himself. He was born on 16 June 1912, in a modest home on the outskirts of Stechford, near Birmingham, the only child of a couple who had both been primary schoolteachers before their marriage in 1909.[1] It would appear that the dominant influence in this austere but happy family was Powell's mother, evidently a woman of strong personality with keen ambition for her son. This atmosphere of seriousness, frugality, and happiness has made its mark on Powell's personality. Encouraged warmly by his mother, his education developed into a determined and triumphant progress from King Edward's School, Birmingham, to Trinity College Cambridge, thence to election to a Fellowship in the same College, and appointment, at the age of 25 to the Chair of Greek at the University of New South Wales, in Australia, in

[1] This account is based upon T. E. Utley's study of Powell, Andrew Roth's *Enoch Powell – Tory Tribune*, Powell's own writings, public speeches, and broadcasts, and interviews with some of his associates.

1937. In 1939, he was appointed Professor of Greek and Classical Literature at Durham University. He was, then, twenty-seven years of age. He had won virtually every classical prize worth winning at Cambridge, and his published work demonstrated that he was a scholar of painstaking care and meticulousness. His shyness and severity, which had earned him the reputation of an alarmingly earnest recluse at Cambridge, concealed the fact that he had written much poetry, of a certain stern romanticism but some of real quality, and had become deeply impressed by German culture and literature, particularly Nietzsche. His industriousness and determination had also been buttressed by a quite exceptional capacity for learning and comprehending languages. It is not surprising to discover that he had made few close friends in this solemn and impressive advance. We have the portrait of a solitary and frugal man, with a passion for order and accuracy, sensitive, nervous of human contact, yet a romantic under stern self-control. We do not, however, have the impression of a cold academic. We see the cool exterior; but we should also note the smouldering fires beneath it. Although the differences between his early years and those of Heath are very striking, the similarities are close enough to be worthy of note.

On the outbreak of war, Powell at once resigned his Sydney Chair, postponed dreams of Durham, and returned to England to enlist as a private in the Royal Warwickshire Regiment. He has himself said that, 'I am essentially an institutional man. I have a natural liking for male institutions, the college, the regiment, the Commons; they are all *corporate*', and that 'I sometimes think I should have made a good monk. I don't feel that it would have got on my nerves to be living an ordered life with others. On the contrary, an ordered life – and the emphasis is on ordered – with others seems to me to be an almost basic condition of happiness. At any rate, male happiness.'[1]

In the Army he was clearly happy and his rise was swift. His period in the ranks was brief, and after he had passed out of Aldershot he was posted to the Middle East, where he characteristically taught himself Urdu, in both the Persian script and the Devanageri script. He rose to Brigadier, and one can well believe the comment of a fellow-officer that, 'if he had a failing it was an overbearing intolerance of inefficiency'.

[1] Quoted in Roth: *op. cit.*, p. 31, and in ATV broadcast 10 November 1970.

The experience in India was clearly a very deep one. He developed a powerful ambition to serve the Empire, by which he meant India, in an important capacity. He has made no secret of the fact that his ambitions were centred on the Viceroyalty itself. At the end of the War he returned to London and offered his services to the Conservative Party. He was appointed to the Parliamentary Secretariat, and went to the cramped but pleasant house in Old Queen Street, Westminster, where the Conservative Research Department has lived since its establishment in 1929 and to which it returned in 1947. But, although he was in physical proximity with the group of young men attracted by R. A. Butler – and which included Iain Macleod and Reginald Maudling – his approach was very different. By training and intellectual conviction he was a fundamentalist, and a profound believer in Logic. The Tory romanticism of a Macleod or the relaxed pragmatism of a Maudling held little deep attraction for Powell. His shock at the granting of independence to India in 1947 was intense, and it sowed the seeds for his slow-moving but profound subsequent lack of interest in, or feeling for, the Commonwealth. India was, in his eyes, the keystone; without it, the rest was irrelevant. For some time these views were kept to himself so thoroughly that their emergence in 1964 startled even those who thought they had known him best.

Powell's first Parliamentary contest was a hopeless battle at a by-election at Normanton, in Yorkshire, in 1947, where he went down to inevitable defeat in spite of an extremely vigorous campaign. He then had to endure, as had so many other Tory hopefuls, the long and infinitely depressing round of constituency selection meetings. Eventually, in December 1948, he was selected for the Labour-held seat of Wolverhampton South-West. His application to this constituency was characteristically thorough and determined, and he was elected by 691 votes in the 1950 General Election. In this period of waiting he had continued at the Research Department and had broadcast for the BBC foreign service, sometimes in German and Urdu, until his selection for Wolverhampton.

Powell's principal work in the Research Department was as joint head of the Home Affairs Section with Iain Macleod, where he specialized in housing, local government, and town and country planning. He was exceptionally good at grasping the complex minutiae of local government, and impressed his colleagues by his assiduity. His efforts and energies were concentrated on his work, and a stream of very able and well-researched Party papers and pamphlets testified to this; one of the most remarkable was the pamphlet, published in February 1949, on Conservative policy for Wales and Monmouthshire, which Powell also presented in Welsh. Other pamphlets on municipal functions, housing, sewage, and local government were written very substantially by Powell. But despite his formidable record of work, Powell's departure from Old Queen Street in 1949 occasioned mixed feelings. Powell has a capacity for making real friends, and those who discover the warm heart and gaiety beneath the frigid surface know that they have found something very special. But – and this was particularly true before his marriage in 1952 – he has also a strong capacity for alienating people. In this early period his ambition was itself so overwhelmingly evident that it had, for some, a positively repellent quality. Some of those who came into contact with him were not prepared to accept the lavish praises of Powell's intellectual qualities, and considered that his Logic led him to conclusions that were not merely politically absurd but were intellectually suspect.

It was not long before the House of Commons became aware of the arrival of this strange, earnest, solitary man with white face and burning eyes. He shared with many of the Conservative newcomers an impatience with what they regarded as the unaggressive tactics of their leaders in a situation in which the vast Labour majority of 1945 had been reduced to six. And there was an early indication of future antipathies. Heath made his maiden speech in warm support of the Schumann Plan; Powell joined a small group of Conservatives who deliberately abstained on an official Opposition motion criticizing the Government for its lack of enthusiasm. He joined the 'One Nation' Group, that included Macleod, Angus Maude, Heath and Robert Carr, which was vaguely dedicated to the proposition in Disraeli's *Sybil* that great perils lay in the division of Britain into two nations, the Rich and the Poor. There was not, in fact, much more consensus in the Group than this, and its members approached the political present and future from very different angles. The quite false impression was gained that it was a cohesive group of progressive Conservatives, somehow linked personally and intellectually with Butler; in fact, as is usually the case, there were many fundamental differences between them.

Even at this early stage it was already becoming difficult to place Powell in any of the neat categories so beloved by political commentators. His fundamentalism took him in different directions, so that appellations of 'Right Wing' or 'Progressive' had to be hastily removed, only to be restored again – with comparable inappropriateness – later. He took an active interest in the social services which culminated in the publication of a pamphlet written in association with Iain Macleod, which appeared in October 1951. On this subject he would be labelled as 'enlightened' or 'progressive', yet on defence and imperial issues he would be classified as yet another of those 'Tory Brigadiers' at whose expense the Labour Party made much merriment at the time. The fact that Powell was a man of genuine intellectual and political independence was beginning to be understood, although the extent of his individuality and independence was not, as yet, fully appreciated.

Powell's principal stand during this period was over the abandonment of the Suez Canal bases – although it was not without significance that he strongly attacked the Royal Titles Bill in 1953 on the grounds that it disrupted the unity of the Commonwealth and Empire – and the revelation of his strong latent hostility and suspicion of the United States of America, subsequently made more evident. Although the Suez rebels failed to carry the day, the point was firmly established that Powell was not to be found in the ranks of those who were prepared to contemplate the gradual abandonment of imperial commitments with equanimity; his joint editorship (with Maude) of *Change Is Our Ally* in 1954 also demonstrated to a wider audience what had long been evident in the House of Commons, that his hostility to the economic and social policies of the Churchill Government put forward by Butler was not the consequence of a desire to gain a reputation for contrariness. Powell was not in reality urging a return to *laissez-faire*, but the strong bias against controls and direction of industry was very evident. *Change Is Our Ally* is a serious and important pamphlet, and if the full argument may be difficult to accept, the point that it is not the job of government to rescue incompetence, either in the private or the public sector, has its point. But Powell's views revealed the very substantial gulf between his convictions about the rôle of the State in controlling the economy and the views not only of the Government but of many of his One Nation colleagues.

A House of Commons reputation is a strange thing, and it cannot be culled from speech or by kind words said in debates about speeches. It is something that goes outside and beyond the Chamber and Committee Rooms of the House of Commons, something that is only slowly acquired. Powell may have been resentful that almost all of the 1950 intake of new Conservatives had received office relatively quickly and were embarking on successful ministerial careers while he remained on the back benches. But office gained too early has its disadvantages. Heath was perforce silent, as a junior Whip; Carr was Eden's Parliamentary Private Secretary; Macleod and Maudling had major Goverment posts. Powell had the freedom to establish himself on a number of issues, and he steadily gained the reputation of a hard worker and a sedulous attender of debates. John Strachey was not exactly charitable when he described Powell in 1954 as 'by far the most considerable figure of the lunatic, anti-democratic fringe of his Party', but he was not the only observer who was prepared to take Powell seriously. If he remained a considerable enigma, regarded by some as just another Parliamentary eccentric going his own way, his House of Commons reputation was established by the time he became, in December 1955, Parliamentary Secretary for Housing and Local Government.

The Ministry had developed into one of the most complex and significant in modern British government. Under Duncan Sandys and Powell the first measure of importance was the halving of housing subsidies, an act that was the prelude to the Rent Bill, introduced at the beginning of the Session of 1956–67. But in October–November 1956 the attention of the House of Commons was fixed on other matters, and it was only as the dust and clatter of the Suez operation were subsiding that the impact of this new legislation was appreciated. But before the Bill had entered the prolonged strains of the committee stage the Eden Government had fallen, Macmillan had become Prime

Minister, and Powell was promoted to Financial Secretary to the Treasury.

Powell was already regarded as a political ascetic, whose eyes gleamed at the prospect of sacrifice. One recalls the judgement of Churchill on Rosebery that 'he was unduly attracted by the dramatic, and by the pleasure of making a fine gesture . . . In a wearing ordeal his thoughts strayed to the fine speech he could make on resignation.' Such judgements were certainly freely applied to Powell when the entire Treasury team – Mr Peter Thorneycroft, Mr Nigel Birch, and Powell – resigned in January 1958. The ostensible battle was over £50 million; but the real issue was between the principles of holding Government expenditure down or letting it rise. It could be seen as a struggle between a deflationist or an inflationist policy, but in truth it was a division between those Conservatives who, like Macmillan, were haunted by memories of the 1930s and who believed deeply in the social importance of increased State expenditure to build a happy and undivided society, and those who took the view that such a course was economically and morally ruinous. The Conservatives were, indeed, moving towards an interpretation of the rôle of government in the economy which was in some respects ahead of that of the Labour Party. The movement was hesitant, and resembled a confused groping for new solutions to chronic ills rather than a carefully thought out change in policy, but it was the trend that so alarmed Powell, and which elicited his protest. Those Conservatives who regarded the resignations as hardly less futile than that of Lord Randolph Churchill in 1886 had missed the real point at issue. There is no doubt that Powell's was a powerful voice in the Treasury triumvirate; and although he subsequently served under Macmillan again, his views on that statesman were permanently marked by his attitude on the economic-social question. 'The Conservative in principle denies, in practice minimizes, government intervention in the economic field' was Powell's credo.[1]

In 1960 – after the Conservative triumph of 1959 – Powell returned to the Government, as Minister of Health. By this time his House of Commons reputation had been very considerably

---

[1] 'The Limits of Laissez-Faire' (*Crossbow*, April 1960). See also his pamphlet *Saving in a Free Society*, published by the Institute of Economic Affairs in September 1960.

enhanced by his speech on the Hola Camp affair, which is referred to later. His arrival at the Ministry was regarded with trepidation which did not seem to be misplaced when he announced increases in charges and contributions to the National Health Service. Powell met the attacks from the Labour benches with cold contempt, but there was solid sense in the comment of Mr Kenneth Robinson:

The Minister, in his ten years in the House, has gathered an unusual fund of respect from both sides for his courage, his integrity, and his intellectual capacity. They are all qualities which were very manifest in the speech he made in the debate on the Hola massacre . . . [But] he seems to display a curiously bleak and blinkered attitude to people, as if he regards people as statistical entities and consumers of Exchequer Funds. Austerity fits him like a hair-shirt.

Despite the opposition that Powell's policies aroused, his tenure of the Ministry of Health was highly competent, and his promotion to the Cabinet, in the reshuffle that followed Macmillan's drastic actions on 13 July 1962, when seven Cabinet Ministers – including Selwyn Lloyd, the Chancellor of the Exchequer – lost their posts, was fully merited. Nor, in retrospect, was it at all surprising that he refused to serve in the Home Government in October 1963, although at the time it caused dismay to those elements on the right wing of the Party, who had come to loathe Macmillan. To Powell it was a matter of honour. He has kept public silence on the succession crisis of October 1963, in which Home succeeded Macmillan, but has never attempted to conceal his view that Butler should have been chosen and that he fully agreed with Iain Macleod's subsequent celebrated assault on the 'magic circle' methods which had resulted in Home's appointment.[1] Nor has he concealed his view that, had Butler stood out, he would have been Prime Minister.

Throughout the development of his career Powell had gradually developed a particular style and what we might loosely call persona. He was the Seer, the Forecaster, the prophet who saw matters starkly and explained them thus. His lack of public bonhomie, which initially had so startled, and in many cases offended, loyal Conservatives who were not only used to, but expected, courtesy and friendliness from their leaders, now

[1] *Spectator*, 17 January 1964.

gradually assumed an attractive character. *He* would not attempt to pull the wool over their eyes, or be afraid to tell them the truth. Powell had, by the mid-1960s, established himself in a position to which all politicians aspire – the ambitious politician who appears to be above politics. It was this factor that explained his success, gave him his attraction, and aroused apprehensions in the Conservative hierarchy. An independent maverick is a matter of little concern to a party leadership; a determined, dedicated, and deeply ambitious politician who is courting the party faithful with an independent line is, as the Americans say, another thing again.

Ambition in a politician is, of course, natural and almost inevitable, but it takes many forms. Contrary to some public estimates, not every Member of Parliament sees himself as a Cabinet Minister, let alone Prime Minister. Others, who do at first, quickly realize that the odds are so long and the sacrifices of time and freedom such that they soon lower their sights. Others have gradually to face the fact that they simply do not have the ability to reach high office; some of these decline into querulousness and bitterness, others determine to seek and enjoy the minor pleasures of public life. The man who is fixed with a cold relentless ambition to get to the top is a relative rarity. The man who adds to this ambition a personal conviction of destiny that is virtually messianic is very rare indeed. Churchill's sense of destiny was very real, and sustained him in his darkest moments of political misfortune, but the warmth of personality, his keen sense of humour, and his lusty enjoyment of the political battle saved him from the darker aspects of personal self-confidence. For much of Powell's career, and certainly until 1966, one of his principal characteristics had been his unpredictability. Consistent in certain attitudes, he had been prepared to make abrupt and unexpected turns on policies. But after 1966 one is increasingly conscious of a change that can only be explained – in the judgement of this commentator – by the fact that he believed that his hour was approaching.

The Conservatives had fought the 1966 General Election as the Party of change, an approach that was incomprehensible to many Conservatives who had not discerned the new direction in which Heath had turned the Party. When, in 1970, Lord Coleraine published a pamphlet entitled *For Conservatives*

Only, Mr Robert Blake[1] – the eminent biographer of Lord Coleraine's father, Bonar Law, and Disraeli – described it in a *Spectator* review as 'brilliant', and applauded Coleraine's skill in pointing out 'the folly of the Conservative party posing as the party of "change" in order to attract a largely fictitious minority progressive floating vote . . . Conservatives are there to conserve – and to conserve a set of values in which they believe, not to consolidate the changes made by their enemies.' Although Mr Blake's views were not very different from those of Heath, they were in principle considerably closer to those of Powell. But these opinions were, in 1968, markedly more widely held in the Conservative Party than they were in 1970. For, even at this stage, Heath's position was still insecure. In the eyes of many Conservatives his approach seemed, erroneously, to consist of proposing variations to the Labour policy rather than of proposing a separate policy. The apparent emphasis on 'efficiency' did not greatly enthuse them. Despite the standing ovations at Party conferences and the ritualistic tributes to the Leader, a gulf remained between a significant element in the Party and the Opposition Front Bench. What did the Conservative Party 'stand for'? To this question Heath had not yet produced a reply that truly satisfied the restless element who saw looming before them the appalling prospect of an endless period of Labour rule. Heath's difficulties were inadequately appreciated, and his personal contribution to the new Conservative philosophy was as yet not really understood. This was the impatient constituency to which Powell had begun to appeal.

This appeal had been made earlier but it had not become so persistent or so well planned before Powell's refusal to serve in the Home Government. Thus we find him declaring, at Bridgnorth, on 25 May 1964:

Here is a nation which lives by capitalism; which by means of capitalism achieved standards for its people exceeded only in one other country, the capitalist United States; which depends for its existence on satisfying the demand of customers throughout the world in competition with all and sundry. Here is a party engaged in a life-and-death struggle with political opponents who are pledged and dedicated to Socialism and whose every policy is aimed at eliminating the processes of capitalism from our economy and our society. Yet the same nation and the same party will stop their ears

[1] Now Lord Blake.

and turn the other way if they hear mention of the very word capitalism; and even the various synonyms or euphemisms – 'market economy', 'free economy', 'competitive private enterprise', – etc. – all share to a greater or less degree in the same denigration.

The Conservative Government's attempts to check wages, prices, and profits were dismissed as 'hocus pocus' and 'dangerous nonsense', and he condemned industrialists who attempted to co-operate with the Labour Government; he attacked the siting of industries in areas of high unemployment for reasons which were quite uneconomic. A series of articles signed 'A Conservative' appeared in *The Times* at the end of March 1964, in which the author poured contumely on a number of Conservative sacred cows, including the Commonwealth. Powell has consistently refused to deny or to admit his authorship of these articles. But in speech after speech, Powell preached the gospel of unfettered capitalist enterprise and excoriated the basis of incomes policies, planned growth, and other devices of the Conservative Government, which he dismissed on one occasion as 'some wishy-washy, illogical compromise with Socialism, willing to plan but afraid to command'. 'We can so easily slide into thinking that the only way to be rescued from ruin is by stripping ourselves of all our inherited characteristics,' he said in 1963, 'jettisoning all typically British methods of conducting life, abandoning all our proven systems of selection and decision-making, and consigning our destiny to the hands of a few omniscient technocrats. These attitudes are, in fact, ready-made instruments of persuasion at the disposal of the Labour Party to further its electoral prospects. They oblige even Tory Governments to operate within the framework of an implicitly Socialist public opinion.'[1]

Even after he joined the Shadow Cabinet after the 1964 Election Powell's independence was not abandoned. This was, of course, tolerable. When a party is in Opposition there is a place for the spokesman who relentlessly attacks the Government, even though some of his views may cause some discomfort to his colleagues. Powell certainly did cause this discomfort, and in their view some of his speeches sounded more like indictments of his former colleagues than of the current occupants of the Treasury Bench. They were not greatly concerned – although many were genuinely surprised – when Powell stood for the Party

[1] Quoted in Utley: *op. cit.*, p. 96.

leadership when Home stood down in 1965. The fact that he won only fifteen votes was regarded as a significant indication of his standing in the Party; it was—but only in the Parliamentary Party.

After the Conservative defeat in 1966 Powell's potential constituency was immediately increased, and he proceeded to speak to it with a freedom that was progressively more resented by his colleagues. By now, some were beginning to demonstrate signs of anxiety about Powell's success and the extent of the publicity he was receiving. His candidature for the leadership was now understood to have been not an ill-advised foray but a formal declaration of serious desire for the Party leadership. One of Powell's principal strengths during his long rise to prominence was that few politicians took seriously the proposition that any substantial section of the electorate was interested in extreme proposals relating to the economy. In the general disillusionment that followed the July measures of 1966 and devaluation of 1967, such assumptions could no longer be held.

Not the least of Powell's attraction to Conservative audiences was his deeply-held patriotism, which he has expressed in language of considerable quality. Indeed, Powell's views on England have been expressed with a mystical love that is deeply striking in a period when such expressions tend to be viewed with embarrassment. 'Tell us what it is that binds us together; show us the clue that leads through a thousand years; whisper to us the secret of this charmed life in England, that we in our time may know how to hold it fast' is a characteristic Powell message, as is one that refers to 'the homogeneity of England, so profound and embracing ... the continuity of England, which has brought this unity and this homogeneity about in the slow alchemy of centuries'.[1] We may also note Powell's deep interest in, and knowledge of, aspects of British history, notably church architecture. He is a Conservative who genuinely wishes to conserve, who slowly came to welcome the end of the imperial interlude which had previously dismayed him because 'our generation is like one which comes home again from years of distant wandering'. He frequently asks the question 'What made Britain great?' and comes up with responses which have their root in tradition, in the honour of

[1] Speech to the Royal Society of St George, 22 April 1961.

excellence, in the development of a civilized identity, and in the strength that comes from personal freedom and absence of centralized interference:

We in our day ought well to guard, as highly to honour, the parent stem of England, and its royal talisman; for we know not what branches yet that wonderful tree will have the power to put forth. The danger is not always violence and force; them we have withstood before and can again. The peril can also be indifference and humbug, which might squander the accumulated wealth of tradition and devalue our sacred symbolism to achieve some cheap compromise or some evanescent purpose.

This fierce and profound feeling for England was one of the factors that gave Powell a political third dimension, that element that enables some politicians – Churchill in 1940, or Baldwin in the 1920s – to appeal to deep but hidden emotions in the complex English personality. It was, furthermore, this very patriotism and belief in Britain's cultural development and integrity that was inexorably pushing Powell in the direction of hostility towards alien contamination. 'The unbroken life of the English nation over a thousand years and more is a phenomenon unique in history,' he has said; 'the product of a specific set of circumstances like those which in biology are supposed to start by chance a new line of evolution. Institutions which elsewhere are recent and artificial creations, appear in England almost as works of nature, spontaneous and unquestioned. The deepest instinct of the Englishman – how the word "instinct" keeps forcing itself in again and again – is for continuity; he never acts more freely nor innovates more boldly than when he most is conscious of conserving or even of reacting.'

But perhaps Powell's principal weapon was that he was an *interesting* speaker in a somewhat drab period of political oratory, and it is remarkable that a substantial number of those speeches have been published in book form, a very rare distinction in post-war British politics. It is probable that many of his audiences have been somewhat mystified by some of his allusions and images, as in his opening remarks in a speech delivered in June 1967 to the Eurofines Conference:

A belief in witchcraft is part of the stock-in-trade of government, and has been so since the dawn of human history. In fact, it is a matter for speculation, which cannot be resolved experimentally, whether without a belief in witchcraft men could be governed at all. Whenever misfortunes befall a tribe, or city, or nation, it is indispensable that they should be ascribed to the work of witches. This explanation performs a number of therapeutic functions. It produces a culprit upon whom the emotions of fear and hatred can be discharged. It maintains the faith of the people in their leaders, priests or medicine men, who are seen to be doing their level best in the face of the forces of evil. Finally, it obviates the painful necessity for rational thought, since witches, as is well known, operate by magic and there is no rational accounting for the effects they produce.

Fortunately for mankind, the supply of witches is apparently inexhaustible; human ingenuity has always been equal to discovering new kinds of witches as the old ones have been used up or discredited; and by a special bounty of providence it so happens that a few witches will go a long way. Occasionally, indeed, the witch blows back in the faces of the politicians. There was that deplorable case of Joan of Arc, when the English at Rouen were landed with a royal but illegitimate princess, had to burn someone else instead, and finished up with the worst of all possible worlds.

Happily, this sort of *contretemps* is very rare, and for a most interesting reason, which I suspect to be of profound significance for the survival of our species, namely, that the witches nearly always prove to be most co-operative. They are generally simple, innocent creatures who easily allow themselves to be persuaded that they possess demonic powers. Once so persuaded, they find the whole idea rather flattering. And there is nothing so easy to prove as what one wishes to believe. It may even give the witch a sense of power and importance to be thus regarded as the villain of the piece and the cause of plagues, tempests, wars and changes of dynasty. So applicants for the post – or the stake, rather – have usually been plentiful.

Prior to his speech of 20 April 1968, Powell had not had the reputation of an exploiter of the racial problem, nor even of having taken particular note of the matter. 'It is my experience,' he has said, 'that all the big decisions are ready made when you discover you've made them, or, to put it another way, you open the door one morning and there it is, standing on the doorstep complete, and then you feel somehow that you knew it all the time. The big ones in my life have been like that.'[1] In fact, there

---

[1] 'Enoch Powell' (ATV Network); broadcast 10 November 1970.

had been several indications of the development of his public views since 1964, which only became generally noticed in the frenetic aftermath of the Birmingham speech. Powell had first begun to make speeches drawing attention to the immigration issue in 1965, and in October and December 1967 – at Deal and in his constituency respectively – he had made speeches of considerable force on the right of Kenyan Asians to enter Britain and on the situation in Wolverhampton. But, as so often happens, these speeches were generally unnoticed until after April 1968. A particular example had occurred on 9 February 1968, in a speech at Walsall, which had aroused some members of the Shadow Cabinet to wrath, but which had not substantial attention. The *Sunday Times* picked up the speech, and attacked it with vehemence, but, in the main, the national impact was marginal. But it was sufficient to make it evident that here was an issue worth pursuing. It was pursued at the annual general meeting of the West Midlands Area Conservative Political Centre, at the Midland Hotel, Birmingham.

It is now possible, in retrospect, to see the origins of this speech more clearly, notably in Powell's disillusionment with the Commonwealth, and the increasing emphasis upon the need for the British to 'rub our eyes, wake up, and say to ourselves: "For us the centre of the world, the centre of *our* world, is Britain." ' There was the gradual awareness of the problems caused by Commonwealth immigration – and particularly Asian immigration – in the Midlands, which he had seen with his own eyes, and saw daily. There was the grim experience of his first visit to the United States in the autumn of 1967, and the spectacle of the race problem in New York. These, and other experiences, had a cumulative impact, which, by the beginning of 1968, had confirmed him in his new course.

There is no reason to question Powell's sincerity on the matter of coloured immigration, but it is also significant to note his increasing personal disenchantment with Heath's personality. Although it is not possible to date this with any precision, there is good evidence to support the belief that a major factor had been Heath's expressed enthusiasm in 1967 for the maintenance of a British military presence East of Suez. Powell had accepted the post of Shadow Minister of Defence because he was assured that Heath fully shared his views on the futility of the Imperial mythology and the need for Britain to 'free herself from the long servitude of her 70-year-old dreams', as he had expressed it. Before this crucial episode Powell had said that, 'I am sure that Ted Heath, when he asked me, to my great delight, to speak for the Party on Defence, knew very well what my outlook was on the shape of the present and future world and on Britain's place in it. It's an outlook which I believe to be in close kin to his own.'[1] Powell was accordingly resentful at what he regarded as Heath's *volte face*, which had been undertaken without any prior warning to him. Although this incident may have resulted from a sincre misunderstanding, it was certainly significant, and ominous.

Then, the immediate context of the Birmingham speech must be emphasized. Race, together with Rhodesia, was the most divisive issue in the Conservative Party between 1964 and 1970. The Opposition was now faced with having to take up positions both on the Kenyan Asian issue and the Race Relations Bill currently before Parliament. The tactics to be employed on the latter were causing particular difficulty, and the eventual compromise – a reasoned amendment approving the principles of the Bill but deploring the measures themselves – was a notable victory, only imperfectly concealed, for the anti-immigration Conservatives, and a defeat for men like Boyle. It was a compromise that marked a significant movement away from what might loosely be termed the liberal approach to race relations in the Conservative Party.[2]

This compromise was reached ten days before the Birmingham speech. Throughout the discussions Powell had given no

---

[1] Quoted in T. E. Utley: *op. cit.*, pp. 104–5. Powell gave public expression to his views on several occasions, of which perhaps the most significant was in his speech at the Conservative Conference on 14 October 1965: 'However much we may do to safeguard and reassure the new independent countries in Asia and Africa, the eventual limits of Russian and Chinese advance in these directions will be fixed by a balance of forces which will itself be Asiatic and African. The two Communist empires are already in a state of mutual antagonism; but every advance or threat of advance by one or the other calls into existence countervailing forces, sometimes nationalist in character, sometimes expansionist, which will ultimately check it. We have to reckon with the harsh fact that the attainment of this eventual equilibrium of forces may at some point be delayed rather than hastened by a western military presence.'

[2] The amendment was in the following terms: 'This House, reaffirming its condemnation of racial discord and accepting the need for steps designed to improve the situation, nevertheless declines to give a Second Reading to a Bill which, on balance, will not in its practical application contribute to racial harmony.'

indication whatever to his colleagues, and certainly not to Heath, of the content of the speech which he was proposing to make.[1] Heath had prepared a careful article to be published on the Sunday, attempting to explain the Conservatives' position. This was the essential immediate background to the Birmingham speech, but its complex origins can be traced far back in Powell's background, outlook, and experience.

It would be an over-simplification to state that the Conservative leadership could be neatly divided into two groups on the immigration issue. There was certainly some members of the Shadow Cabinet – notably Boyle – whose view could be loosely described as 'liberal', while there were others who had actively favoured stricter controls for some time. A speech by Home at Hampstead on 3 February 1965 urged tighter controls, checks on evasions, and a Government scheme to assist those immigrants who wished to do so to return to their country of origin. Significantly, on 16 February 1965, Boyle had been replaced as Shadow Home Secretary by Thorneycroft, and on 2 March the entire Shadow Cabinet had voted for a motion in the Commons brought forward by Cyril Osborne which had urged 'periodic and precise limits' to immigration. The Conservatives had opposed the 1965 Race Relations Bill with a reasoned amendment, and the Conservatives' 1966 Manifesto had followed the principles set out by Home in his Hampstead speech, including the principle of voluntary repatriation.

But although this represented an uneasy compromise, and the leadership could argue – with some justification – that the Conservative policy was considerably more fair and human than that urged upon it by a vociferous section of the Party in the constituencies, notably by the Birmingham group. Race was an issue which, like Rhodesia, caused very considerable rifts within the Conservative Party, but until April 1968 it had

---

[1] In a speech at Eastbourne on 16 November 1968, Powell claimed that 'party officials' had been informed of the contents 'in the normal course'; he stated that, 'What is a matter of fact and not of opinion is that neither in making the speech, nor in any of the circumstances attendant upon it, did I neglect or break any of the rules or conventions which govern honourable behaviour between colleagues.' But although the speech was circulated well in advance to the Press and local Party officials, the Conservative leader, the Shadow Cabinet, and Central Office were wholly unaware of it. The head of the publicity department at Central Office first heard of it on the Saturday night when he telephoned the editor of the *News of the World* about Heath's article on race relations.

appeared that Heath had managed to secure general – if reluctant – agreement to a policy which adopted the principle of strict control, accepted the right of immigrants to be treated as ordinary British citizens, and refused to threaten them with arbitrary repatriation. It was this delicate balance that was now put in jeopardy.

Powell's Birmingham speech has been so often quoted and analysed that it seems almost superfluous to go over the familiar ground again. It opened with a highly dramatic account of a conversation with a constituent, who wanted his children to emigrate because 'in fifteen or twenty years the black man will have the whip-hand over the white man' in Britain. Then came the figures: $3\frac{1}{2}$ million Commonwealth citizens in Britain, in fifteen or twenty years' time; 'in the region of five to seven million' by 2000; 'twenty or thirty' additional immigrant children arriving in Wolverhampton every week. And the then assault:

We must be mad, literally mad, as a nation, to be permitting the annual inflow of some 50,000 dependants, who are for the most part the material of the future growth of the immigrant-descended population. It is like watching a nation busily engaged in heaping up its own funeral-pyre.

The most devastating passage, however, concerned the situation of the 'existing population', confronted by this appalling invasion:

For reasons which they could not comprehend, and in the pursuance of a decision by default, on which they were never consulted, they could themselves be made *strangers in their own country*. They found their wives unable to obtain hospital beds in childbirth, their children unable to obtain school places, their homes and neighbourhoods changed beyond recognition, their plans and prospects for the future defeated; at work they found that employers hesitated to apply to the immigrant worker the standards of discipline and competence required of the native-born worker; they began to hear, as time went by, more and more voices which told them that they were now unwanted.

In point of fact, this was grossly exaggerated, except in special cases, and the dominant worry of social workers and local authorities in the areas of major immigration were for the condition of the newcomers, not for the existing population. But the passage played upon two emotions – fear that spreads in an industrial community in a period of increasing unemployment, and basic xenophobia. There was also the highly important factor that, in the Midlands, the influx had been so sudden and so large; the same speech, delivered in other areas where unemployment was low, social conditions reasonable, and the immigrant influx more gradual, would not have had an equivalent response. But the place, no less than the time and the audience, had been carefully selected. The figures themselves were inaccurate. They were based on the answer given to a Parliamentary Question asked by Osborne on 22 June 1967; the question asked for the estimates for 1975 and 1985 based on the assumptions that the current rate of coloured immigration continued and that the current rate of immigrant fertility was maintained. On the basis of these assumptions the answers were one million in 1966; $1\frac{3}{4}$ million in 1975; $3\frac{1}{2}$ million in 1985. Subsequently the Home Office gave a revised estimate of $2\frac{1}{2}$ million immigrants by 1985, but Powell took the first answer – despite the nature of the assumption on which the answer had been given – and then formed a calculation of the probable figures of the year 2000. They were far, far above the estimates given by any authority in the field, but their impact on the audience and the wider public beyond was immense.[1]

There came then the celebrated account of the old lady in Wolverhampton who was threatened by black men to rent rooms to immigrants, and who had excrement thrust through her letter-box, and who was 'followed by children, charming, wide-grinning piccaninnies' bawling 'racialist' at her. Subsequent attempts to discover this unfortunate person were unsuccessful, and examination of Powell's text reveals that the letter was written from Northumberland *about* the constituent,

---

[1] Mr Roth has commented: 'As a Cassandra warning of impending danger, Powell was subordinating accuracy to impact. He wanted immigration stopped and reversed' (Roth: *op. cit.*, p. 347). In doing so, Powell was following the precedent of Churchill in the 1930s, when broad effects were regarded as being of greater significance than strict adherence to the facts. But, in both cases this approach lost each man the confidence and respect of those who were in possession of the facts.

not *from* her.[1] But no matter. Then came the peroration, carefully built on what had gone before:

As I look ahead, I am filled with foreboding. Like the Roman, I seem to see 'the River Tiber flowing much with blood'. That tragic and intractable phenomenon which we watch with horror on the other side of the Atlantic but which is interwoven with the history and existence of the States itself, is coming upon us by our own volition and by our own neglect. Indeed, it has all but come. In numerical terms, it will be of American proportions long before the end of the century. Only resolute and urgent action will avert it even now. Whether there will be the public will to demand and obtain that action, I do not know. All I know is that to see and not to speak would be the great betrayal.

Powell himself has described that speech as 'a seismic event for me personally'. It can be seen either as the moment of his real rise, or that of his fall. Perhaps it is too early to say. In the short run it brought him an overwhelming vocal support, and made him an international figure. This commentator was then temporarily living on the outskirts of San Francisco, writhing under an existence dominated by what are possibly the two worst major newspapers in the western world, the *San Francisco Chronicle* and the *Examiner*. The United States itself was passing through a year of violent trauma, which had opened with the Tet offensive in Vietnam, and had already been followed by the McCarthy triumph in the New Hampshire primary, the entry of Robert Kennedy into the contest for the Democratic candidacy, the withdrawal from the Presidency of Lyndon Johnson, and the assassination of Martin Luther King. Even if the San Francisco newspapers had not been dismal models of mediocrity and parochialism, they would have been justified in

[1] Powell subsequently stated that he had checked the source – i.e. the Northumberland correspondent – but not the existence of the old lady. This was bad enough; what was worse was his insistence that this episode was 'the typical situation of the last and usually elderly white inhabitant of a street or area otherwise wholly occupied by immigrants' (Eastbourne, 16 November). In support of this allegation he quoted cases from the Milner Holland Report on Housing in Greater London (Cmnd 2605). When, in the Eastbourne speech, Powell quoted other cases put to him by a Dr Bamford, investigation confirmed that only one of them had any discernible basis in fact.

keeping attention close to home. Yet Powell's speech and the aftermath swept all else aside, and the national television news programmes gave a prominent rating to Powell. No one could doubt that he had unquestionably arrived – but at what price?

To Heath, the shock of the Birmingham speech was intense. It is impossible to begin to understand that complex personality without making strong allowance for a moral sense of right and wrong and a feeling for decency in human behaviour which is perhaps rare in politicians, and is usually unsuspected in former Chief Whips with a justly-earned reputation for determination. As has already been emphasized, Heath did not rise to the leadership of the Conservative Party by accident. It is also the case that Heath has a tendency to over-value both personal and collective loyalty. Furthermore, he has a long and not always forgiving memory. But on this occasion all considerations were insignificant when compared with the palpable sense of moral outrage which Heath experienced when he read Powell's speech. It has been frequently alleged that if Heath had not disassociated himself from Powell he would have had at least two major Shadow Cabinet resignations. It is true that there *was* a choice, and that a refusal to denounce Powell would have created grievous divisions in the Conservative hierarchy. But these were not the decisive factors. From the moment he read the speech, Heath had no doubt about what course he would take. Subsequent discussions had no effect upon the first decision. In a curt telephone conversation later that day Heath informed Powell that he was no longer a member of the Shadow Cabinet in view of the 'racialist' tone of his speech. In a written response, Powell dismissed the charge, and in effect accused Heath of having bowed supinely before 'fear of clamour from some sections of the press and public'.

Heath's action was followed by substantial and impressive demonstrations of popular support for Powell and a deluge of letters to the newspapers and politicians. Powell received some 110,000 letters, of which the overwhelming majority were in strong approval. Diana Spearman, who has analysed a sample of these letters, comments that 'the words foreign or black or coloured invasion are freely used. A sense of being overwhelmed by an unforeseen, unplanned event is expressed. There is no suggestion of expulsion; even the racialists wish to pay the immigrants to leave rather than force them.'[1] These letters, the demonstrations in Powell's support, and the fevered discussions that followed the Birmingham speech, demonstrated clearly enough that Powell had touched on a subject that was a matter of deep general concern. One of the letters to Powell made a point that was fundamental to this concern:

No Briton wants to see his traditional way of living, the country he has loved and fought for, lose its identity and particular character through the over-great acceptance of too many peoples of quite different cultures and ways of life.[2]

So strong was this reaction that it seemed for a few days that Heath's leadership was in peril, but in the Parliamentary Party there was only isolated support for Powell.

This was the decisive factor. It would be to over-simplify the matter to claim that Heath's reaction of moral revulsion was shared by all Conservative Members, although it was certainly shared by many. Hostility to Powell was the result of other factors. In the first place, it was considered that he had behaved with monstrous disloyalty to his colleagues, and this, in the Conservative Party, is a high crime and misdemeanour. Despite its electoral successes, the Party was going through a highly uncomfortable period, faced by the combination of the Kenya Asians Bill and the new Race Relations Bill. The real core of Powell's message was contained in one short paragraph:

The natural and rational first question with a nation confronted by such a prospect is to ask: 'How can its dimensions be reduced?' The answers are equally simple and rational. By stopping, or virtually stopping, further inflow, and by promoting the maximum outflow. *Both answers are part of the official policy of the Conservative Party.*

It was the last claim, in the context of the speech as a whole, that was the really significant one. The official policy was to *limit* immigration, not to stop it, and there was a very substantial difference between assisting voluntary repatriation and 'promoting the maximum outflow'. Thus, Powell's considerable and deliberate extension of the Party's official policy could not, in itself, be permitted to stand.

Then, Powell had appealed directly to the Party in the

[1] *New Society*, 9 May 1968, pp. 667–9.
[2] *Ibid.*, p. 668.

country without any warning to his Parliamentary colleagues, and had made the position of many of them extremely difficult. Life is not always easy or placid for a back-bencher in Opposition – and particularly a Conservative back-bencher in Opposition. His supporters are unhappy and often querulous, and always disappointed. Why, they indignantly ask, is the Government getting away with it? Why is the Government not being harrassed out of existence? Why is there not more 'bite' in the Opposition? And now, on top of all this, came the question about the Member's stand on Mr Powell. Is he for him or against him; and, if the latter, why? The immediate reactions to the Powell speech demonstrated one salient and remarkable fact about the race question which has already been mentioned – that it is in those areas where there are no coloured immigrants that the fears are often greatest and the pressures most severe. As the Race Relations Board was to assert, it was from Cornwall, Westmorland, Surrey, Sussex, Devon, Dorset, and Somerset that the pro-Powell noises were the most shrill and vehement. More than one Conservative Member, sitting on a quiet and safe seat, found himself under severe and strident assault from his association for his alleged Socialistic tendencies on the race issue because he was dutifully following the Party line and the Party leadership.

For some Conservative Members, of course, there was little problem. Either they announced themselves well satisfied with Powell's courage and plain-speaking – which only emphasized what they themselves had been thinking (if not saying) for years – or they hurriedly accommodated themselves to the new situation by declaiming that, although they might not agree with all of Powell's comments, he had rendered a notable public service by bringing a major issue into the blazing light of day. There would then follow an attack on the Labour attitude to the 1962 Act and a glowing account of the rôle played by the Conservative Party in checking the headlong flood of Africans and Asians into the country. For those Conservatives with strong ambitions and well versed in nimble changes of direction, this exercise caused little difficulty.

Nonetheless, even these felt resentment at the necessity for this performance, and also for the dreary chore of replying to the letters that descended upon them in a dreadful cataract. And they could not fail to note the gleeful exploitation of the issue by their opponents. And then, what if Enoch had got it wrong? Perhaps, for every letter of support for him, there were ten outraged electors who remained silent? Such grim reflections were far from uncommon at the time among Conservatives.

Then, there were some who were immediately in very serious trouble with their supporters, of whom Boyle – who had refused to vote for the reasoned amendment on the Race Relations Bill – was the most conspicuous. In many instances, this was but one more episode in which they had demonstrated perilous leftist views; first, the abolition of capital punishment; then, support for Rhodesian sanctions; then, that inexplicable support for – or absence of positive hostility to – reform of the law relating to homosexuals; and now – weak on the blacks!

As a profession, politics has many compensations. The life of the House of Commons can be wonderfully congenial and exhilarating, and is especially exciting to any man or woman with even the most faint sense of history and tradition. There is always the hope of fame and position, but, if even these chimeras disappear, there is the Smoking Room, and the wonderful camaraderie of the House of Commons. But we all have our vanities. Most of us are buttressed by a system or an organization against too-painful exposure to major humiliations. And, if we suffer them, we usually suffer them in private. But the politician, if he crashes, crashes before an audience. If he has risen high, the audience is large, and the publicity proportionate. The businessman who suffers a severe reprimand and a stern warning as to his future conduct does not read of the fact bruited abroad in the evening newspaper as he journeys homeward. The report on an official's errors is filed and noted in the Civil Service, but is known to a limited few. The army officer who fails to make the grade is destroyed, but not in public. Modern society provides elaborate precautions that ensure that our personal vanities are not brutally and publicly mocked. Such protection is not vouchsafed to the politician.

The hazards and discomforts of the politician's existence are ill-appreciated. The distant observer has not experienced the agonies of a Selection Committee, nor looked into the eyes of the grim and sceptical Faithful, who hold his future in their hands. Nor has he writhed in a suffocating room, coping with hostile and querulous demands which he cannot supply. Nor has he ever stood on rainswept street corners soliciting votes. He has not travelled for five hours at his own expense with a burning oration in his bosom, only to discover that the audience consists of three persons (of whom one is belligerently and intelligently from the Opposition), or, even worse, that the Secretary meets him at the station with the tragic admission that he has failed to book the hall, and that the meeting has been abandoned. All this – and much besides – may be acceptable if one is winning, and the prize is the ticket to Westminster and, hopefully, to Whitehall. But the electorate is fickle, and the politician may find himself making a bitterly grateful speech in some crowded and unsavoury Town Hall, congratulating his victorious opponent, knowing that his supporters will blame him personally for numerous offences of commission and omission, while all the time he is wondering how he is going to feed and educate his children.

Thus, for all its compensations, it is a rough calling. And perhaps the most disturbing aspect of it is that the politician may find himself, utterly without warning, in dire jeopardy. It may be over a local private Bill, whereby some remote and ignored valley is to be flooded to make a dam; the Member has accepted the arguments of the local authority, and supported the project – only to discover in his mail a petition signed by 20,000 constituents expressing outrage and fury, of which the first signature is that of his Constituency Chairman. The experienced Member learns caution in such matters, but he cannot anticipate all eventualities. Powell, at the end of April 1968, was such an eventuality. Thus many harrassed Conservative MPs found themselves unexpectedly faced with a new problem, and were intensely resentful of the man who had created the problem.

In a sense, this was Powell's major achievement and contribution. It cannot be denied that many politicians had shrunk away from the race issue, or had thankfully ignored it as having no relevance in their areas. Unquestionably, many of them had not thought much about it, and had concentrated on other matters.

Indeed, perhaps the most fundamental cause of Powell's sudden acclamation was the widespread feeling that the issue of immigration had been deliberately ignored by 'the politicians', who spoke with a collective patronizing manner to citizens who expressed alarmed concern about what they sincerely believed to be a drift towards catastrophe. Thus, Powell's appeal was also an appeal of the citizen against the aloof and distant politicians who had lost touch with the people they were supposed to be representing. There was just enough validity in this charge to give it a remarkably widespread strength, and gave Powell an additional constituency. If the positive reaction to Powell was, to quote an American adjective, 'visceral', so was the negative reaction. His opponents were shaken to discover certain basic facts, of whose existence they had previously been unaware. They may have believed that Powell had grossly exaggerated the problem, but he had drawn public attention to the fact that the problem did exist and that it aroused profound emotions. It may be charged that Powell rendered a gross and lamentable disservice to community relations in Britain by the Birmingham speech, but it can also be argued that that speech was in some sense overdue. It undoubtedly aroused some unpleasant, normally hidden, aspects of the British character; but it also brought officials, politicians, and citizens face to face with grim realities.

To say this is not to condone the Birmingham speech. What it did was to make the subject respectable politically; by mentioning the unmentionable Powell had opened the way for race to become a major topic. If it had been discussed in terms of reason and knowledge[1] there would have been little harm in this, but the nature of the issue and the inflammatory nature of Powell's own speech made this impossible.

Powell was appealing to a very basic and elementary emotion, the fear of the indigenous citizen of an influx of unwelcome strangers, and he was appealing to it at a time of very considerable social unease in Britain. The unwelcome stranger is always a threat, because he is an unknown quantity, and the indigenous citizen can swiftly be persuaded that his own failures

---

[1] One of the shrewdest thrusts in the Birmingham speech was the attempted differentiation between worthy and unworthy coloured immigrants; his proposed controls, he emphasized, had nothing to do with the immigrants who came for purposes of study or improving their qualifications 'like (for instance) the Commonwealth doctors . . . These are not, and never have been, immigrants.' But when the figures were examined, it was seen that out of a total of 7,500 vouchers issued in 1965, 5,180 had gone to persons with medical or professional skills; it would appear, therefore, that the furore was over the remaining 2,320 per annum and their dependants.

and the inadequacies of his circumstances are not his fault, but those of the alien. We live in tribal communities, and we resent intrusion from other tribes. Thus, it is less a colour question than a community question. The elementary point of colour is that the alien is instantly recognizable and immediately classified as an alien.[1] Thus, a chronic failure to provide adequate housing in the Midlands can be very easily sloughed off into the allegation that the provision is adequate but that the aliens have expropriated it.

Heath was justified, yet at the same time was not justified, in describing the Birmingham speech as 'racialist'. The fundamental popular appeal of the speech was that it spoke for a frightened community that saw its community threatened and was clinging to what it knew, understood, and could accept. Powell's language, although shocking to sophisticated politicians, journalists, and social workers, had a directness which was attractive, and there is some truth in Maurice Cowling's statement that Powell's 'current doctrines ... are in fact the expression of a feeling, which is to some extent present in all classes, that the language used by politicians is not the language which the body of the people understands, and that the distance between the politicians and the public is great and growing'.[2] It is doubtful if many read Powell's Birmingham speech, but they received the broad message; and it was to that message that they reacted so positively and with such enthusiasm. The reaction was, and was not, racialist; it was the visceral reaction of the citizen who feels his community is threatened by an alien element.

The Birmingham speech dramatically projected Powell into a position of considerable prominence. 'I can only say that, from

[1] For further attention to this question see W. W. Daniel: *Racial Discrimination in England*, D. Eversley and F. Sukedeo: *The Dependants of the Coloured Commonwealth Population of England and Wales* (Institute of Race Relations, 1969); P. Cori: *West Indian Migration to Britain* (1968); J. Rex and R. Moore: *Race, Community and Conflict* (Oxford, 1967); Paul Foot: *Immigration and Race in British Politics* (1965); and Nicholas Deakin: *Colour and Citizenship* (1969). For two vigorous counter-attacks on Powell's immigration speeches see B. Smithies and P. Fiddick: *Enoch Powell on Immigration* (1969) and Paul Foot: *The Rise of Enoch Powell* (1969). For support of Powell see George K. Young: *Who Goes Home?* (Monday Club, 1969).
[2] John Wood (ed): *Powell and the 1970 Election*, p. 13.

that moment onwards, everything was changed,' he has said, 'like a geological fault, all the rocks are at different levels, everything is in a different relationship to everything else.'[1] The problem was how to exploit this position without running the danger of becoming a politician with only one issue. In the event, he never escaped from this dilemma. Powell had never been short of subjects on which to express his disagreements with the Conservative leadership – it could be said of him with justice that he is a natural questioner and challenger – and his freedom from what restraints he had laboured under in the Shadow Cabinet could now be – and was – fully utilized. Thus, 'Powellism' was developed further into a very wide-ranging political programme. It appeared for a time that this very fact would be its strength. A good Conservative might abhor his stand on the immigration issue, but could admire Powell's stern speeches on the economy, or *vice versa;* thus, he had, in a sense, 'bought Powellism', and Powell's speeches covered such a wide area of public affairs that it would have been very difficult for a Conservative *not* to have agreed with parts of his philosophy. But the fatal weakness in the Powell programme was that it did not add up to a 'package', and it was only on the immigration issue that he had any solid political support. In particular, Powell's antagonism to the Common Market, the Commonwealth, and East of Suez alienated many Conservatives who were supporters of his immigration views. His refusal to serve under Home in 1963 was also not forgotten, nor his 'liberalistic' attitudes to such subjects as capital punishment on which the Right has views. His fundamentalist economic arguments were also viewed with considerable reservation by many rank and file Members. They might privately agree with these views, but they could also see exactly where, politically, Powell was leading them, and they did not relish the prospect of courting the floating vote on some of Powell's policies.

The Conservative Party has its enthusiasm and its zeal, but it has a shrewd concept of political realities. The great men may thunder and roar, and the multitudes applaud or excoriate; the faithful Party worker has to canvass door to door, and attend to all the chores in the long periods between elections. Powell, for all the claims by his associates of his links with the rank and

[1] ATV broadcast, 10 November 1970.

file and his own constituents, moved on an entirely different plane. Powell and Heath are both aloof men, who deliberately keep their distance. Neither have many really intimate friends, inside or outside politics. Ability at small talk and the brand of personal charm which Home, Macleod, Maudling and Carr effortlessly – and unconsciously – exercised could never be claimed for either. But Heath had always kept close to the Party workers, and he had a sensitive awareness of their rôle, their importance, and their problems. Heath may have dazzled no one, but the Party knew that he was determined to maintain a close identification between the Party's policies and the men and women who had to do the hard slogging work in the constituencies. Barber had only been Chairman for seven months, but he had already established close links with the Party leaders and workers in the constituencies.

Thus, Powell's position in 1968 and subsequently was nothing like as strong in the Conservative Party as his admirers, and many observers, assumed at the time. His personal following in the Parliamentary Party was miniscule, and the hostility against him was very substantial.

Perhaps the most significant paradox of all in Powell's position lay in the fact that whereas he consistently refused to debate race matters in Parliament – despite numerous opportunities – and mounted his campaign entirely outside Parliament, he indignantly repudiated the inevitable accusations that his approach evoked to the point when he made explicit claims that he was being calculatedly persecuted. In this context, it is important to remind oneself of the kind of language that Powell was using and the kind of emotions he was intent upon stirring up. As one opponent put it: 'To use the language of the streets, and then to complain about its use in retaliation, seems to me to argue a very curious form of self-righteousness.' Even his popular appeal on the immigration issue was an uneven one, generating immense enthusiasm in some areas, disgust in others. In the Party as a whole he occupied no position of real power, and its mistrust of intellectuals and zealots did not assist him. Even on the Right, as has been emphasized, he was viewed with strong reservations. The Powell 'package' never developed into a coherent and practical programme that might have captured the imagination of the Party. He was clearly a man to be watched, and after the

Birmingham speech and its extraordinary aftermath no one could be sure where, and on what issue, he might do it again. It was this factor above all that made Heath and his lieutenants eye him with such wariness and unease, and it was only gradually that they appreciated the insecurity of the foundations of Powell's political base. But before then, and despite protestations to the contrary, the Conservative leadership perceptibly edged towards many of Powell's positions.

What was 'Powellism'? It is impossible to categorize it succinctly, because the creed, with all its perplexing variations, was of less significance than the man, for it was something that was intensely personal and individualistic. Powellism was – and is – whatever Powell happens to say at any given moment, even though it totally contradicts what he has been saying before. 'The politician is employed by society,' he has written, 'to reconcile it to the inevitabilities of the world around, by dramatizing them and so making them appear human, explicable, and amenable to management and manipulation.'[1] It is not the business of popular demagogues to be consistent. What matters is the aura, the impression of personal power and magnetism, rather than the words themselves. One leaves a Powell meeting with little recollection of what he has said, but an overwhelming impression of personality. While he is speaking one looks at the face and at the gestures and the gyrations of this extraordinarily mobile orator; the arresting eyes set in the ashen face; the accent itself, with its rasping gentleness, has a compulsive quality. But how does one explain this to those who have never beheld him, save on television? It is impossible, because the relationship between orator and auditor cannot be adequately conveyed either by television or by verbal report.

An excellent example was his speech on the tragedy of Hola Camp in Kenya, delivered at 1.15 a.m., on 27 July 1959. It was a speech of extraordinary simplicity and power, in one of the most memorable debates in the House of Commons since the War. The words themselves retain their force on re-reading, but

[1] Article on 'Truth, Politics and Persuasion' in the *Advertising Quarterly*, Spring, 1965.

were of lesser impact than the orator. Rising after several hours of attempting to gain the Speaker's eye, speaking from one of the most remote back benches, he held the House of Commons in a thrall from his opening sentence. Only those who heard it can adequately testify to the impact of that speech.

It is this factor that renders rational analysis of Powell an impossibility, as it is in the cases of Parnell or Gladstone. His facts may be – and often are – wrong, and his conclusions may be intellectually and politically unacceptable, but the impress of his personality is the important factor. One may read and re-read the words, but they tell one very little if they are not immediately transferred into the voice and the image of the speaker. For a time, people become 'Powellized' not by reason or intellect, but by collective hypnosis. When one is in his presence, reason tends to disintegrate. That link between speaker and the individual in the audience – however large the audience – is created, and, once created, is ineradicable. He possesses, in short, a 'something' that is beyond definition or rational explanation – but is there. Historical comparisons are never exact; but it is not wholly inappropriate to recall a contemporary's account of Gladstone's comparable power:

I can only tell you that, profoundly as I distrusted him, and lightly as on the whole I valued the external qualities of his eloquence, I have never listened to him even for a few minutes without ceasing to marvel at his influence over men . . . when I am assailed through eye and ear by this compacted phalanx of assailants, what wonder that the stormed outposts of the senses should spread the contagion of their own surrender through the main encampment of the mind, or that against my judgement, in contempt of my conscience, nay, in defiance of my very will, I should exclaim, 'This is indeed the voice of truth and wisdom. This man is honest and sagacious beyond his fellows. He must be believed, he must be obeyed.'[1]

The distant observer, however, is required to furnish a cooler approach. By 1968 Powell's speaking technique appeared complex, yet it was in fact basically simple. It consisted of an opening allegation put forward as a straightforward statement of fact. He then made further allegations, also stated as facts, which led back to the original allegation, so that it appeared that he was adducing evidence whereas in fact he was usually

[1] Quoted in John Morley: *Life of W. E. Gladstone*, (London, 1908) vol. II, p. 248.

making further allegations which, collectively, appeared to support the principal one. An admirable example – indeed, almost a classic – is to be found at the outset of his speech at Northfield, Birmingham, during the General Election campaign, on 13 June 1970:

> *Britain at this moment is under attack.* It is not surprising if many people still find that difficult to realise. A nation like our own, which has twice in this century had to defend itself by desperate sacrifice against an external enemy, instinctively continues to expect that danger will take the same form in the future. When we think of an enemy, we still visualise him in the shape of armoured divisions, or squadrons of aircraft, or packs of submarines. But a nation's existence is not always threatened in the same way. The future of Britain is as much at risk now as in the years when Imperial Germany was building dreadnoughts, or Nazism rearming. Indeed, the danger is greater today, just because the enemy is invisible or disguised, so that his preparations and advances go on hardly observed. When Czechoslovakia was dismembered or Austria annexed or Poland invaded, at least one could see that a shift of power had taken place; but in the last three years events every whit as pregnant with peril have given no such physical signal.
>
> As we prepare to elect a new Parliament, the menace is growing, as such dangers do, at an accelerating pace. Other nations before now have remained blind and supine before a rising danger from within until it was too late for them to save themselves. If we are to escape the same fate, it is high time we opened our eyes; for the first condition of self-defence is to see what it is we have to fear.
>
> I assert, then, that this country is today under attack by forces which aim at the actual destruction of our nation and society as we know or can imagine them . . .

This is only the beginning. By taking some very disparate examples – university unrest in the United States and Britain ('we have seen the institutions of learning systematically threatened, browbeaten, and held up to ridicule by the organizers of disorder') – the racial problem, the decision on the South African cricket tour[1] (compared to the sinking of the battleships *Prince of Wales* and *Repulse*) – and the Northern Ireland crisis, he creates the impression that these episodes are part of a gigantic pattern of organized subversion by 'the enemy within' – an enemy that is never identified.

[1] See pp. 240–241 below.

Have you ever wondered, perhaps, why opinions which the majority of people quite naturally hold are, if anyone dares express them publicly, denounced as 'controversial', 'extremist', 'explosive', 'disgraceful', and overwhelmed with a violence and venom quite unknown to debate or mere political issues? It is because the whole power of the aggressor depends upon preventing people from seeing what is happening and from saying what they see . . .

The audience is left with the impression of having been vouchsafed a privileged glimpse into the murk, a dramatic flash of penetration from a brilliant light, which reveals all. It is only perhaps later – and the word 'perhaps' should be emphasized – that some may ponder on the fact that no evidence whatever had been brought forward, that there has been no case, no identification of the menace. It remains vague, sinister, and fearful – and all the more fearful because of its vagueness. 'They' are watching Us. *They* will swoop ruthlessly if We lower our guard. *They* have already been at work in the United States, subverting universities and exploiting the blacks, and in Northern Ireland, subverting and exploiting the peace-loving Catholics and Protestants. ('That the enemy has utilized the materials of religious division is almost as fortuitous as that a mob should use missiles from a nearby building site'.) If We do not bestir ourselves, *They* will do it here, and We shall be lost.

If it can be said that only Powell could have made such a speech, it is even more to the point to emphasize that the same speech, in the mouth of another man, would have had infinitely less impact. We have to recall the orator, bearing on his shoulders the repute of an untainted and untaintable integrity, the outcast who was cast out because he had to speak the truth, the 'sea-green incorruptible of the Right', as one admirer has described him. 'I trust Powell,' one local Conservative dignitary informed this commentator, 'because he says what he feels and thinks. It may all be very inconvenient; some of it may be rubbish; but what he says are the views of a sincere man who does not tell lies in public. And that is more than you can say of most other politicians.' We also have to recall his physical presence; that unique, unparodyable voice; those burning eyes; the taut and incessant gesticulations; the haunted face; the tone of utter sincerity and passion; the Leader come among us. Perhaps the speech itself, as an intellectual and political argument, can be swiftly dismissed. But by his audience it is not dismissed. He has touched their hidden fears, the hidden fears that lurk in all of us, and which are most aroused when we cannot easily identify its cause. Powell himself has said that, 'We all have things which we fear, and we all fear things which we don't fully understand, and forces which we apprehend may be perhaps bigger than ourselves.'[1] We all of us remain children in the inky black, hearing noises which we imbue with hideous fantasy into monsters intent on our destruction. Thus, Powell's menacing account of the enemy within, amongst us, close at hand, all-powerful and all-knowing, touches a deep and responsive chord. We go out shaken and exhilarated. It is only some time later that some of us emerge from the trance, retrace our steps, and are appalled at our credulity. We have been mesmerized, if only temporarily; but, for others, was it temporary?

But behind Powell's remarkable public emergence in 1968 there lay another, and perhaps deeper factor – that perilous longing for a Real Leader, that dream of the strong, single-minded charismatic Saviour who would turn the Conservative Party and the nation away from the drawling drift into nothingness and back towards its old glory. The Conservative Party had never felt really comfortable with Churchill, Eden had become a disaster, and the relationship with Macmillan had been one of mutual wariness, not untinged with aversion, but there had been moments in each case when it had seemed that the Saviour had arrived. Hogg had fleetingly appeared in the rôle, but only very fleetingly. Home, for all his charm and integrity, had not satisfied this yearning; Heath certainly did not. Powell, with his very weirdness and frightening passion, his intense articulateness, his burning zeal, was the closest available approximation to the fulfilment of this aspiration. Thus it was that although Powell's arguments and policies could be assailed and denied by other politicians and political leaders, this fact was not relevant, for the words were of far less significance than the man and what, to his fascinated admirers, he seemed to represent to them. If, therefore, 'Powellism' defies rational analysis it is simply because it was a wholly irrational phenomenon. And, for a time, it transformed British politics.

[1] ATV broadcast, 10 November 1970.

The most interesting dilemma about Powellism is whether it had any durable effects. In the Conservative Party, although it was apparent, after the initial shocks,[1] that Powell represented no serious immediate threat to Heath's leadership, the longer-term possibilities were disturbing, and particularly because there was in existence an already thriving and active section of the Conservative Party which shared many of Powell's views. It is accordingly important to examine what was one of the most significant developments in British politics in the 1960s.

The Monday Club had been founded in 1961 on the initiative of a group of young Conservatives who had been particularly dismayed by Macmillan's 'Wind of Change' speech and who considered that the Party's drift to the Left had gone far enough. 'Only in the last three years,' this small group declared, 'has Conservatism seemed to drift without ideas or purpose under an aura of secrecy and condescension', having lost sight of the fundamental purposes of the Party, of which the most central was 'the unfettered development of the individual ... The State is a servant of the people; it should be neither a domineering nor an interfering body.'[2] The founder-members initially met informally on Monday evenings, but, as the size grew, more formal machinery was established; subsequently the administration and general policy of the Club was controlled by an Executive Committee and the Club's director. The Club produced some thirty-six pamphlets between 1962 and 1970, and established branches throughout the country. Its membership in 1961 was 25; by 1964 it had grown to 140; between 1966 and 1970 it further increased from 400 to over 2,000. It had regular meetings, became a highly active organization, and established a small and efficient headquarters office in London, in Victoria Street. The annual subscription is three guineas, with lower rates for applicants under 25 and students. All applications for membership have to be sponsored by a member, and all applicants go before the Executive Council for approval – a very necessary precaution, in view of the possibility of infiltrations from extreme organizations such as the National Front. Its funds come from membership subscriptions, fund-

---

[1] Some five thousand London dockers went on strike in sympathy with Powell; there were sympathy strikes in other ports; 39 Immigration Officers at London Airport sent a letter to him 'heartily endorsing' his speech, and there was a move to prosecute Powell under the Race Relations Act of 1965.

[2] *Conservatism Lost? Conservatism Regained* (Monday Club, October 1963).

raising activities, profits on sales of literature, and some personal donations (the latter, the Club states, do not constitute a significant element in its resources).

The avowed aims of the Club are essentially to 'evolve a dynamic application of traditional Conservative principles. It is committed to advocating a policy based on belief in individual initiative, free enterprise, and a strong and independent Britain. This means recasting our whole society and reducing the power and influence of the State whilst elevating the responsibility and dignity of the individual and the status of the family.' The importance of individual freedom (with an appropriate quotation from John Stuart Mill), is heavily emphasized, and there is a very definite moral note:

Advancement in society must be open by merit to all who seek it. An egalitarian society is a contradiction in terms. Our social fabric must foster decency, responsibility, and wholesome family life. Our constitutional heritage of Monarchy, representative government, and bicameral legislature must be rescued from debasement. The Prime Minister is the Queen's First Minister, and not a Head of State. *Ich dien*, the motto of our Royal succession, must also be the ethos of society.

In more practical terms, the Monday Club advocates substantial reduction in State interference in the economy, encouragement to personal savings, a foreign policy that accepts international responsibilities and associations, the abandonment of sanctions against Rhodesia ('If a decision has to be taken between a small Commonwealth which believes in the rule of law, respect for human rights, and the sovereignty of fellow members, or some larger grouping which includes governments which disregard these principles it can only be the former'), an independent defence capability, stronger law and order, the repeal of the Race Relations Act, and the establishment of a commission to examine repatriation of 'immigrants of non-European origin'. Much of this was official Conservative policy, or was close enough to it to evoke little difficulty. The important aspect of the Monday Club is less its specific objectives than its general political philosophy.

This philosophy runs as follows: After 1945, largely as a result of the growth of influence of men like R. A. Butler, Iain Macleod, and Harold Macmillan, and in its eager search for office, the Party moved too far to the Left, with the result that by the late 1950s and early 1960s the two major parties were virtually indistinguishable. Admittedly, this opportunism brought short-term advantages, but at a cost of the real *raison d'être* of the Conservative Party. The Empire had been abandoned. The State had been permitted to intrude into every detail of the national life. Initiative and independence had been stifled. Public expenditure had been allowed to soar to unacceptable heights. Personal taxation remained much too high. A 'dear money' policy meant that small businesses could not prosper. Capitalism and private enterprise, on which Britain's wealth and greatness had been founded, had been abandoned. National independence in foreign and defence policy had been lamely surrendered, mainly to the Americans. Office, in short, had been purchased at a terrible price by the cynical betrayal of the fundamental tenets of Conservatism – a betrayal not merely of a party but of the whole nation.

The remarkably swift success of the Monday Club demonstrated that the handful of original members were not alone in their views. The Club regards itself as a 'ginger' rather than a 'splinter' group, and points to its careful screening of applicants to ensure that no extremist right-wing group infiltrates as proof of this. The Club claims that its main body of support comes from the 'grass-roots of the Conservative Party', and, while it willingly concedes that what it calls, with some contempt, 'the intellectual elite' favours the Bow Group, is not deeply concerned on this account. The Monday Club is an officially recognized element in the Conservative Party, and its members include MPs,[1] constituency officials, and even staff of Central Office. The Club always encourages its members to join, and be active in, local associations – not, it avers, for the purpose of causing trouble or intriguing, but to ensure that the 'true Tory' point of view would not be unheard.

If this were all, the scepticism and suspicion with which some elements in the Party hierarchy eyed the Monday Club for some time would have seemed somewhat excessive. But it was not all.

[1] Some of whom, interestingly enough, have asked that their membership of the Monday Club should remain secret. Seventeen Conservative MPs were declared members in the 1966–70 Parliament; in the 1970 Election the total rose to twenty-six. These included Mr Julian Amery, Mr Geoffrey Rippon, and Mr John Peyton who became Ministers in the Conservative Government.

On the purely ideological level, many Conservatives contemplated with horror the bland desire of the Monday Club to return to a form of vague, lost Toryism of some distant, ideal, past, and particularly those Conservatives who had spent their active political careers in building the Conservative Party into what they regarded as a viable, attractive, progressive party of ordered change – those who believed, in short, in the Conservative national coalition. Such men – who included Butler, Macmillan, Heath, Macleod, Maudling, and Carr – tended to be dismissed by the Club either as misguided or as 'opportunists', who had, either through negligence or design, let crash to the ground the Holy Grail of what they imprecisely describe as 'pre-war Conservatism'. When pressed for further definition of this latter ideal – Baldwinite Conservatism? Chamberlainite? – the Club's members disappear into an acrid cloud of generalities and protestations.

In fact, the heart of the Monday Club is a strange and interesting brand of the Tory Democracy of Lord Randolph Churchill, a politician for whom they profess high esteem but whose political career and objectives they do not appear to have studied very closely, or in any depth. Tory Democracy may have been in Rosebery's phrase, 'an imposture'; but it was a brilliant imposture, in that it was a direct assault both on the then Conservative leadership and on the Liberal grip on the newly enfranchised artisans. It is difficult to judge which was the first priority in Lord Randolph's mind, and it is probable that Lord Randolph would have found it difficult to explain himself. But the glamour of Tory Democracy lay in the possibility of an aristocratic-artisan coalition against the bourgeoisie, the owners of 'pineries and vineries' on whom Lord Randolph heaped his withering invective and scorn. Tory Democracy itself had more than a tinge of Disraelian Young England in its mixed origins, and it was this aspect in particular that has so attracted the Monday Club. Maurice Cowling has expressed one part of this emotion very clearly:

Over the last thirty years a morally conservative, hard headed and patriotic electorate has been persuaded to defer to an eccentric element amongst the progressive intelligentsia with which it has nothing in common with the rest. This has produced fear and intellectual uncertainty in the Conservative party and the presence in its higher reaches of a widespread belief that care should have been taken to avoid a direct assault on the feelings and prejudices of this wing of the intelligentsia, however absurd the opinions to which it may be committed.[1]

The fundamental tenet of the Monday Club is the Tory Democratic faith that the working classes are basically Conservative. They are hard-headed, realistic, patriotic, proud of their country, love their Queen, and have nothing in common with the bulk of the Labour and Liberal leaders. Thus, as Lord Randolph had seen the same signs in the 1880s, and had spectacularly driven a wedge between the Liberal leadership and the artisans, so could the same wedge be driven in the 1960s.

Although the circumstances of the period 1880–85 were not strictly and completely analogous to those of the 1960s, the Monday Club's leaders and members firmly believe that The People will return to the Conservative Party when that Party returns to its hallowed principles and stops attempting to compete with Labour in a progressively socialistic direction. It is a very deeply held belief; it is held with great sincerity; and it is not to be lightly dismissed.

It might have been thought that Heath's philosophy and policies were not uncongenial to the Monday Club. Up to a point they were, and the Club has not been slow to claim due credit for its contribution to this process. But Heath was regarded as unsatisfactory in other respects, and most of his Shadow Cabinet colleagues were considered by the Club to be very unsound on true Conservative principles. The Club did not desire any open confrontation with the Party leadership; its ambition, it declared, was to educate that leadership through giving prominence to those grass-root sentiments in the Party which had been ignored and unheard for so long. It did not establish itself as providing an alternative set of policies and philosophy; it wished to articulate those fundamental Conservative attitudes that had been forgotten. Thus there were no unseemly public disputations or clashes. The Club lay low, worked hard, and steadily increased in size and influence.

The Monday Club's problem was that it lacked a leader of sufficient national prominence who could articulate its member's fears and concerns. Lord Randolph had been a leader without an organization; the Monday Club was an organiza-

[1] John Wood (ed.): *Powell and the 1970 Election*, (London, 1970) pp. 14–15.

tion without a leader. For a brief period in the early summer of 1968, it seemed that it had found one.

For, by 1968, despite its steadily rising membership, the Monday Club could claim only a limited degree of success in its avowed objective of putting the Conservative Party, literally, back on the right track. In part, this was the result of an instinctive mistrust in the Party of organizations that call themselves 'ginger groups'; experience has shown that such groups tend to have a divisive effect, and the Party has a deeply ingrained apprehension of division. Then, the Monday Club's formally declared aims and purposes had an ideological whiff that aroused suspicions. The fundamental factor about the grass-roots Conservative is that he does not *need* ideology. He knows instinctively why he is a Conservative, and he views with scorn the tortuous writhings of the Labour Party as it battles over ideological quandaries. To the rank-and-file member the earnestness and precision of the Monday Club's objectives – even though he might agree with all of them – had, collectively, a faintly uncomfortable flavour.

For, at some stage in its development, which it is now difficult to date precisely, the character of the Club had changed. Some observers mark the turning point as the appointment of Mr Paul Williams as Chairman when Paul Bristol, the original founder, went abroad in 1964. Paul Williams had been elected to Parliament for Sunderland South in 1953, when he had been the first victor for the Government in an Opposition-held seat since before the War. He had subsequently been a conspicuous member of the 'Suez Group'; he lost his seat in Parliament in 1964. Whether or not Williams was personally responsible for the very definite shift in the approach of the Monday Club after he became Chairman, or whether this trend would have happened in any event after the defeats of 1964 and 1966, the Club took a very marked step further to the Right on almost all issues, and the language of its pamphlets and statements become increasingly vigorous. The Monday Club avers that it has no quarrel with the Party, and that it is a loyal section of it. The last thing it desires, it declares with indignant virtue, is to cause divisions and strife. It is not the case, however, that all its members see their rôle in this light, with the result that in certain constituencies there was, by 1968, an unconcealed tension between elements in the local association and the

Club. Certainly, the Party leadership believed that in some areas its members were more preoccupied with challenging the established Conservative organization than with fighting the common enemy. Thus the relationship between the Party hierarchy and the Monday Club became an uneasy one. No party can afford to turn away activists without very good cause, and particularly activists who are prepared to work as enthusiastically as many Club members did, but no party could view with equanimity the expansion of what looked suspiciously like a faction intent on occupying a dominant position.

In one respect the Monday Club had a value, if only as a counterweight to the Bow Group, which had been founded in 1951, and which was heavily university-orientated from its inception. The Bow Group was intended as 'an effective counter to "intellectual" Socialism and the Fabian Society', and its value to the Conservative Party was very considerable. It certainly attracted to the Party young people from the universities who might otherwise have drifted elsewhere, and it provided an important opportunity for original thinking. The Group's publications, which include the quarterly *Crossbow*, have been of good quality, but although it emphasizes that its membership is not confined to university graduates and that 'the interests and backgrounds of members are numerous and diverse', the dominant character of its activity has been what might be called university-based progressive Conservatism. The Group's members, furthermore, tended to be more aloof from the dreary chores of politics, and there was a certain atmosphere of condescension towards those whose involvement in politics was less cerebral than theirs. The heavy Oxbridge influence, also, was not universally esteemed. The Monday Club was not a deliberate competitor to the Group at its inception, but as it developed the contrasts between the composition and approaches of the two bodies became increasingly sharp. A subtle polarization between the Bow Group and the Monday Club was significant of something more than two elements within one political party. They stood for two entirely different views of Conservatism, for entirely different sets of values, and had very different social and intellectual bases. And because the Club's members became increasingly active in the constituency associations, its influence with the Party structure at the rank-and-file level steadily increased.

Further indication of why so many of the Conservative leadership came to mistrust the Monday Club may be gleaned from its publications. In particular, the reiterated claim of the Monday Club that it is a loyal element of the Party is hardly borne out by an examination of perhaps its most celebrated publication, *Who Goes Home? Immigration and Repatriation*, written by Mr George K. Young, and published in 1969. The pamphlet bears, as do all Club pamphlets, the disclaimer that the views expressed are those of its author alone, and 'are not intended to represent in any sense the official views of the Monday Club'. Nonetheless, it was this pamphlet that resulted in the isolation and resignation of the Club's founder-member, Paul Bristol, that appeared to establish a close ideological connection between the Monday Club and Powell, and that seemed to make feasible a much closer liaison.

Paul Bristol's dismay at this publication is explicable.[1] Apart from the fact that it warmly supported Powell's views, the dominant characteristic of the document was its sneers at 'the Liberal neurosis' – which, the author claimed, afflicted the Foreign Office no less than *The Times* newspaper – and the very thinly-veiled attacks on the current Conservative leadership. It is perhaps sufficient to quote one passage to give a fair presentiment of the calm and ordered logic of this document:

> The active members of the various bodies claiming to be experts on race relations, their faces distorted by hate as they talk about the brotherhood of man, could perhaps be discussed as characters in Peter Simple's *Daily Telegraph* column. But the same persons appear as manipulators in propaganda campaigns and pressure groups, penetrating strategic studies, sitting on race 'conciliation' boards, leading cultural exchanges, packing Chatham House discussions, securing preferential treatment in BBC current affairs commentaries, calling for war on terrorism against overseas European communities. The fragmentation of our society facilitates their task.[2]

Here, indeed, is 'the enemy within'! There are few identifying features given, and certainly no names; the impression of a vast conspiracy that includes the permanent officials of the Foreign and Commonwealth Office, the newspaper editors (particularly

---

[1] Bristol in fact resigned over the draft, which was even more extreme than the published version. Lord Boyd of Merton, a former Conservative Colonial Secretary, also resigned at this time.

[2] George K. Young: *Who Goes Home?*

of the *Guardian* and *The Times*), and others whom can be conveniently described under the general heading of 'the liberal neurosis' ('If men really become the things they fight against, the liberal neurotic is well launched on the storm trooper's path') is created and, because of its very vagueness, has a considerable impact of sinisterness. Although the concept of 'penetrating' strategic studies or of 'packing' Chatham House discussions may be regarded as utterly ludicrous by those with some knowledge of these affairs, the less informed reader is left with the strong impression of some enormous subterranean organization that is sedulously worming its way into the soul of the Body Politic. Nor is the reader left in any doubt of the hero of the hour: 'The vicious attacks on Enoch Powell reveal the malice and hatred which the liberal neurosis evoke', and a Conservative Research Department pamphlet on Immigration and Race Relations was condemned out of hand as containing 'certain inaccurate figures and tendentious conclusions'. The Labour Government received its fair share of abuse, but the Conservative leadership was implicitly condemned on the basis of guilt by association. After the Birmingham speech 'a sense of self-interest – however short-sighted and muddled – has become increasingly evident in the Tory leadership as the pressure of public opinion made itself felt', although this was evidently preferable to the previous situation in which the arguments of officials 'fitted in with the mood of surrender and cynicism encouraged by the Party leadership of the time and suited the pharisaical element of the Tory Party moving comfortably along the safe side of the Jericho road'.

In the main, the Monday Club's publications – which are well printed and produced – have a certain quality, which may not be apparent to their opponents, but which must be respected. The Club is not a lunatic fringe group, publishing frenetic rubbish to a fanatical and ignorant clique. If it were, there would be little point in examining it. One does not have to agree with the arguments set out in the pamphlets to deny their value and seriousness. But there are exceptions.

The emotional link between Powell and the Monday Club was by 1968, very close. Both had been arguing for several years that the Conservative Party was slithering towards an indeterminable and spineless 'liberalism', and was doomed unless it rediscovered its true principles and faith. Each had acted independently, but their fundamental complaint was common, and their success demonstrated that a significant element in the Party shared their concern. In these circumstances it was very fortunate for Heath that there was no serious chance of an alliance between Powell – who never became a member – and the Monday Club. This was partly the result of Powell's own individuality which makes him an uncomfortable political associate, but the main cause was the incompatibility of his views on several subjects which are particularly dear to the Monday Club. Here, the very width and extent of 'Powellism' was its principal political weakness. And there is some validity in the comment of one observer that 'while the Monday Club is Tory, Enoch is a Whig'. Nevertheless, the closeness in outlook between Powell and the rapidly expanding Monday Club was a factor that the Conservative leaders had to take into serious account, and particularly on immigration; on the Third Reading of the Race Relations Bill forty-five Conservative backbenchers defied their Front Bench and voted against the motion.

Heath's position by this stage was a very difficult one. He knew that there was no real danger of a Powell–Monday Club coalition, and he suspected that the Parliamentary Party was outraged by Powell's performances. But he also sensed a feeling in the Party at large – and in the country – that required action that went beyond the 1965 Home guidelines. Viewed in retrospect, it was not suprising that, in a major speech at York in September 1968, Heath declared new guidelines for Conservative approaches to immigration which were close enough to Powell's position to arouse comment and concern. In this speech Heath laid down the new Conservative policy. The first emphasis was on the need for racial harmony, but this was followed by the declaration that Conservative policy was now to bring the Commonwealth immigrants under the laws relating to aliens. Entry for immigrants should be conditional and related in all cases to a specific job, to be negotiated before departure from the country of origin; the right to decide would only be conceded after four years' satisfactory residence; in the initial period, any change of employment would have to be approved; UK citizenship would no longer be granted as of right after five years, but conferred only after procedures similar to those for aliens; heads of households intending to bring dependants would have to register their intention before departure for the UK; repatriation of those immigrants who had failed to settle down and who wished to return to their country of origin would be assisted.[1] These new guidelines were emphasized by later statements by Heath at Folkestone on 17 November and at Walsall on 25 January 1969. That even this movement towards Powell was insufficient was seen when the majority against Powellite opposition to the official Party in the 1969 Party Conference was only 1,349 to 954. Thus, although Powell had not succeeded in taking the Conservative leadership all the way, he had taken it a considerable distance. One of the first acts of the Conservative Government elected in June 1970 was to announce further restrictions on immigrant work permits for Commonwealth citizens. But to what extent was this an abandonment of the 1965 policy? At first glance it might seem possible to accuse Heath of firmness in April and capitulation in September. But this would be a superficial judgement. On this point it is important to be reasonable. Many commentators had hoped that Heath's stand against Powell was to be one of principle, and was to be vigorously maintained. The fact that the point of principle was quickly obscured, to the point when Heath was in effect arguing that the differences between himself and Powell were essentially of degree,[2] was a profound disappointment to all engaged in the positive aspects of race relations, and it would be difficult to describe Heath's performance in heroic terms. Heroism in politics, as in war, is usually demanded by individuals who have no personal involvement in the action nor in its consequences. But the contemporary commentator does not have to reduce himself to the laborious dragging forward of the tawdry chariot of political prudence in order to emphasize that Heath's position was very difficult. Whatever one might think of Powell's motives and language, he had exposed a raw nerve in contemporary British society; he had also exposed a fundamental schism in the Conservative Party. Of practical necessity Heath had to take note of these facts, and to limit his objectives to the preservation of the 1965 position. The fact that he was successful in doing so was, in itself, a form of victory so far as the Conservative Party

[1] For the full text, see *The Times*, 3 September 1968.
[2] It is perhaps significant to note that Heath's statement on Powell's dismissal from the Shadow Cabinet stated that the action had been taken 'with the greatest regret'.

was concerned. The possible movement of the Parliamentary Party towards extreme policies on this matter by the Party at large was resisted and defeated.

The most important point to emphasize is that this resistance went beyond the issue of race relations itself. Its success confirmed that the programme established in 1964–5 would be maintained and preserved. For behind the challenge to the Party's race policy there lay other challenges which Heath was determined to resist. By his movement towards Powell's attitude on immigration controls, Heath was fighting the other and deeper political menaces of 'Powellism'. By meeting some of the points raised by Powell on immigration he was defeating the other radical tenets of the Powellite 'package'. A number of concessions on the most heated issues removed pressure from others. Thus, Heath was able to defeat the collective thrust of the challenge of 'Powellism' by judicious concessions on one particular front. In immediate terms it was totally successful. The sudden challenge to his leadership was resisted with complete success. From September 1968 Heath's leadership was not in question. But the bad effect which his performance made upon the leaders of coloured minority groups in Britain represented a very serious deficit in the balance, and opened the question as to whether the price for Heath's victory will not turn out to be, in the long run, a very heavy one for the Conservative Party to bear.

But it is also important to emphasize that, while Heath was obliged to move some direction in making the Conservative line on immigration much firmer than it had been, he was absolutely determined not to permit the Party policy to be contaminated with racialism. On 17 November, in reply to a question put to him at the conference of the Kent group of Young Conservatives at Folkestone, he condemned 'the character assassination of any racial group in this country' and the treatment in emotive terms without constructive proposals of a complex and sensitive human problem. He described a Powell speech at Scarborough on 17 January 1970 as 'an example of Man's inhumanity to Man which is absolutely intolerable in a Christian civilized society',[1] and he clearly spelt out the limits of

[1] It appears that there was a misunderstanding over what Powell said and meant to say. The implication of the speech was that government assistance to areas with high immigrant populations should be checked, so that conditions

the Party's repatriation policy at the Party Conference at Brighton on 11 October 1969:

We shall make funds available to assist immigrants who wish to return to their own country of origin. But we are not going to press them; we are not going to harry them; we are going to do everything to prevent a climate being created which will make them wish to leave against their own free will.

To maintain his position, and that of the leadership as a whole, Heath had had to take serious note of the feelings in the Party, which were by this stage running vigorously in favour of a much tougher line – as the 1968 and 1969 Party Conferences demonstrated. But he was able to keep that movement within the 1965 Home policy, particularly on dependants. This was, in the circumstances, a not inconsiderable achievement.

One observer has compared this entire story to an old Hollywood film run backwards, in which the happy ending is at the beginning, and everything thereafter goes wrong. Very few politicians emerge from the story with great credit, and the most depressing aspect of all was the relative failure to attempt to solve the problem with positive measures. The establishment of the Race Relations Board, the Institute of Race Relations, and the Community Relations Commission, have not been sufficient. By 1971 the basic problem is no nearer solution than it was in 1961, and in most respects the situation has actually become worse. It sleepeth, but is not gone.

Although two of the three major steps in this story were taken by the Labour Government, the Conservatives had definitely moved towards a much harder line on immigration even before the Powell speech, as the reasoned amendment to the Race Relations Bill demonstrated, and the pressure came from the Party as a whole – and from the Midlands in particular – rather than from the leadership. The tail came to wag the dog. In his attempt to maintain balance, Heath and his colleagues were

would become so intolerable that the immigrants would depart on their own accord. This was certainly Heath's understanding, and that of others, but for once Powell's language was ambiguous, and too extreme an interpretation on what Powell was arguing may have been placed.

forced gradually into a more firm line than they would have desired. This was an issue on which the Party could have divided catastrophically – and very nearly did so. In the circumstances, Heath's qualified retreat was inevitable. And he was careful to stop that retreat far ahead of the position which a substantial element of the Party – and probably the majority – would have wished.

Such episodes can be interpreted in one of two ways. They can be seen as clear evidence of a weak leadership, which is not prepared to stand on a matter of fundamental principle, and which – while protesting loudly that it is doing nothing of the sort – is bowing to the clamour of its more extremist supporters. But they can also be seen in the light of the duty of a party leader to take serious note of the clearly expressed will of at least a large number of his supporters, and also in the light of that leader's duty to prevent splits in the party developing into irreparable divisions. Regarded in the latter light, Heath's actions in the second half of 1968 made sound political sense. The forty-five Conservative MPs who defied him on the Third Reading of the Race Relations Bill represented, after all, some 18 per cent of the Parliamentary Party; it was evident that they had other sympathizers who did not defy the Whips; it was even more evident that they spoke for a substantial element in the Party outside. In these circumstances, Heath had no real choice but to take up his new course.

There can be little doubt that the forces in the Conservative Party for which Powell had spoken – but which he had not created – on 20 April 1968 had propelled the Conservative leadership further and faster on a course which it wished to take more cautiously. It is more difficult to assess the general impact of Enoch Powell on the Party's policies as a whole. The problem is made more difficult by the fact that, despite many differences of outlook and temperament between the two men, Heath and Powell had, politically, much in common. It could be argued that, the differences being mainly of degree, there was no difference in emphasis in Heath's approach after April 1968 than before. But although any movement towards some Powellite attitudes was accompanied by vigorous denunciations (principally in private) of Powell personally by the leadership, these could not disguise the fact that a new insecurity was evident in the Conservative Party after April 1968. Heath himself was concerned by the pressures from the Right, and took steps to reduce them. He could claim – and does – that the basic policies of 1966 were those on which the 1970 Election was fought, but there was a very distinct sharpening of certain points after April 1968. It was less the policies themselves than the new *note* that struck an ominous sound for what must be loosely categorized as the liberal Conservatives. They found themselves under increasing pressure in their own constituencies, and one, Nigel Fisher at Surbiton, faced an overt attempt to remove him as a candidate; the threat against Terence Higgins at Worthing was a less serious affair, but was also indicative of the changed temper, as were the pressures against Boyle in Handsworth, Birmingham.[1] The case of another liberal Conservative candidate, who had to change his tune very sharply on certain issues – notably immigration and Rhodesia – in order to calm his association cannot have been unique. The pattern was not general, but by the end of 1968 there were many Conservatives who were very troubled indeed by developments in the Party. The manifest satisfaction of the Monday Club at these developments was an ominous sign.

The Powell eruption was important because it exposed Heath to the charge of not being 'Conservative' enough from the Right, and it distressed his more liberal supporters through what they regarded as his lack of moral courage. They had thought at first that he was going to stand and fight Powell as Gaitskell had fought the unilateralists in 1959–61. When he did not, several were disillusioned and dismayed. In certain non-political – but by no means unimportant – groups this disillusionment was much stronger, and this was most evident in universities and higher education circles generally. This alienation of a numerically small but highly articulate and influential middle-class group from the Conservatives may well become permanent. They did not adequately appreciate the latent strength of the forces with which Heath had to be content; nor the substantial measure of his success.

Powell did not initiate the movement towards a 'harder'

[1] Boyle announced his departure from politics in October 1969, to become Vice-Chancellor of Leeds University.

Conservative policy. That process had been developing since 1964, and in certain areas had been initiated by Heath himself. But the collective significance of the activities of the Monday Club and Enoch Powell, even though they did not coalesce and were incompatible allies on many issues, was to accelerate this process, with the consequence that, by the end of 1969, a new and important polarization between Labour and Conservative was apparent. It was this polarization that Wilson was to attempt to exploit in the early spring of 1970. Thus in any analysis of the gradual erosion of the 1950s consensus politics, the contribution of Enoch Powell can hardly be over-emphasized.

Part Four

THE GENERAL ELECTION OF 1970

WHETHER in Office or in Opposition, the prospect of a General Election looms over every politician with a terrible finality. In the historical perspective, five years is not a long time; but in the lifetime of a politician it is an eternity. The observer may argue that the political future of the nation is at stake; but to the politician what is at stake is his own future for the next five years. For the victors there will be office, satisfaction, and influence, and the glow of success; for the vanquished there will be a period of frustrated impotence and the sour taste of defeat. Thus to those whose personal prospects and careers are at hazard a General Election is an ordeal made tolerable only by the excitement that is created by the very magnitude of the stakes. This tension gradually communicates itself to the electorate. In 1970 this was slow to develop, but certainly by the final week of the campaign the natural drama inherent in any general election was plainly evident. It is probable that the General Election of 1970 will be remembered principally because of its unexpected outcome, but for the political observer it possessed an exceptional interest for other reasons.

Few politicians doubted that the Election would come in 1970. The power of timing General Elections is one of the most significant advantages enjoyed by the governing party, and it was clearly highly probable that Wilson would allow the Parliament to run its full course into 1971, and thus deprive Labour of this advantage. While the power of dissolving Parliament at a time best suited to the interests of the governing party should not be exaggerated, it is not entirely without significance that before 1970 a governing party with a Parliamentary majority has been defeated only five times this century.[1]

In contrast, the Opposition parties have to guess, analyse hints, and gaze hopefully or fearfully towards the forthcoming months, their plans being of necessity contingency plans. By the beginning of 1970, although the Conservatives and the Liberals were convinced that the Election would come in 1970, there were several important incalculables in the situation. They could read the trade figures and study the economic trends, but they did not have all the information available to the Government that might make the crucial difference between a spring, summer, or autumn election. They could not know what the Budget would contain, nor what part – if any – this would play in the Government's strategy. They could not overlook the possibility that the element of recklessness in Wilson's political character might tempt him to a gambler's throw at an unexpected moment and virtually without warning. They knew that all the decisive initiatives lay with the Government. The Conservatives had a healthy respect for Wilson's electioneering skills and remembered the perfect timing of the 1966 dissolution. They knew, furthermore, that there had been a distinct movement back to Labour of disgruntled supporters, and they had been apprehensive of the possibility of an election in the previous autumn; but they could not determine whether Wilson would take a chance on a sudden swing towards the Government in the opinion polls and by-elections, or whether he would await longer confirmation of the permanency of such a swing. Thus, by the beginning of 1970, the balance of tactical advantage still lay with Labour, and this fact was keenly appreciated by the Conservative leaders.

The Conservatives were technically as well prepared as they could be, and were certainly in an infinitely stronger position

---

[1] In 1923, 1929, 1945, 1951, and 1964. In 1924 the Labour Government did not have an overall Parliamentary majority, and the Election came after a defeat in the House of Commons. It should also be noted that in 1923, although the Conservatives lost their overall majority, they remained the largest single party in the Commons; in 1951 Labour secured a majority in the national vote, although it lost its Parliamentary majority; and 1964 was, as has been noted, a very close contest.

than they had been in 1964 or 1966. The first draft of their General Election arrangements had been written by Fraser in July 1969, and covered all the administrative details. Although the paper was subsequently amended – principally in minor changes of the rôles of certain individuals – the essential features were retained. The Manifesto was well in hand, and successive drafts had been considered and amended by Heath's steering committee and the Advisory Committee on Policy. The elaborate Campaign Guide was also well advanced, and posters and leaflets were ready for printing as soon as the election was announced. Heath's tour programme had been arranged.

There were no difficulties over the Party programme, which was in essentials the same as that of 1966, now amended in some areas, more deeply researched in others, and hardened in some places. The 1966 programme had looked somewhat tentative and hastily prepared; by 1970, although there had been no major changes in strategy or principle, the appearance was more convincing. The changes were of emphasis, and although they indicated evidence of a slight but significant movement towards a more radical and doctrinaire approach since 1966, these changes were only evident to close observers. The presentational weakness in the programme was that it looked ominously like the mixture as before. The question that concerned the Conservative leaders was whether this very fact would not be counter-productive, and give the Party a too-familiar appearance. Would the radical package of 1966 not seem somewhat familiar and unexciting by 1970? Might it not be alleged that, after four years of Opposition, the Conservatives had emerged with nothing new, and were stuck with their old cries, their old men, and their old policies? These apprehensions were not assuaged by the threat of a Labour poster campaign on the theme of 'Yesterday's Men (They failed before)' in which unflattering models of the Conservative leaders were to be shown.

But despite the readiness of the Conservative machine, the basic dilemma of timing remained. Tactical considerations – to say nothing of financial factors – argued strongly against any major national publicity campaign early in 1970. But the publicity which a Government and a Prime Minister naturally attract – and particularly a Prime Minister as publicity-conscious as Wilson – gave Labour such an advantage that it is probable that the Conservatives were excessively cautious.

In contrast to this somewhat muted approach, Wilson was beginning to attract considerable publicity and attention, and it was evident that he was determined to seize the political initiative. On 6 February, at Nottingham, he launched a major assault on the new Conservative philosophy in a speech which contained charges which, although exaggerated, were close enough to the reality to be damaging:

This is not just a lurch to the Right, it is an atavistic desire to reverse the course of twenty-five years of social revolution. What they are planning is a wanton, calculated and deliberate return to greater inequality.

The new Conservative slogan is: Back to the free for all.

A free for all in place of the welfare state. A free for all market in labour, in housing, in the social services. They seek to replace the compassionate society with the ruthless, pushing society. The message to the British people would be simple and brutal. It would say: 'You're out on your own.'

Wilson in full cry is an exhilarating spectacle for his supporters and one that arouses bitter passions in his opponents. The historian finds himself comprehending both emotions. One example – Camden Town Hall, on 21 February – may be noted:

It is [the Conservatives'] purpose to force up the cost of living, deliberately to force up prices, and especially food prices, in Britain. It is nothing to do with negotiations for entering into Europe. It is irrespective of these negotiations. They would put up prices, they would eliminate food subsidies – for the sheer hell of it.

Although the Conservatives responded to such allegations, the responses attracted much less attention than the original assault. As in 1963-4 the Conservatives found themselves on the defensive throughout the spring, and by April it was clear that Wilson had succeeded in his purpose of seizing the public initiative from the Opposition. Unquestionably, the Government had won the first round, and, with the other advantages, which it possessed as the governing party, Labour was well situated.

Thus, although the Conservatives were technically very well

prepared, 1970 had opened ominously. In Macleod's words: 'Everything that hard work can do has been done. Everything that sophisticated modern analysis can do has been done. Everything that dedication and determination can do has been done.' But not all observers were as satisfied. They found it difficult to establish exactly why they were unimpressed, but one suddenly became aware of a growing feeling that the Conservatives were going to lose again. From the Labour viewpoint the Conservatives had become very predictable. There seemed little call for Ministers to lie awake of nights, fretting over what the wily Tories might unexpectedly spring on them on the morrow. Thus, no doubt, did the German commanders on the Western Front in the Great War feel when a major British offensive was imminent. They knew that it would be massive, most formidable, meticulously planned. But they knew exactly what the enemy would do. In politics, as in war, the fear lies in the unknown and the unexpected, the eventualities that cannot be foreseen, the unpredictability of a foe adept at dodges, contrivances, and subterfuges. Labour knew that they would have to meet a determined but straightforward frontal attack, with the greatest force being applied to certain easily identifiable points. The most important of these was the economy, and, by the late spring of 1970 there was a mounting confidence in the Government that an attack here could be turned back without difficulty.

The Conservative leaders believed that the reiteration of their programme since 1966 had established a public awareness of what the Party's policy objectives were. Their own researches revealed the existence of a firm movement towards them that was sufficient for a working Parliamentary majority. They were convinced that disillusionment with the Labour record was such that there would be heavy abstentions among former Labour supporters. They still believed that Labour's handling of the economy was its weakest point. But the high confidence of a few months before had been replaced by a sober realization of the difficulties of unseating a Government headed by a man of infinite resource whose national popularity remained high. The Conservatives, furthermore, were very much in the same position as Labour had been in the 1960s. A third electoral defeat in a row would be bound to have devastating effects on the Party. The Conservatives were, in short, in a 'now or never' situation, and could see all the tactical advantages moving towards their opponents.

But if the Conservatives had their problems, the Liberals' predicament was much more unenviable. Between 1960 and 1964 the Liberals had believed that their long-awaited revival was at hand. The by-election victory at Orpington in 1962 and the evidence of the public impact of Mr Jo Grimond had indicated that organization and money are not everything in politics. In 1964 the Liberals had increased their Parliamentary representation to nine, and had come second in fifty-four constituencies, and had won over 3 million votes, their highest figure since 1929.

But the 1964 Election had been in reality a disaster for the Liberals, for it exposed their fundamental predicament – were they a party of the Left or of the Right? The dream for many years had been of a new revitalized 'Radical' party which would attract disillusioned moderate members of the Labour Party, and this dream had been based on the confident expectation that the Labour Party was on the verge of final disintegration. The 1964 result meant that this event was going to be postponed and, in the meanwhile, the Liberals found themselves in the position they had long publicly desired but which many had secretly feared – that of holding the balance of advantage in the House of Commons. They could not bring down the Government, but their votes made the issue perilously close.

Grimond, after lengthy consideration, made what was in effect a public offer to Labour of an alliance in the summer of 1965. He had not flown this *ballon d'essai* without consulting his colleagues, and he can hardly have expected to have secured complete approval. But the furore that the suggestion made in the Liberal Party served to emphasize that its members held very different opinions on where their principal balance of allegiance (or balance of hostility) lay. Were they, in short, Liberal–Conservative or Liberal–Labour? – or, to put it in another way, did they hate the Tories more or less than Labour? As the debate raged, the split in the Party became increasingly sharp, and was greatly complicated by the feverish activities of the Young Liberals, who at times seemed to occupy a position too far to the Left to be tolerable in the Labour Party, let alone the Liberals. Wilson was not, at that stage, prepared to come to terms with Grimond. The failure of the Grimond initiative was demonstrated in Wilson's scathing comments on the Liberal Party in the course of his speech to the 1965 Labour Party Conference, and the sweeping Labour victory in 1966 relegated the possibility to oblivion. The Liberal vote fell to 2,327,533 even though their Parliamentary representation rose to 12 – the highest since 1945. But the position to dictate terms, or even to negotiate them with any realistic expectations, had gone. The Labour Party was evidently not in a disintegrative frame of mind, and Grimond's elaborate political house of cards abruptly collapsed. He himself resigned the leadership at the end of the year, and was succeeded by Mr Jeremy Thorpe.

Although his general strategy may have been proved by events to have been at fault, Grimond had been the Liberals' principal public asset, and his departure placed a very severe load on the shoulders of his successors. Thorpe had won North Devon in 1959, and had quickly become the *preux chevalier* of the diminutive Parliamentary Party and the new hero of the faithful in the country. His problem was that he was a difficult man to take very seriously, despite his ability and quickness and (or perhaps because of) his wit. The gravity that is deemed suitable to a British politician sat uneasily on Thorpe's shoulders, and we may recall Disraeli's celebrated comment that the British, being a nation subject to fogs and possessing a large middle-class, require grave statesmen. Despite many personal and political qualities Thorpe seemed to lack that of *weight* – of all political attributes the most difficult to describe.[1] He was certainly the outstandingly best equipped successor to Grimond in the Parliamentary Party, and he had some political qualities that Grimond had lacked, but he could not equal the public position which Grimond had acquired, nor his respect in the Party at large.

Much might have been salvaged if there had been a significant shift to the Liberals in by-elections during the 1966 Parliament, but with some momentary exceptions it became apparent that disillusioned Labour voters were staying at home, or voting Conservative, or – even more ominously – voting for Welsh and

[1] The Latin word *gravitas* is perhaps the best equivalent.

223

Scottish Nationalists. The solitary exception was a gain from Labour in Birmingham, Ladywood, in June 1969.[1] This was but a glimmer of light in a long, dark night. The Liberals found themselves trapped between the two main parties, evidently gaining little new support, and in danger of losing what support they had.

This was partly the result of a chronic shortage of money and inadequacy of organization, but it was perhaps principally the consequence of a hesitant and divided leadership. Thorpe was not in a sufficiently strong position to lead with vigour, and that position itself was under constant – if clandestine – harassment. The fundamental problem of whether the Party was Conservative- or Labour-inclined, or merely wandering in the middle crying 'Radical' at suitable moments, was not resolved. And so the Party drifted unhappily towards what most Liberals gloomily realized was bound to be a miserable Election, whenever it came.

It is difficult to see how Thorpe could have done better or other than he did, given the situation which he inherited, and given also his own limitations as a public personality. It might have helped if he himself had determined on a course which represented something easily identifiable as different from that of the major parties, and had staked his position on the outcome. Perhaps that was to ask too much. But the fact remained that, whereas in 1964 – and to a lesser extent in 1966 – the Liberal Party had seemed a viable and respectable alternative to the main parties, by 1970 it had fallen almost out of sight. But this was also very substantially due to the fact that both major parties had stolen what few clothes the Liberals had possessed. In 1964 the cry of 'If you think like a Liberal vote like a Liberal' had had some relevance; by 1970 it seemed to have less. In the Labour–Conservative contest for the political area loosely described as 'the middle ground' the one easily identifiable casualty was the Liberal Party. Even in the 'Celtic Fringe' the old faith seemed to be wobbling and in the isolated outposts of Liberalism in England the indications were that the Liberals were doomed to be crushed between the two main parties.

The Liberals had managed to survive since 1945 principally because they had continued to appeal to a section of the

[1] Labour recovered the seat in 1970.

electorate that found decreasing attraction in the doctrines and leaders of the two main parties. In the late 1950s and early 1960s they had been the principal beneficiary of the new volatility in the electorate that these disillusionments had created, and in Jo Grimond they had had a leader of considerable ability and national attraction. In the period when the party had been under the dead hand of Mr Clement Davies the Liberals had relied upon traditional support and votes from those voters who had left one of the major parties but who could not bring themselves to make the long leap to the other. But the Liberals could not remain for ever the collector of random votes from the disgruntled supporters of the Conservative or Labour Parties. Sooner or later they would have to commit themselves to one side of the political spectrum. They were bound to lose some support when they did so, but they were also bound to lose support if they hovered unhappily in the middle. This was the insoluble Liberal dilemma.

By 1970 the Liberals did not present an impressive spectacle. The Young Liberals were hardly likely to appeal to an electorate that was becoming increasingly resentful of long-haired self-appointed experts, and even less likely to appeal to a leadership which the Young Liberals publicly regarded with unconcealed derision. The great Liberal figures of the 1950s were either gone, or had aged, or had lost their impact, and their successors did not give the impression of being capable of storming the Tory or Labour bastions and sweeping them aside in a glorious assault. The new Liberals seemed sadly surplus and ineffectual, a peripheral group of no serious account. By this stage their activities were almost completely ignored by Labour and Conservative, which was eloquent commentary on their declined position. Just before the General Election the Party announced that its overdraft had been paid off, but the Treasurer subsequently reported that 85 per cent of the money subscribed to Party funds in the eight months before the Election had come from less than twenty-five individuals.[1] They had been forced to move out of their Smith Square headquarters two years previously, and by 1970 had only seventeen full-time agents. It was apparent that on any normal assessment the Liberals were painfully ill-equipped to fight the Election.

[1] *Liberal News*, 9 July 1970.

It is doubtful whether there is a place in modern British politics for a third party. But it would appear to be the case that there is no place for a third party which has no real identity. The Liberal Revival, which had seemed so significant and exciting in 1962–5, slowly faded until, by the beginning of 1970, it seemed to belong to a distant political history, as remote from contemporary reality as Mr Asquith's by-election victory in 1919. The history of the Liberal Party had been, since that event, one of false dawns.

The part played by the national opinion polls on the timing of the Election was crucial. In general, the Conservatives had enjoyed a very substantial advantage in these polls since the summer of 1966, and at times their lead had reached dizzying proportions. The more sober Conservative calculation, based on their sample survey, was that their lead was in the region of 4–6 per cent, and there was not too much concern when it began to fall steadily between January and the end of April 1970, when Gallup gave them a 4.5 per cent lead. But it was at this moment that the Harris Poll actually gave Labour a national lead, and was confirmed by Marplan; Gallup swiftly followed with polls giving a real Labour lead which, to the consternation of the Conservatives, was put at 7 per cent by the middle of May.

If most Conservatives were baffled by this development, Wilson was not. The well-publicized meeting of the Shadow Cabinet at Selsdon Park in January was regarded by the Conservatives as a great success; Wilson calculated that it was a major error, and he was swift to pounce on the character of the meeting with his scathing depictions of 'Selsdon Man', a hard-headed, flint-hearted, and reactionary enemy of the social services and a planned economy and cold advocate of a 'law and order' policy. He believed, like Cromwell when he saw his foes coming down from the mountains at Dunbar, that, 'the Lord hath delivered them into my hands'. For the Conservatives had provided him with a target, and one which could be used to unify his followers and distract public attention from Labour's difficulties and deficiencies. By February, with the Conservatives remaining rather quiet, Wilson was up and running; by March and early April he was in a gallop. What was particularly significant was Wilson's use of television – including an appearance on a sports programme (on the very dubious grounds that Heath had been interviewed following his victory in the Sydney–Hobart sailing race)[1] and a tour of Chequers which showed him at his most patriarchal and benevolent – and exploitation of other non-political occasions, of which one example was his speech to the United Nations Association at York in April, in which he injected the clear insinuation that the Opposition was engaged in secret negotiations with the Smith regime. This should have been a period in which the pressure was coming from the Conservatives, but despite Wilson's new aggressiveness the Opposition was uneasily passive. The argument that the more the public saw Wilson the more would they turn to the Conservatives was not being confirmed by the opinion polls which, as in the previous autumn, were showing the Conservative lead once again 'going down like a lift'.

Wilson had had his eye on a June Election ever since Selsdon Park – and, indeed, for some time before that event – and the evidence of what can be reasonably described as the Spring Offensive gradually confirmed him in this view. At this stage a majority of the Parliamentary Labour Party, whose morale was rising swiftly, favoured October, as did a majority of Ministers; the factor that made them change their minds and agree to a June poll was the startling evidence of the opinion polls.

Political polling on the basis of sample and quota surveys had been one of the more intriguing post-war growth industries. The Gallup Poll Organization had done some work in this field

---

[1] This had been a most remarkable achievement, rather comparable to that of a novice winning the Grand National in his first season. Heath's qualities of planning, team selection, toughness, and nerve were well exemplified. But on strictly political terms it is doubtful whether the triumph had any real effect outside enthusiastic sailing circles. Indeed, it is even possible that it might have done the Conservative leader some harm. It is doubtful whether many electors would grasp the magnitude of Heath's achievement; what they could grasp was that taking a sailing boat to Australia for one race is an expensive undertaking which is limited to very few persons. And it may be questioned whether the reference in Heath's introduction to the 1970 Manifesto to 'endless backing and filling' had a very widespread comprehension. But it was certainly the case that the achievement was extremely popular in the Conservative Party, and it gave Heath much personal satisfaction at a difficult time.

in Britain before the Second World War, but their prediction of the 1945 General Election – correct, as it happened – was generally ignored, even by the newspaper (the *News Chronicle*) which published it. The comment of Professor McCallum was indeed prophetic:

> In future, no doubt, more attention will be paid by journalists and others to Gallup Polls and other similar devices for estimating public opinion, and the nature of our electoral system may be better understood. With this exception [Gallup] in 1945 the forecasting can only be described as reaching a very high degree of political ineptitude. The General Election of 1945 . . . was the Waterloo of the political meteorologists.[1]

The fact that Gallup forecasted accurately the winning party – although not the majorities – in the Elections of 1950, 1951, 1955, and 1959 increasingly restored confidence in, and made politically respectable, a technique whose credibility had been gravely disrupted by the inaccurate prediction of the 1948 Presidential Election in the United States. There were, before 1959, some competitors to Gallup – most noticeably two somewhat erratic polls published by the *Daily Express* and *Daily Mirror* – but the arrival of National Opinion Polls in 1959 was the first serious one, and the fact that its founder (Mr Michael Shields) had been trained by Gallup was not without significance. In 1959, 1964, and 1966 both Gallup and NOP were accurate in predicting the winner. NOP used some random samples before the 1964 Election, but Gallup stuck to quota sampling.

In 1966 the two most serious polls were Gallup and NOP; in 1967 the *Evening Standard* began publishing the results of the work of a new organization, Opinion Research Centre; in 1968 *The Times* followed suit with Marplan, and in 1969 the *Daily Express* abandoned its previous poll and started to publish the polls of Louis Harris. NOP, Harris, and Marplan used random sampling, while Gallup and ORC stayed with quota sampling.

Until 1970, the polls had enjoyed complete success in that the winner of a General Election – and, in several cases, of by-elections – had been correctly predicted. The fact that the predictions had often been wrong on the percentages attracted

[1] R. B. McCallum and A. Readman: *The General Election of 1945* (London, 1964), p. 243.

less attention than the rightness of the prediction. If a tipster declares that a horse will win by five lengths and in the event wins by two, the punter is not very aggrieved. But these errors – which in some cases were quite sizeable – should have alerted more people than they have to the crudeness of the technique.

The problem of the political opinion poll is fundamental. However carefully selected, and on whatever basis it is conducted, a sample *is* a sample. Some enthusiastic zealots of the technique have been rash enough to compare it with a blood sample; it is quite correct that, in order to ascertain the proportion of red and white corpuscles in the body, it is only necessary to take a minute speck of the patient's blood and analyse it. But the body politic has certain fundamental differences from the human equivalent. The human blood sample literally cannot lie; the electorate sample, albeit unwittingly, can. And a red corpuscle cannot subsequently decide to become a white corpuscle!

To take one important instance; since 1945 between 16 per cent and 28 per cent of the electorate has not voted at all, whereas the polls had very rarely picked up a non-voting intention of more than 6 per cent. Many explanations have been put forward to explain this inconsistency, but they are reduced to the relatively simple point that a voting intention is not a vote. The polls have attempted to meet this problem by attempting to identify the strength of the propensity to vote in each party, to produce the compensating 'differential vote'. In the 1970 Election campaign NOP operated a panel system, whereby on the last weekend they reinterviewed the sample they had interviewed at the outset. But the intricacies of quota-sampling and random-sampling, the differential turn-out, and so on, were lost on the mass of the electorate and most politicians. All they knew was that the polls had been 'right' every time since 1945, and the American débâcle of 1948 had been satisfactorily explained. Certain very curious episodes – of which the polls' prediction of an easy Labour victory in the Leyton by-election of January 1965 was a classic[1] – were ascribed to technical deficiencies or unpredictable circumstances that occur between general elections. The respectability of election polls was established in the Nuffield study of the

---

[1] The forecast was a 20 per cent Labour lead; the Conservatives won the seat.

1966 Election, when it was stated that politicians 'now have more accurate tools for measuring what public opinion really is. What they still need is education in how to use these tools – and how not to use them.'[1] Before 1964 there were still many politicians in both parties who mistrusted the opinion polls; afterwards, they became noticeably fewer, and those who remained sceptical were usually dismissed as being out of date. Even Iain Macleod, who good-humouredly derided the psephologists not only on the grounds that they were making a science out of something very unscientific but were also taking the fun out of politics, became persuaded of the value of close inspections of polls and their implications.

Wilson was, like President Johnson, a committed devotee of opinion polls, which he followed with close attention. He was cautious about individual polls but convinced by trends. At the bleakest moments in the fortune of the 1966–70 Government, when the Labour inferiority in polls was reaching cataclysmic proportions, he drew much comfort from the fact that his personal rating remained high, and was usually much higher than that of Heath. At one point in the 1970 Election campaign he asked a questioner at a press conference, with much scorn, whether he could recall an occasion when a party had lost an election when its leader was favoured by a majority of two to one in the opinion polls. In the manner of that remark there was something more than enjoyment of discomfiting Heath; he believed it.

The polls played, accordingly, a vital role in the plans for the 1970 Election, and were watched with eagerness and attention by both parties. The Conservatives, with their own massive operation in progress, could view them principally as a guide to what Wilson was likely to do; Wilson, with no such comparable machinery at his disposal, had to use them as his principal source of information. Thus, when, in the early spring of 1970, they began to move in Labour's direction, the date of the Election perceptibly edged closer.

The important point was that the opinion polls showed the same trends as the by-elections, and particularly the South Ayrshire by-election in March. Here, the swing to the Conservatives was only 2.9 per cent in a remarkably high poll (over 76 per cent), and the Scottish Nationalist did much less

[1] Butler and King: *The British General Election of 1966*, p. 177.

well than had been expected. Since December, therefore, the by-election movement to the Conservatives had fallen from 14.3 per cent to 2.9 per cent. Wilson's confidence that he could repeat his triumph of 1966 against all the odds had never wavered, but the majority of his colleagues and the Parliamentary Party had never seriously shared it. But by March the mood had changed. Every indication to hand was that there was a definite movement back to Labour, and the discussions increasingly became about timing in order to maximize this new and exciting trend. Some Ministers and Party officials, who already had uncomfortable experience of Wilson's over-optimism, advocated caution, but as the evidence accumulated their voices became fainter.

It is not difficult to determine the principal cause of this shift back to Labour. The balance of payments in 1969, despite a bad first quarter, had been in surplus by £387 million, as compared with deficits of just under £400 million in 1968 and £461 million in 1967. This fact was perhaps of less significance than the upsurge in wages that had followed the abandonment of prices and incomes controls in April 1969. This had removed one of the most powerful sources of grievance against the Government. It is somewhat over-dramatic to claim that the trade figures in themselves transformed the political situation 'in a single stroke'.[1] It was the combination of a more hopeful economic climate and the leap-frogging of prices by wages that had restored the battered image of the Labour Government, and to this should perhaps be added the aggressiveness of Wilson's assault on the Conservatives in the early spring.

Wilson took good care to involve the Cabinet and the NEC in his decision – and to publicize the fact – but the decision itself was necessarily his. As he has written, and with evident feeling: 'A decision on election-timing is a lonely one. Whatever the consultations, it is one man's decision, and if things go wrong he is as likely to be criticized for missing a favourable tide as for plunging in too early.'[2] Some of his colleagues may have had strong reservations about Wilson's capacities as Prime Minister; few had doubts about his formidable capacities on electioneering matters. Some resented his personal seizure of the credit for the improved situation, but they had to recall

[1] Butler and Pinto-Duschinsky: *The British General Election of 1970*, p. 118.
[2] Wilson: *The Labour Government 1964–1970*, p. 201.

that he was to be again their leader in an election campaign.

By early May the message of the opinion polls seemed clear. What was even more significant was that it was confirmed by the local election results. Every known indicator pointed in the same direction. When Wilson decided on a June Election, there were very few in the Labour Party who seriously questioned the rightness of his judgement. It was to be 1966 all over again.

It is important to remember what the political opinion polls had done. They had replaced the old haphazard methods of judging what the electorate was feeling. The predecessors of the polls had been by-election results (notoriously unreliable),[1] canvass returns (highly suspect), the Press (very untrustworthy), agents' reports (variable, although often accurate), and the opinions of Party managers, which were reached by methods of calculation that reduced themselves in the final analysis to little more than an informed guess. Those who guessed right became, like the Conservative manager Captain R. W. E. Middleton in the 1880s and 1890s, legendary figures, to whom Party leaders turned respectfully for oracular guidance; the less successful disappeared into that limbo reserved for false prophets. As the world had progressed, and new political weapons and techniques had been forged, the arrival of the pollsters – at first ignored, then mistrusted, and finally gratefully accepted – seemed a natural event, part of the process whereby the element of gambling in politics had been reduced to a carefully calculable level. Science had triumphed again. Wilson was not, therefore, foolish or irresponsible in accepting the polls; he was relying on a new method of estimating the same thing that other techniques had tried – and usually failed – to do beforehand. If it was to be his misfortune that he was to be the first British politician to prove that this particular science had its limitations, he was not alone. And it is worth emphasizing again that the polls had been confirmed by by-election and local election results. The only contrary indicator – and it was, of course, secret – was that of the

[1] Perhaps the most famous example is that of 1880, when two good by-election results wrongly persuaded Beaconsfield that the time was ripe for a dissolution, but the Conservative victory at Newport in 1945 just before the General Election was another false pointer. The Labour victory in Hull just before the 1966 Election was an opposite example, but the perils of regarding by-elections as significant indications of the result of a general election are confirmed by many celebrated instances.

Conservatives' panel, which still pointed generally towards a Conservative victory. But even that gleam was dulled by the surveys of ORC. With such evidence at his disposal, and as he himself has said, Wilson would have been 'mad' not to have dissolved. If he had not, and had gone down to defeat in October, he would have been seen as the man who had missed his opportunity – much as Disraeli had been criticized for not going to the country in 1878 after the Congress of Berlin.

But there were other factors. Wilson and his advisers saw the choice as between June or October, and there were virtually none – if, indeed, any – who seriously considered the possibility of waiting until the last possible moment, the following spring. The case for October was that there would have been time for the sudden movement to Labour to be confirmed (to use the Conservatives' image) as a 'tide' and not a 'ripple'. There was also the point that in May Labour did not have a manifesto and that the Party organization was not ready (to which there was one retort to the effect that it was never, and never would be, ready, however long the warning). Against this was the evidence of the economy. The collapse of the wages freeze meant that wages were rising faster than prices, but it was clear that the latter were already in the hunt and would soon be level and perhaps even ahead. If the Labour theme was to be the economy – and in fact it had to be – the case for October looked much less strong than June. It is difficult to decide which was *the* determining factor in the choice for June, but this must have been a substantial one.

No serious student of polling techniques, and no serious practitioner, has ever claimed that they are infallible. Before the 1970 Election the major polling firms went to considerable trouble to explain their methods and to emphasize the vital statistical qualification. Mr William Gregory, who formerly was in the Gallup organization, pointed out in the *New Statesman* on 29 May that the figures available on 18 May, although all giving Labour a lead, were also capable of an entirely different interpretation of the range of tolerance (up to 6 per cent) in any decisive direction. Thus the NOP-published Labour lead of 3.2 per cent could produce a Conservative win of 2.8 per cent or, at the other extreme, a Labour lead of 9.2 per cent. It was Mr Gregory who made the most prescient of all warnings when he wrote that, 'when polls go

seriously wrong they tend to go wrong in the same direction. . . .
The polls guarantee no certainty of victory for Mr Wilson,
only a probability.' The Gallup organization itself, in the
Gallup Election Handbook, emphasized that past and future
failures were 'inherent in the nature of sampling'. The pollsters
could reasonably claim that the public had been warned, but
only a very small fraction of the public could have noticed, and
it is questionable whether even that fragment fully understood
the warnings.

The effect of the polls on the calling of the General Election
was clearly considerable although not, in this commentator's
judgement, decisive by itself. It is very questionable whether it
had any impact whatever on voting intentions of the electorate.
But it certainly affected the party workers of all parties, most
candidates, and virtually the whole of the army of political
journalists. Thus, from the outset, the Conservatives were cast
as the losers, and Labour as the winners. As one Conservative
candidate (Sir John Eden) remarked: 'When a lead which we
have held for three years appears to have vanished in three
weeks for no clear reason at all, it is hardly surprising that we
are reeling a bit.'

And there was another element in the complex equation. The
Conservative Party has to face the fact that, as the 1961 Census
clearly demonstrated, some two-thirds of the working population of England and Wales are manual workers. The increase
in the proportion of non-manual workers since the War has
been considerable, but it still represents only one-third of the
working population. We have already noted that 72.6 per cent
of family incomes were under £1,000 a year by 1965.[1] The
Conservative Party depends for its existence upon receiving the
active voting support of a substantial part of the manual
workers, but several indications – notably the work of Dr
Butler and Dr Stokes, published in 1969 – were to the effect
that it was not succeeding as effectively in the 1960s as it had
in the 1950s. Thus, in addition to the polls, the weight of
expert opinion – which Wilson fully shared – was increasingly
tending to the view that there was a built-in Labour advantage
in the electorate which could only be overtaken by circumstances in which the appeal of Labour was so exceptionally
weak and that of the Conservatives so exceptionally strong that

[1] *Annual Abstract of Statistics, 1967*, pp. 286–7. See also pp. 88–89.

the 'natural' situation could be reversed. It was Wilson's conviction – in which he was far from alone – that those special circumstances did not exist in the early summer of 1970. Wilson's decision was not without its risks, but few British political leaders in modern times can have entered into an election with such a multitude of favourable indications.

But behind this new confidence there lay some serious weaknesses in the Labour position. In contrast with the Conservatives' organization – for all its imperfections – that of the Labour Party had deteriorated since 1966. Transport House had found that its separation from the leadership had increased sharply after the 1966 victory, and that proposals for reform were shelved. Matters were not improved by the events of July 1968 when the National Executive chose a successor as General Secretary to Mr Len Williams. The principal candidate was the Minister of Housing, Anthony Greenwood, who was known to be favoured by Wilson. Somewhat late in the day Mr Harry Nicholas, a distinguished official of the Transport and General Workers' Union and a former Treasurer of the Party, emerged as a rival candidate, supported by George Brown. Greenwood had been recommended unanimously by a sub-committee of the NEC of which Nicholas had himself been a member, and Wilson and political commentators were not unjustified in assuming that Greenwood would be easily elected. But it appeared that Brown and Callaghan were not alone in their hostility to appointing a man who – despite Wilson's vigorous protestations to the contrary – seemed to be the nominee of the Party leader. In the event, Nicholas was elected by fourteen votes to twelve. This episode, which was given considerable publicity as a rebuff to Wilson, was not calculated to improve relations between the Prime Minister and Transport House.[1]

It could be argued that the decision of the NEC was significant in that it denied to one man complete control over the Party. But on the other hand it could equally be argued that the Conservatives' principle of complete personal confidence between the leader of the Party and the head of the Party organization is a good one. The traditions and customs of the two parties are so different that it would be very unwise to assume that the practices of one would be applicable to the

[1] For two very different versions of the episode, see George-Brown, *In My Way*, and Wilson, *op. cit.*

other. Nonetheless, a situation of the kind in which Labour found itself after July 1968 could hardly be regarded as efficient or desirable.

Once again, the historian is reminded of the importance of personality. The Conservative reforms were possible essentially because of the experience and personality of Sir Michael Fraser, a highly efficient, shrewd, and experienced man who is absolutely dedicated to the Conservative Party, and in whom successive leaders of the Party have had complete trust. Fraser became in effect the 'Permanent Secretary' of the Party because of his unique qualifications to fill such a rôle. No comparable individual had emerged in the Labour Party, and neither Greenwood nor Nicholas can reasonably be compared with Fraser. Nor was there a position comparable to Barber's. The hierarchy at Transport House was of a rather lower calibre than that in the Conservative Central Office, and the relationship with the Party leadership was substantially less close.

This is not to say that Transport House lacked individuals of considerable ability. The differences lay in the combination of the quality of leadership, administrative cohesion, and the links between that leadership and the respective Leaders of the two parties. And it was here that the Conservatives had a substantial advantage.

The other evident discrepancy was seen in the proportion of party revenues that each party was prepared to put into organizational activities. By the end of 1969, despite severe financial problems which had been overcome by sheer hard work, the Conservative national organization was in good shape, and it had even been possible to restore the 'cadet agent' scheme which had to be temporarily abandoned. The Conservatives not only had many more agents and active local organizations but, in general, much better ones. Salary levels in the central and local organizations of the Conservative Party were at least roughly comparable to those in other professional fields; those of the Labour Party were not. It was, accordingly, not surprising that although both parties lost men and women of ability during this period, the Labour loss was substantially more significant than that of the Conservatives, both numerically and qualitatively. When the 1970 General Election took place, only 128 constituency Labour parties had full-time agents, as opposed to 439 Conservative associations.

There was something more in this than money, organizational ability, or tradition. The Conservatives were still attracting and retaining men and women dedicated to working for the Party. The Labour Party was not. In retrospect, this was the real importance of the contrast between the condition of the parties' national organizations by the beginning of 1970.

Wilson's task was, in the words of one senior Conservative strategist, to walk on eggs for three weeks. So long as he broke none, by dexterous footwork and much care and gentleness, he would probably win. But if he slipped, he was done for. The Conservative strategy, accordingly, was to harry, jostle, and hopefully rattle him into this situation. There were many Conservatives who, remembering everything that had happened since 1964, were sceptical of the potentialities of this strategy, and the difficulty of the Conservative position was well summarized by Mr David Wood in *The Times* on 15 June:

> The truth is that Mr Heath and the Shadow Cabinet prepared through the years to fight an election in a time of economic crisis, and Mr Wilson managed by luck and audacity to bring on the election at a time when hardly any voter could believe there is a present crisis.

The Labour strategy was strikingly similar to this but – not surprisingly – was expressed in somewhat different terms. All talk of financial or other difficulty was to be contemptuously dismissed. The advantage of being the Government was again to be played to the full, with the Conservatives portrayed as somewhat tedious and mildly dangerous despoilers of an established competent administration. It was to be, as the *Sunday Times* remarked, Harold Baldwin against Ramsay MacHeath, as in 1966. Then Heath's stiffness and brigadier-manner were to be exposed in great contrast to Wilson's warm, humane, and good-natured approach. Labour's own calculation was that the more the public saw Heath the more would they turn to Wilson.[1] The exact nature of the policies need not

[1] It was a curious feature of the 1970 General Election that each side regarded its opponents' leader as one of their most important assets. In the event it is very doubtful whether the personalities of the party leaders played a part of any real significance in the electors' calculations.

be too precisely delineated. Heath had chosen to fight the Election on 'style', and the Labour organizers were more than pleased to conduct the battle on those terms. Thus, it was argued, while Heath ranted away and bored everyone to distraction, a calm, serene, sympathetic Prime Minister would tour the country radiating compassionate benignity. 'The idea is the electoral equivalent of those impulsive "walkabout" dashes into the crowd pioneered by General de Gaulle, and used with such success by the Queen during her recent Australian tour,' in the words of one newspaper.[1] This activity would, moreover, be concentrated on the Labour-held marginals whose retention would be vital. But when Wilson attacked, he would give the Tories hell.

This was far from an aggressive strategy, and it was soon apparent that the formula was very close to that of 1966. It was to be the 'You *know* Labour Government works' campaign all over again, with minor innovations. But the danger of repeating a successful electoral formula is that its appropriateness may have changed. In 1966 the Conservatives had been still in some disarray as a result of divisions over Rhodesia, the psychological difficulties of switching from Government to Opposition, and the establishment of a new leader and pro-gramme. In contrast, Labour had been confident, fresh, and united, and had been still profiting from the reaction against the Conservatives after their long period of domination. In 1970 these circumstances did not obtain. Given the conditions as they were, with a record that was less than impressive, an organization that had been permitted to decline, strong evidence of Party disillusionment, and a certain lack of cohesion in the hierarchy, a more dynamic and forward-looking strategy would have seemed to have been much more ap-propriate. By returning to the 1966 formula Labour had opted for a campaign strategy that was excessively static. The crux of the matter was that Labour did not have any agreed and carefully planned policies. The lack of preparatory planning, the gulf between the Government and Transport House, and clashes of personality and philosophy had created an almost completely bare policy cupboard. Labour accordingly ad-vanced with what was in effect a request for a renewed mandate

[1] *Sunday Times*, 31 May 1970.

without specifics, with dire warnings of the disaster that would ensue if their opponents won. It was somewhat reminiscent of the Conservatives' 1929 'Safety First' campaign. The real point was that in 1966 the claim that 'You *know* Labour Government works' had had real validity; by 1970 it was considerably more controversial.

Labour got off to what it regarded as a flying start. On the afternoon of the day of the dissolution announcement (18 May) Wilson was filmed in the garden of 10 Downing Street, replying gently to some very gentle questions put to him with much deference by the courteous Mr Hardiman Scott of the BBC, whose selection for this honour by the Prime Minister had been far from coincidental. 'I don't think that they (the electorate) want a lot of change and disturbance,' Wilson declared, thoughtfully, squinting in a statesmanlike and considerate manner in the sunshine. Immediately after this somewhat awe-inspiring interview, in which Wilson's regal tolerance was very evident, Heath was exposed to some very rough handling from Mr Robin Day on 'Panorama'. Day stands high in the Tory demonology, and his standing was not lowered by an inquisition which opened with the brusque request for information about Heath's future plans if he lost the Election. Some Conservative managers were pleased, arguing that Heath had been stung into a thoroughly aggressive performance; the Labour counterparts were equally pleased, as this was precisely what they had wanted. But it is doubtful whether anything was gained or lost; it was a beautiful evening in an exceptionally beautiful May, and perhaps the British public has better things to do with its summer evenings than watch politicians on television. This commentator watched the announcement in a London public house. It was thinly patronized, and the few customers evinced no interest whatever in what the Prime Minister was saying against the background of early summer flowers in the garden of Number Ten. Perhaps the rest of the nation was agog, but it appeared improbable.

In any event, the lines for the contest had been drawn, and were to be adhered to. Labour was immensely confident that it had found what one enthusiastic candidate described as 'an assured recipe for victory'.[1] Lord Byers' comment was more sardonic: 'Harold Wilson is determined to play it cool and to give the impression that the election is a minor inconvenience which the Labour Party has to suffer every four years to indulge the grateful peasants.' Robert Carvel summarized the Labour strategy in similar terms: 'Vote for honest Harold, continuity and safety first. That is to be Labour's theme. And as a corollary don't vote for Edward Heath and his tired, half-experienced crew of wild men out to disturb the nation with turbulent divisive policies in such fields as the unions and law and order.'[2] The Conservative leadership was convinced that Wilson could not keep this up for three weeks, and could be harried into an error that would send him crashing through the egg-shells. But this confidence was no longer universal. 'Wilson's real achievement,' a depressed Conservative candidate remarked, 'is not that he has made Labour regard itself as the natural governing party, but that he has made us regard ourselves as the natural opposition party.' Each side looked – both with some trepidation, but in the Conservative case with real apprehension – towards Wolverhampton, to see what unexpected developments could emerge. It was virtually the only foreseeable unpredictability in the campaign.

Between the announcement of the Election and the opening of the campaign the Government reached a belated decision which generated a certain amount of political heat at the time. The tour of Britain by a South African rugby team in the previous winter had been marked by anti-apartheid demonstrations and incidents, few of them serious but most of them vexatious. Now, a South African cricket tour was impending, and the problems of protecting sports arenas from protesters, relatively simple in the case of a rugby match, assumed serious implications for three-day and five-day cricket matches. The Cricket Council decided that the tour should take place, despite the private urgings of organizations concerned with

---

[1] Christopher Price, *New Statesman*, 29 May 1970. Mr Price, who had a majority of 3,665 in 1966, lost his seat by 1,266 in 1970, the victim of a 6.3 per cent swing to the Conservatives.

[2] *Evening Standard*, 14 May 1970.

community relations in Britain. When an organization to stop the tour was created the intransigence of the Council increased. The Council could have been persuaded by a firm word from the Government, but none came until 21 May, when Callaghan officially requested the Council to call off the tour, which it did on the following day.

Although the performance of the Cricket Council throughout this affair had not won the admiration of all close beholders, that of the Government had been much more reprehensible. In a television broadcast on 16 April, Wilson had described the decision to continue with the tour as 'ill-judged', but his subsequent remarks betrayed a certain ambiguity:

They are coming. Therefore, I say they should be allowed to play their matches. I do not believe they should be disrupted by digging up pitches or violence. I believe that everyone should be free to demonstrate against apartheid. I hope people will feel free to do that. But not by violent methods ... Let's all express our detestation of apartheid in any peaceful way – let the matches continue.

Callaghan's intervention could – and should – have been taken months before. It was difficult to escape the conclusion that the Government had been playing somewhat juvenile politics with the issue. Perhaps the only individuals who had emerged with any credit were those whose quiet and reasoned case to the Council had been summarily dismissed. One does not have to be overendowed with cynicism to express doubts as to whether the Government would have made its belated intervention if there had not been a General Election pending. And it was perhaps significant that the First Test had been due to open on 18 June – polling day.

The phrase 'a new style of Government' has been ascribed to Mr David Howell, the Member for Guildford since 1966 and a former director of the Conservative Political Centre, and the phrase had been the title of a CPC pamphlet written by Howell and published in May 1970. In the Conservative Manifesto Heath had taken the phrase further, to present a stark choice between the alleged gimmickry and triviality of the Wilson approach and the practicality and honesty of the Conservatives.

> Decisions have been dictated simply by the desire to catch tomorrow's headlines. The short-term gain has counted for everything; the long-term objective has gone out of the window. Every device has been used to gain immediate publicity, and government by gimmick has become the order of the day ... I am determined therefore that a Conservative Government shall introduce a new style of government and that we shall re-establish our sound and honest British traditions.

The decision reflected something more than a tactic. Heath – and perhaps to an even greater extent, Barber – had reached an opinion of 'the little man' which was rancorous and contemptuous, and they assumed that their feelings were shared by the electors. As so often happens in politics, they made insufficient allowances for the recognition of Wilson's qualities – real or imagined – which existed among all but the most dedicated Conservatives.

The tactical objective – and it certainly existed – was to attack what the Conservatives regarded as Labour's greatest asset. If Wilson could be cut down to size, then the destruction of his position would destroy that of Labour. That was the objective. In fact, by making the Election very much a personalized contest the Conservatives were taking a major – if calculated – risk. Thus, the Conservative leadership opened the campaign by deliberately inviting comparisons between the two leaders and their styles. Those Conservatives who were uneasy at this decision soon seemed to have solid evidence for their apprehensions.

While Wilson was embarking on what he depicted as this 'happy, enjoyable Election' in Yorkshire, Heath was off to Cardiff in a chartered aircraft. The journalists accompanying him travelled to the airport in a bus provided with a bar and television, but on the flight the Conservative leader stayed in chilly seclusion with his aides. His speech that evening was delivered in what one account described as 'his stiff, crisp manner, the military bark, the staff officer lecturing the troops'.[1] The pattern each man set was faithfully adhered to throughout the campaign, with some variations that will be

[1] *The Economist*, 6 June 1970.

described. Each style told one a great deal about each man. Wilson's task was to avoid any recollection of the events of the previous four years, to create an atmosphere of benign warmth and comfort, to avoid discussion of policies, to make a few vague prophecies of the gleaming future of the nation under his leadership, and generally to spread happiness and content-ment. Heath's campaign was planned to enable him to deliver a morning press conference, make at least one major speech, and be in bed in his flat by midnight; the speeches were carefully prepared, and were intended to flush the Prime Minister out of his avoidance of discussing past errors, present misfortunes, or future policies. Heath's strategy was very well planned and very worthy in content, but no sparks were struck, nothing memorable was said, and although the faithful cheered loyally, the general impact was not substantial. The contrast was, as Peter Jenkins put it, between The Entertainer and The Vicar.[1]

Apart from the reiterated theme of 'Labour's broken promises', Heath hammered away at the price issue, many of his advisers being convinced that the housewife's vote described in one Conservative television broadcast as 'the hidden majority who traditionally have voted by habit but now seems determined to vote by conviction',[2] could be caught thereby. In the previous two years the cost of food had risen by over 13 per cent; drink by 14.4 per cent; tobacco by 12.4 per cent, clothing by 8.8 per cent, and so on. But the reactions seemed less than encouraging. The Conservative strategy resembled one of those careful set-piece battles when every-thing goes exactly to plan except that no impact is being made upon the enemy. It was exactly like 1966, and the journalists had an eerie sense of *déjà vu* as they accompanied Heath on his flights and listened to his worthy speeches. The Conservative Manifesto – *A Better Tomorrow* – long prepared and with a vigorous introduction by Heath, was published on 26 May without fuss. The Labour Manifesto, which appeared a day later, bore all the hallmarks of very hasty and belated prepara-tion. Here, the nature of the Labour Party's policy organiza-tion was most painfully exposed. The principal difference of opinion in the National Executive was over any reference to a

[1] *Guardian*, 1 June 1970.
[2] But see p. 278.

Wealth Tax, which many Ministers wanted included. Jenkins refused this, and also fought against commitments to specific financial policies and undertakings. The final document, given eventually to an exasperated group of journalists at Transport House on the evening of 27 May, was entitled *Now Britain's Strong Let's Make It Great* (a better title, one disgruntled critic suggested, would have been 'Life's Better Under Labour. Don't Let Socialism Ruin It').[1] It was all rather a shambles, but it did not seem to matter very much.

It was at this moment that Powell intervened. Powell's Election address was a direct challenge to the official Party line on immigration and entry into the Common Market. The language was characteristically vehement: 'The greatest danger Britain faces is Commonwealth immigration and its consequences. It carries a threat of division, violence and blood-shed of American dimensions, and adds a powerful weapon to the armoury of anarchy.' The Conservative leadership was convinced from that moment that Powell's tactic was to go as far as he dared to disassociate himself from it and to stake his own claim to the leadership in the probable event of a Conservative defeat. Powell's subsequent actions did nothing to persuade Heath and those around him that their first interpretation of what he was up to had been mistaken.

From this moment Heath was in the position most dreaded by party leaders. He was fighting an Election against what seemed to be a winning opponent while simultaneously having to beat off an attack from his rear. 'He has failed to achieve public affection or even, in some parts of the country, acceptance as a personality,' *The Economist* declared censoriously – and almost contemptuously – of the Conservative leader on 30 May, 'and he cannot blame Mr Wilson for that.' He came under very strong pressure from some of his colleagues and many candidates and Party workers to disassociate himself totally from Powell.[2] Heath chose not to do this, but to attempt to play down Powell's significance. At the time this seemed a major error, as the publicity given to Powell was such that it was impossible to pretend that he did not exist; it was also inevitable

[1] *Sunday Times*, 31 May 1970.
[2] Contrary to one account (A. Alexander and A. Watkins, *op. cit.*) the pressure on Heath to associate himself positively *with* Powell was negligible.

that the Press would make Powell's position a major item in Heath's daily press conferences.

For Labour, Powell's dramatic re-emergence was a doubtful advantage. There were some who were delighted, and were eager to exploit the issue to identify Heath with Powell, or, alternatively to depict him as a weak leader without the courage to disown a violent and disloyal colleague. There were others, however, who were uneasy for one of two reasons; first, an attack on Powell could seriously affect Labour's chances in the Midlands, or, alternatively, pressure on Heath could lead to a sympathetic public reaction. In the event, what happened was what looked suspiciously like a trial balloon floated by Mr Wedgwood Benn, which was undertaken on the evening of 3 June.

In this speech, delivered in London, with full television coverage, Benn in effect accused Powell of racialism, Heath of supine weakness, and the Conservative Party of guilt by association. It was a very curious occasion. The most interesting feature of the speech was the contrast between its content and its actual delivery, which was halting and mild. The suspicion that Benn was not the 'true and onlie begetter' of the speech was created by the impression that he was carefully reading from a text with which he was not completely familiar. The phrase that was particularly striking was that 'the flag of racialism which has been hoisted in Wolverhampton is beginning to look like the one that fluttered twenty-five years ago over Dachau and Belsen'.

As the Conservatives saw the incident, Labour's objective was to discover what mileage there was in this issue without involving any major Government spokesman. If it worked, Benn could be warmly endorsed and the matter pushed forward; if not, the word would go out that Wilson was much displeased, but that Ministers could not be gagged on a matter of such deep moral importance. In the event, the Labour leadership concluded that the speech had been a mistake, particularly as it had provoked a dignified and contemptuous rebuttal by Powell, who had confined himself to the point that in 1939 he had come home from Australia to enlist as a private in the British Army in order to fight Fascism. Many Labour candidates were also unhappy about stirring up fires which they wanted banked down. On the grounds that more harm than advantage was liable to arise from highlighting the issue, Wilson backed off. On the morning following the Benn speech Heath had had a rough passage at his Press Conference, during which he had attacked Benn for attempting 'to smear the whole Conservative Party with Nazism and anti-semitism' and had made plain his differences with Powell. That evening, in Birmingham, he had been obliged to deal again with the Benn speech. The Conservative managers, by this stage very alarmed, were profoundly relieved when the Labour pressure on the Powell issue faded away. Some of them subsequently regarded this as a major error of tactics by Wilson. Powell continued to be a thorn in Heath's flesh, his speeches continued to attract very considerable attention from the press and television, but the moment of real peril had passed.

This gradual diminution of the Powell problem was assisted by the fact that Powell's speeches, and, above all, their style, diminished their impact. Under stress, the frenetic aspect of Powell's oratory became increasingly pronounced, his vehement emphasis on his abandonment by his leader seemed at times to border on persecution mania, and the impression was created of a man who was temporarily unbalanced. The most striking instance was the speech delivered at Northfield on 13 June, on the 'enemy within', and to which reference was already made in Part Three, but the most bitter speech of all was that delivered in Wolverhampton on 16 June, when he complained that he had not received, 'even the ordinary loyalties and courtesies that prevail generally between colleagues in the same cause'.

On the final Sunday of the campaign – 14 June – the Conservative leaders met at Barber's London house, and agreed to issue a firm and final statement on Conservative immigration policy, and then to concentrate on other matters. At his press conference on the following morning Heath made a brief reference to the statement, and then refused to discuss the matter further. On that day the trade figures for May – showing a deficit of £31 million – were published, and the Powell issue vanished.

Heath has been accused, in the course of a vehemently pro-Powell section of a book which was evidently written in the conviction that Labour was going to win,[1] of 'over-reacting' to

---

[1] Alexander and Watkins: *op. cit.*, p. 194.

Powell, and of attacking 'the people's darling' for reasons of personal animosity. Such arguments omit to note the fact that the pressure had originated from Powell, and that it had to be met; it was, furthermore, the persistence of the Press rather than personal inclination that had forced Heath to deal with it. There was also the factor that Heath, with his sincere belief in 'educative' aspect of politics, would not sidestep questions put to him on Powell. Nonetheless, the decisive factor was that Powell went too far, and thereby destroyed his own challenge. He had been under a very heavy personal strain since his speech of April 1968. To this was now added the tensions of a major Election campaign. His relationship with the Party leaders was as bad as it could have been. In these circumstances, and despite the support which he still aroused – and which was evidenced by the size of his daily post – his political judgement seemed to be seriously impaired. There was certainly an impression of desperation and isolation in his Election speeches, as though he realized that he had got on a course which was personally disastrous and yet which he could not abandon. This commentator was sadly reminded of the question posed and answered by Lord Beaverbrook on the abdication of King Edward VIII: 'Who killed Cock Robin? Cock Robin.'

It appeared to most observers that the first week of the campaign had been near-disastrous for the Conservatives, and the confidence of all but the most convinced had been badly shaken. The *Financial Times* – whose reporting of the campaign had a notable style and perception – described the situation on 6 June:

After a week of the election campaign it is clear that the Conservatives are getting rather the better of the argument, but decidedly the worse of the war. In so far as serious issues have been raised it has been the Opposition which has raised them, and to the extent that the discussion has risen above the 'ouch-you-beast' level it has been the Conservatives who have made the more telling points. Yet the opinion polls show an obstinate tendency to edge, if anything, towards Labour ... No attempt is being made [by Labour] to outline, far less justify, the policies which a renewed Labour Government would pursue. The positive appeal that is being offered the voters is a vague sense of security and continuity presided over by a genial, pipe-smoking father figure. The negative appeal is the fear of the return of a bunch of fascist worker-bashing monsters led by a chilly nonentity.

On Sunday 7 June the Conservative leaders had analysed the situation at Heath's London flat. The general conclusion was that the message was the right one, and that the problem was how to get it across more effectively; the meeting did not seriously consider any major switch in tactics, but a more aggressive emphasis on Labour's economic record, unemployment, and housing. The real significance of the meeting lay in the refusal of the Conservative leadership to be rattled, and to stick to the chosen course.

Nonetheless, in the gloom there had been some shafts of light. In a BBC television programme on 1 June Lord Cromer had said that, 'there is no question that any government that comes into power is going to find a very much more difficult financial situation than the new Labour Government found in 1964', and had made the point of the trade surplus that, 'when you take a closer look at it, as bankers do, the figures are not so glamorous as they appear on the surface'. Cromer was a known Conservative supporter, but Lord Kearton, chairman of Courtaulds and a known Labour supporter, generally agreed with his analysis. Subsequent Labour attacks on Lord Cromer – of which the most incongruous and visually farcical was a statement read by Wilson leaning out of a first-floor window in Nottingham a week later – were perhaps a mistake, but it was a difficult matter for the Government to handle. Some Conservatives felt that Heath had not made sufficient use of the opportunity, and although Heath was very concerned not to repeat Wilson's mistake of 1964 in overstating the case, it is probable that more use could have been made of this important intervention.

Another hopeful sign was the quality of the Conservative television propaganda, which was the result of the work of Geoffrey Tucker and James Garrett, a professional producer of television commercials; the directors of the broadcasts were Mr Bryan Forbes, Mr Richard Clement, and Mr Terence Donovan. The first task was to make the Party's political broadcasts interesting and the technique adopted was to adopt that of the successful ITV 'News at Ten' programme. Two

Conservative MPs who were accomplished and experienced television performers – Geoffrey Johnson Smith and Christopher Chataway – were the 'newscasters' and there was even a 'commercial break' with advertisements, of which the most effective was a pound note being snipped away with a commentary to remind the viewer of the declined value of money since 1964. The second half of the programme was a straightforward presentation by one of the Conservative leaders. It was a stimulating format, handled with skill and fluency, and was unquestionably more interesting than the somewhat conventional and dull Labour broadcasts. On sound radio, undoubtedly the most successful broadcast was by the playwright, Mr Ronald Millar, on 14 June, in which Wilson was attacked with a remarkable personal virulence.

The Labour and Liberal television broadcasts were certainly never of comparable interest, and Wilson's last television broadcast before the polling was notably ineffective. By far the best was by Callaghan, talking to a group of young voters, but even this looked somewhat fustian when compared with the Conservatives' spirited performance.

It is doubtful whether the parties' television strategies and techniques had a decisive effect, but, unless all political observers are completely wrong, the superiority of the Conservatives' programmes must have had *some* effect, if only to improve Party morale, and the constant reiteration of the point that the economic situation was far worse than Labour proclaimed must have made a contribution to the inexorable erosion of the foundations of Labour's case.

Television must not be seen in isolation. The Conservative technique was one part – albeit a very major one – of a general strategy, and it was flexible and professional enough to seize new factors and exploit them with skill. It is very doubtful whether any British political party had previously used the medium with comparable success to entertain and explain, and there is no reason to doubt the findings of the Conservatives' research organization that the Party's television programmes enjoyed a considerably larger viewing audience than those of the other parties.

The irony of the situation lay in the fact that Wilson had insistently argued that the Election would be won on television, and he had had no doubts about his superiority over Heath in this field. (Nor, may it be remarked, had most Conservatives.) But, as events turned out the Prime Minister had a very bad television Election indeed. On 28 May he appeared on a BBC programme called Election Forum, on which he and the other Party leaders answered questions sent in on postcards by viewers. The first question to him was: 'Since you have lied and broken promises, do you expect the electorate to place any reliance on your word?' Wilson was rattled, and his answers were poor; Heath and Thorpe, in marked contrast, had a much easier time, and emerged in better shape. Then, Wilson's campaign strategy itself, with its sudden unannounced forays, was not very good television material, and in some instances seemed rather trivial, thus giving the Conservatives' jibe that he was running away from the issues an added emphasis. His own performance on party political broadcasts – particularly his last one – were poor by his previous standards, and on 11 June he was treated with contemptuous condescension by Mr Robert Kee on an Independent Television interview that can have done Wilson no good at all.[1] If television was a major factor in the 1970 Election, then the judgement must be that the Conservatives won the battle decisively. It is possible that the glorious weather negatived some of this advantage, but the number of viewers seems to have been high enough for the political historian to place at least some importance upon it.[2]

Then, there was the factor of the marked imbalance in scale and quality of organization between the parties. The Conservatives, particularly in the selected marginals, were well-prepared and well-equipped. The condition of the Labour organization, in contrast, may be seen from the fact that the number of local agents fell from 204 in 1966 to 144 in 1970, and

[1] This was a very remarkable interview. This commentator's impression mirrored that of Mr Anthony Sampson, who subsequently wrote (*Observer*, 14 June) that Mr Kee, 'relaxed and amused, took up the unusual position of a psychiatrist who was having a difficult session with a congenital liar'.

[2] Striking confirmation of what was this commentator's strong impression came in an enquiry of an electoral sample conducted by the Conservatives after the Election. This enquiry placed the two parties' television effectiveness in terms of very effective, moderately effective, and ineffective. Two Labour and one Conservative broadcasts were in the first category (the two Labour being those of Jenkins and Callaghan, the Conservatives' being Heath's last broadcast): the second category was filled by the four Conservative broadcasts; the third was filled by three Labour broadcasts, of which two had been by Wilson (the third was by Edward Short).

that in 468 constituencies this work was done by volunteers.[1] These statistics, do not, however, tell the full story of the weakness of the Labour organization, at local and national level. 'At the announcement of the General Election date,' the subsequent report of the NEC commented, '135 consultations had been held with marginal constituencies and in every case these consultations confirmed how badly the constituency organization had been hit by the events of the last two or three years.'[2]

No Labour Campaign Guide was issued for the Election, and the 'Today' unit at Transport House – which in the course of the campaign issued fifteen editions and four supplements – consisted of five people. The situation was therefore one of declining Party membership, low general morale, and a weak organization. All this was known to the Conservatives. A final factor, of even greater encouragement, was the nature of the reports from the constituencies. Conservative candidates and associations were reporting a far better reception and greater enthusiasm in the Party workers than they had experienced in 1964 or 1966, and could not understand why the national situation seemed so cheerless. They did not know that the Labour experience was exactly the reverse – excellent national optimism and local concern.

Thus, the confidence shown by the meeting at Heath's flat on Sunday 7 June was based on something more than an obstinate refusal not to become downcast. Some of the Conservative leaders – perhaps, most of them – believed that they were heading for another defeat. But now, unlike 1966, there were strong indications that the picture was not as dark as it appeared.

In his perceptive and amusing portrait of Britain in the 1960s[3] Mr Geoffrey Moorhouse took up the observation made by *The Times* in February 1964 that, 'the world of Westminster, Whitehall, the West End clubs and even Fleet Street, seems curiously remote from what goes on in the rest of the country'.

[1] Report of the 69th Annual Conference of the Labour Party, 1970.
[2] *Ibid.*, p. 11.
[3] Geoffrey Moorhouse: *The Other England* (Penguin 1964).

To a remarkable extent, Britain remains an island of different communities, obstinately refusing to follow the pattern of the United States, where regional characteristics have declined dramatically. Fears, which were often expressed after the War, that local accents and intonations would disappear and be replaced by what was called 'BBC English' have not – thankfully – been justified. London and the South-East contains the largest concentrations of people, wealth, industry, and commerce; London is the capital of England in a very complete sense that is not so in the case of other national capitals, for example, Washington DC. Nonetheless, it is dangerous to consider London to *be* Britain, and one of the perils of a London-based national Press is that it has a strong tendency to make this major, and wholly erroneous, assumption.

In most constituencies the first signs of an Election are the new posters going up, the party labels appearing in the house windows, and in the evenings, the evening ritual of television interrupted by the party political broadcasts. Then, hitherto aloof Members of Parliament – Ministers, even! – may be actually seen in the flesh, bedecked with their favours like prize bulls, advancing eagerly on electors. Village halls, theatres, and cinemas are hastily booked up. The canvassing teams are marshalled, and each evening are sent out with their lists of electors and instructions.

The cardinal rules of canvassing are to steer clear of houses bearing the enemy's favours ('Don't wake up the Opposition'), to be courteous, and not to waste time arguing with the incurably committed hostile elector. Canvassing has its attractions and puzzles, as this commentator discovered when he followed a canvassing team in a particularly poor part of South London. One redoubtable Labour lady lamented that military conscription had been abandoned; a household of West Indian immigrants proved to be fierce Conservatives, and proudly flaunted their Tory posters; a Labour father sadly said that his son and daughter, both voting for the first time, were Conservatives, shaking his head mournfully at the apostasy; very few of the electors had any idea of the names of the candidates, and one of the canvasser's most important tasks is to get his candidate's name registered in the elector's subconscious. It is no good declaring that he is canvassing for this or that Party; he must declare that, 'I am canvassing on behalf of Mr BLANK, your Conservative / Labour / Liberal / Nationalist / Flat Earth / Anti-Common Market / Independent Candidate.' If he achieves naught else but establish his candidate's name in the elector's mind he has achieved much.

For the candidates, it is a gruelling period of their lives. The principal pressure is on the defender, for whereas for his opponent the Election may be the beginning, for him it may be the end. Some politicians profess to enjoy Elections; most abhor the whole wretched business with, in Churchill's words, 'its disorderly gatherings, its organized oppositions, its hostile little meetings, its jeering throng, its stream of disagreeable and often silly questions'. It is very good for the politician to be obliged to seek his job in the market-place, and a rowdy Election meeting is a considerable test of a man's fluency and quickness – to say nothing of his temper and nerve – but it is not surprising that so many politicians loathe it.

But the value and charm of a British Election is that so many chickens unexpectedly come home to roost. As Robert Carvel observed during the campaign: 'One of the greatest things about elections is that they remind the politicians in a physical way that they are answerable to the people. Too many forget it too soon.'[1] The General Election may be about all sorts of weighty national matters, but the candidate may find that an angry meeting in a church hall is obsessed by his failure to provide a decent school bus service, or by the fact that the third old age pensioner that year has been killed at a dangerous crossing that ought to have had traffic lights. Then, in the excitement of a previous campaign the candidate may have made some handsome promises about local amenities. Why had they not been honoured? Many of the questions may be unfair, and should have been directed more appropriately to local councillors, but the candidate has to answer them and to endeavour to give satisfaction. Most candidates – and particularly defending candidates – would privately warmly echo the lament of the late Lord Norwich (Duff Cooper):

There are people who enjoy Elections. I am not one of them. The combination of anxiety and tedium is very trying. The solitary subject of conversation, to which, however hard one may try to avoid it, one always returns, the good ideas which suddenly strike

[1] *Evening Standard,* 17 June 1970.

one's supporters, their hopes and fears and petty quarrels, the rumours of one's opponents' successes, the one thing that should have been done and has been forgotten, the great mistake that has been made and that it is too late to rectify, the vast accumulation of daily annoyances culminating in the evening's speeches, which are followed by sleepless nights of pondering over possibly unwise utterances, all these build up an atmosphere of nightmare through which the distant polling day shines with promise of deliverance.[1]

In modern British General Elections the issue is settled nationally, or, as it has been put more precisely, 'the remarkable uniformity of swings in party support across all constituencies offer persuasive evidence of the importance of national political issues and events as opposed to more local influences on the choice of the individual elector'[2] – but there is strong evidence to support the claim that a candidate *can* make a difference in a close fight, in certain conditions. The 1970 Election gave further evidence of this in seats where a defending Labour Member survived against the national trend. There are also important negative factors. A candidate who has been a bad Member of Parliament can, and frequently does, actually lose a seat, and the 1970 campaign contained one constituency where the personality of the Conservative candidate so dismayed the Party workers that the collective effort to win a very winnable seat was fatally lacking. Although it is very dangerous to generalize, there is solid evidence to prove that in a constituency with a stable electorate – a vital factor – personality and organization can stand against the national trend. It is in any event important for candidates and their workers to believe this, and for those who do the personal pressure of an election campaign is heavy. In these contests what is being said or done in London has remarkably little relevance.[3] The candidates work in their own areas, rightly obsessed by the small world of their own constituencies, and often rather worse informed about the course of the national campaign than the average newspaper reader.

[1] Duff Cooper: *Old Men Forget*, pp. 134–5.

[2] Butler and Stokes: *Political Change in Britain*, p. 6.

[3] An interesting example of how perspectives can become distorted occurred in the 1970 campaign. A Conservative candidate, convinced that his Party was going to lose, watched a preview of Heath's final television broadcast in London. He thought it not very effective. He then travelled back to his constituency, where he found his wife and his supporters enthusiastic about the broadcast. Travelling around his constituency he met the same reactions.

A General Election provides a convenient opportunity for the observer to take stock of what has happened, or is happening, in his own country. One of the most striking impressions made on this commentator in 1970 is that although so much has happened over the past twenty years, how relatively minimal these changes have been in most areas of Britain. In the period 1951–70, out of the ten principal areas of the nation, the population had increased substantially (i.e. by over 400,000) in only three (the South-East, and the East, and West Midlands) despite the national increase of over seven per cent. If one looks further back, to 1931, it will be seen that the populations of Wales, Northern Ireland, Scotland, Northern England, North-East England, Yorkshire and Humberside, and East Anglia have remained – relative to the national increase of over nine millions – virtually static. A flight from Gatwick airport in Sussex to Edinburgh graphically demonstrates what has happened. The flight takes the observer over the South London suburbs, spreading remorselessly into the infinite, over the West London sprawl, and then up the thickly populated industrial spine of England. But beyond that spine and the South-Eastern mass, where live and work nearly half of the total population of the United Kingdom, there is verdant emptiness, and one realizes that Britain is a country which is severely over-populated only in certain areas; elsewhere it is thinly populated, and in some areas hardly populated at all. On the ground, in South London, or in the Midlands, or on Tyneside or in Glasgow, one has the impression of a dispirited, endless, meaningless jumble of mean houses, identical shopping centres, by-passes, fly-overs, stunted trees, petrol stations, and gloomy women in headscarves. In Manchester, Liverpool, Glasgow, and Birmingham the old heart of the city has been literally torn out, to be replaced by characterless structures of concrete and glass. At the centre, an empty and soulless nothingness; on the periphery, 'Subtopia', equally uniform, dreary, and sterile. So much for the new God, Planning! and the even mightier one, Progress! But, thankfully, all this is physically but a fraction of the country.

The 1970 General Election was peculiarly agreeable in that it was held in weather so glorious that one excited Conservative candidate compared it with the golden and tense summer days of 1940. The warm evenings made canvassing almost enjoyable, and the weather gave the campaign what was at times almost a carnival air. In these circumstances of sun and cheerfulness it was all too easy to forget what had really happened since 1960. Although the general standards of living had risen, it was evident that the pace of the 1950s had slowed sharply. It was also apparent that the rise in the national well-being had been very unevenly distributed throughout the country and the population. For all the high and ostentatious prosperity in some areas, the old, half-forgotten spectre of unemployment was abroad in the land. In July 1951 the total had been 210,000; in July 1961 it was 259,000; in June 1966 252,000; by June 1970 the total was over half a million, the worst summer figure since 1940.

Thus the issue of the Election was being resolved silently, by the private calculations about the unemployment statistics, the increases in prices, the economic and psychological disappointments of the previous decade, and the myriad of factors that were troubling the people. It has always been thus, but in the sunshine, with the attention given by commentators to the national contest, the press conferences, the pat answers of the leading politicians, and the prognostications of the pundits, the simple fact that elections are settled by the private decision of the anonymous elector was forgotten.

At some moment, which it is difficult to mark with any exact precision, the Labour strategy faltered. During the second week, from 8 June until the 13th the indications continued to flow in Labour's direction, reaching its culmination with the NOP forecast of a 12.4 per cent lead, a forecast that momentarily shook Heath's confidence in victory. But the Conservatives, despite the ominous portents, were now making all the running.

Heath's principal message was contained in a passage in a speech at South Croydon on 13 June:

What is wrong is that, as a people, we are in danger of falling asleep. As a people we have been flattered and lulled far too long by a trivial Government. The real problems, the real issues, have been kept from us as if we were children . . . And meanwhile the world is passing us by . . . My warning, which is given with all the force at my command, is this: As things stand, we are contracting out of the twentieth century . . . And my message is this: Unless Britain wakes up, Britain will lose the future.

The one exception to the muted Labour campaign was George Brown's almost traditional grand tour of hamlet, village green, and street corner, a pilgrimage which was old-fashioned and exhausting for the orator, but in stimulating contrast with modern electioneering techniques. There was about the venture an endearing pre-Campbell-Bannerman air that wrung pleasure and sympathy from all who beheld it. Thus, one felt, did the Germans at the Battle of the Marne view with respect the white-gloved cadets of St Cyr charge across the wide fields into the rising sun and the machine-guns. But if George Brown on the stump was fun, and followed an older and much better tradition of electioneering, it was difficult not to come to the conclusion that it was poor employment for a man of such ability and spirit, who enjoyed so wide a personal popularity and respect.

By this stage, and despite the glowing expectations offered by the opinion polls, some Labour activists were becoming uneasy. A national newspaper strike, which lasted from 10–13 June, revived the old fear that any strike in an Election period helps the Conservatives. Then the doctors, with consummate timing, put strong pressure on the Government to meet the award of the Kindersley review of a 30 per cent increase to general practitioners, consultants, and dentists. What appeared to be a hint by Callaghan that Labour would have to give attention to the wages issue after the Election revived the possibility of another wages freeze. The television debate was not going well for Labour, and some Ministers were looking surprisingly unimpressive in competition with their opposite numbers. The relative lack of volunteer support was alarming some candidates, and the enthusiasm of the Students for a Labour Victory to fill the gap was not invariably appreciated.[1]

[1] Students for a Labour Victory (SLV) was the creation of Hugh Anderson, President of the Cambridge Union, and one of the most promising recruits to the Labour Party, but who died soon after the Election. SLV was created specially for the Election campaign, and was disbanded thereafter. It is difficult to estimate its impact outside the student electorate, and certainly one Labour agent regarded the activities of the students – particularly in working-class areas – as seriously counter-productive. It may – or may not – be significant that in the 1970 Election the Conservatives did very well in all the university cities with the exceptions of Hull and York, notably Oxford, Cambridge, Brighton Kemptown, Edinburgh, Loughborough, Lancaster, Exeter, Reading, Bristol, and Leeds.

The determination of the Conservatives to fight to the end, when contrasted with evidence of apathy in the usual Labour activists, was disconcerting. Without being able to decide what was going wrong, many in the Labour movement were becoming worried by the close of the second week.

The final three days of the campaign opened with the announcement of a deficit on the balance of trade of £31 million for May. At an early stage of the campaign it had been evident that the emphasis was less on the general state of the economy than on prices, but the Conservatives – and particularly Heath – had linked this with the health of the nation's economy. Charges of 'sham sunshine' and the prospect of four more years of austerity and inflation if Labour won had forced Labour on to the defensive. But the counter-attack, when it came, had been weak, and even before 15 June it appeared that the Conservatives had regained the tactical initiative. Whether this really mattered seemed doubtful at the time. Mr John Mackintosh seemed quite justified in writing in *The Times* (16 June) that, 'since it seems unlikely that any new factor will emerge to prevent the Labour Party from winning the Election, it is possible for the leading politicians to raise their sights a little and consider some of the other functions of an Election campaign'. But the significance of the announcement of the trade deficit was that the whole basis of the Labour strategy was undermined.

The announcement was not, in itself, sufficient to destroy the Labour case but, perhaps as a result of tiredness, Wilson did not handle the matter dexterously. In his last major speech, on 15 June, he emphasized the importance of the purchase of two Boeing 747s for BOAC, in distorting the May figures. The psychological effect was exactly the opposite to that which he had intended, a fact that was well analyzed by Mr Jon Akass in the *Sun* on 17 June:

Now I don't know about you, but I get a shade glazed when it comes to visible trade gaps. I have no idea what £31 million looks like.

I know what aeroplanes look like though. I have seen some. I have even seen some very big ones.

Mr. Wilson was trying to be reassuring. But what he was saying was that the British economy is still so fragile it can be knocked askew simply by buying a couple of aeroplanes.

This struck me as immeasurably more disturbing than the gap itself. And it struck a lot of people that way, too, as I found out afterwards.

On the next morning, after Heath's press conference, a lengthy statement on the economic situation was issued. It had been written by an able and persistent party official. But although Macleod had used it, Heath was only vaguely aware of its contents. It was, however issued under his name. It contained two statements that were important – one at the time, and the second later.

The first passage ran as follows:

The danger in complacency now is that it will mean a further four years of austerity which in all probability will lead, as happened in the aftermath of the 1966 freeze and squeeze, to a further devaluation. Worst of all, such a development would leave our problems unsolved and our basic situation even more difficult.

This statement had some impact, but it was considerably increased when, that afternoon, Wilson solemnly repudiated the charge that the return of a Labour Government would lead to another devaluation. The Conservative document had not said this explicitly, although the implication was clear; but Wilson, standing incongruously in a field in Oldham to read out his repudiation, himself mentioned the fatal word. It was at this moment, the Conservative strategists later considered, that Wilson fell through the egg-shells. His claim on his final television broadcast that, 'no Prime Minister in this century has fought an Election against such a background of economic strength as we have got today' accordingly lacked real credibility.

The other statement in the Central Office paper did not receive so much publicity at the time. It came in a passage on economic strategy, and referred to reducing 'those taxes which bear directly on prices and costs, such as the Selective Employment Tax, and taking a firm grip on public sector prices and charges, such as coal, steel, gas, electricity, transport charges, and postal charges. This would, at a stroke, reduce the rise in prices, increase production, and reduce unemployment.' Subsequently, when the Labour leaders were casting around for malpractice by their opponents, this passage was given much prominence. After a certain distortion had taken place, it became a major feature of Labour tactics to claim that Heath had promised to cut prices 'at a stroke' if the Conservatives were elected. In fact, Heath had never made the statement, and the passage in question – although somewhat rash – did not contain any pledge to cut prices. And the relatively scant attention given to this passage at the time provides a very slender foundation for the subsequent charge that the Conservatives won the election as a result of a disreputable promise by their leader to cut prices at a stroke.

The real blow to Labour's credibility had fallen before this, and there were other indications of the slump in the Labour campaign.

One sign that might have been noted at the time was the surprisingly easy ride that Conservative candidates were generally having. When the Labour movement is in an aggressive and boisterous mood one indication is a desire to ensure that the Conservative enemy is made aware of the fact. When the Labour movement is crestfallen these manifestations are absent. Before the Election both main parties had been concerned at the possibility of violence, and the decisions not to announce Wilson's movements in advance and to make Heath's meetings all-ticket affairs had been the result of these apprehensions. In the event there was no repetition of anything approaching the howling down of Home in Birmingham in 1964, and the Election was so devoid of incidents of this kind that the throwing of occasional eggs at the Prime Minister and a scuffle between a university student and George Brown at the conclusion of a meeting were given somewhat excessive prominence. The Labour managers seemed pleased by the quietness of the Election, which not only fitted in very conveniently with Labour strategy but appeared to indicate public satisfaction at the condition of the nation. To be fair, other observers drew similar conclusions. It was only subsequently that interpretations of the significance of this calm came to be amended.

An interesting indication of Wilson's tiredness and loss of touch occurred on the 16th, when he made lengthy reference at his Press Conference to an OECD Report which had emphasized that inflation was a general phenomenon, and not confined to Britain. The reference caused considerable mystification, as no Report could be traced, and OECD officials, indignant at being brought into a British Election campaign, had no knowledge of such a document. It transpired that Wilson was basing his statement on a report by Mr Anthony Harris in the *Guardian*, which had referred to 'reports from OECD'. It struck the Conservatives as odd that a Prime Minister, with all the resources of Whitehall to hand, had relied upon a misreading of a newspaper article as the basis for a major statement.

Subsequently, the announcement of the poor trade figures and Wilson's over-reaction seemed to have been of very major importance. The Conservatives, who had battled away on the economic issue without apparent reward for two weeks, certainly began to feel that they were making headway at last. But perhaps a much more significant factor was that the Labour campaign as a whole suddenly seemed to stop. Mr Hodder-Williams has drawn a comparison between the loss of the World Cup match to West Germany on 15 June – when England lost 3–2 after being two goals ahead – and Labour's collapse in the days before polling: 'In both instances, the initiative was surrendered and the late runners, by being allowed to attack consistently, ultimately exploited the weaknesses in their opponents' defences. Having lost the initiative, neither England nor the Labour Party found the momentum or the luck in the time available to regain the advantage they had squandered.'[1]

Certainly the Conservatives finished considerably more vigorously than their opponents, a feature that particularly impressed this commentator when he visited two marginal South London constituencies on 17 June. Once again, what was evident was the activity and confidence of the local Conservative workers, combined with a baffled depression about the probable national result. Canvassing was being energetically conducted, students were handing out pamphlets to London commuters as they left the railway stations, Conservative loudspeaker vans were operating, helpers from safe Conservative seats arrived to assist, the candidates were being briefed on local issues for their eve-of-poll meetings, and there was a general air of bustle and energy. In contrast, the reports of Labour activity were nil. A visit to the Labour offices found it deserted at 8 p.m.

[1] R. Hodder-Williams: *Public Opinion Polls and British Politics*, p. xvii.

This situation, although far from universal, was also far from unusual. But it could not make many observers or participants doubtful about the eventual result. By this stage the Conservatives had been decisively written off by every political commentator. The *Sunday Mirror* (14 June) declared that, 'the public have already hanged [Heath] before his trial at the polling booths', and on the following day *The Times* said that, 'the Conservatives are on the defensive along the whole front of men and measures, and even if they have an all-in counterattack left it is too late to recover lost ground. All their reserves were committed long ago.' David Watt was more charitable:

> Mr Heath has really fought the election very well, and far above the level which his gloomier detractors expected ... It is impossible to hear him these days without feeling respect and immense sympathy for his predicament.[1]

The conclusion was that the Conservatives, locally and nationally, had fought the campaign with far greater skill and enthusiasm than their opponents, but without effect. The evidence of the opinion polls was overwhelming, and the judgement of the political commentators unanimous.

On 17 June ORC gave a prediction of a 1 per cent Conservative lead, but this forecast was so wildly out of line with the other predictions that it was generally dismissed. ORC had never undertaken a General Election poll before – it had been founded in June 1966 – and its connection with the Conservative Party was (quite unwarrantably) taken into account. The picture on June 18th, when the polling-booths opened and the silent multitude began to vote, was as follows:

	ORC (Quota)	HARRIS (Random)	NOP (Random)	GALLUP (Quota)	MARPLAN (Random)
Conservative	46.5	46.0	44.1	42.0	41.5
Labour	45.5	48.0	48.2	49.0	50.2
Liberal	6.5	5.0	6.4	7.5	7.0
Others	1.5	1.0	1.3	1.5	1.3

Thus, the very best the Conservatives could hope for on the basis of the opinion polls was a tiny majority. If Harris was right, there would be a modest Labour majority; if NOP,

[1] *Financial Times*, 15 June 1970.

Gallup, or Marplan was right, the Conservatives were going to be heavily defeated. The more cautious commentators anticipated the Labour majority at between 20 and 50. Other commentators were less cautious, and one – an hour before the first declaration – put the Labour majority between 70 and 90. Wilson had recently delighted his associates with the comment that 1975 was going to be a difficult Election.

It seemed that Fate was determined to spare Heath nothing in his humiliation. He had held Bexley since 1950, but in 1966 his majority over Labour had been reduced to 2,333, and he had in fact been elected on a minority vote. His seat was accordingly highly marginal, and his problems had been compounded by his inevitable absence from the constituency during the campaign and by the intervention of a Mr Edward James Robert Lambert. Mr Lambert had changed his name by deed poll to Heath, and stood as Heath, E.J.R.L. (Conservative and Consult the People). This was a deliberate 'wrecking' candidature, inspired by Powellite influences (although Powell himself was totally unaware of the move, and had no knowledge whatever of it). Heath's closest aides – Mr Robert Allan and Mr Douglas Hurd[1] – spent polling day outside polling booths in Bexley bearing banners urging voters to beware imposters. But despite this, and the feverish publication of thousands of official Conservative leaflets, Heath's Bexley headquarters received a stream of agitated telephone calls from Conservatives who had in fact voted for the wrong Mr Heath. 18 June was darkened for Heath by the very real apprehension that even if his Party had won the Election – which he still firmly believed had happened – he himself might have been defeated by a malicious candidature.[2]

It is said that every American alive at the time can remember with absolute clarity what he was doing, where he was, and

---

[1] Heath's political secretary since March 1968, the son of a former Conservative MP, and who served in the Foreign Office before resigning to take up a political career. He is the author of *The Arrow War*, an historical study of serious value, and, with Andrew Osmond, of three admirable works of fiction – *Send Him Victorious*, *The Smile on the Face of the Tiger*, and *Scotch on the Rocks*.

[2] In the event, Heath's majority over Labour was 8,058; Mr E. J. R. L. Heath secured 938 votes.

with whom he was, on the day that the Japanese bombed Pearl Harbour, or when President Kennedy was assassinated. Englishmen, also, have their vivid recollections, and, to a certain extent, the night of 18–19 June 1970 comes into this category. One was reminded of the celebrated Election night in 1922, when Lloyd George, Birkenhead, and other former members of the Lloyd George Coalition dined with Sir Philip Sassoon at his house in Park Lane, 'along with intimate supporters, including wives', in Lord Beaverbrook's incomparable account.[1]

And the scene of that occasion was very similar to that on Election night in 1970. To quote Lord Beaverbrook again: 'The brandy flowed around and around. Then the news from the constituencies also flowed. Gaiety departed. And gloom entered.'[2]

Or, of course, the other way round. For, on 18 June the Tories watched and waited with despairing fortitude, foresworn to an early bed; their opponents awaited in cheerful authority for the formal confirmation of their victory. And then, with the very first declaration, everything started to go wrong – or right, depending on the viewer's outlook.

Wilson retired to his suite at the Adelphi Hotel, Liverpool, with several journalists, who were politely asked to leave at 10.30 when the first results were due. Wilson, his wife, and two close associates sat together watching the television screen. The first declared result was at Guildford, and showed a heavy Conservative swing. Then came Cheltenham, with the same indication. But it was not until the two Salford results and the news of the first Labour loss – at Exeter – that the message began to sink in. Across the nation, others were watching the same results, with equal amazement.

George Brown and Jennie Lee were the most conspicuous in the ranks of the fallen; among junior Ministers who lost their seats were Evan Luard (Oxford) and David Ennals (Dover); among the more promising younger Labour MPs who fell were David Anderson (Monmouth) and Christopher Price (Perry Barr). Douglas Houghton was among those established Labour MPs who only narrowly survived defeat. Throughout the land on that extraordinary night, and on the morrow, stunned

[1] *The Decline and Fall of Lloyd George*, p. 221.
[2] *Ibid*. p., 221.

Labour candidates and exultant – and equally amazed – Conservatives found themselves making very different speeches to returning officers than those which they had envisaged. Heath's buoyancy under severe pressure had rarely faltered – the only outward sign had been on the evening of 13 June, when he had been told of NOP's prediction of a 12.4 Labour lead – but he was a realist, and he had steeled himself for another grim Election night. Wilson had not made this mental preparation, and, as the results unfolded, the shock to him personally was palpable. When he eventually emerged from his room to go to his own declaration 'he looked as if he had seen Banquo's ghost', in the words of one not unsympathetic observer. He entered the Town Hall as if in a trance, and seemed to have difficulty in undertaking the task of the traditional speech of thanks to the returning officer. He and his wife then returned to the Adelphi before setting out on the long drive back to London. A photographer followed them, and as his car overtook the Prime Minister's he took a heartless and melancholy photograph of the Wilsons slumped in the back, the Prime Minister's head on his wife's shoulder.

After a brief sleep, he faced the television interviewers on the following morning, strained, tense, and weary, and still with the shaken look of a few hours before. He conducted himself with dignity, taking care to emphasize that his successor would have a better economic inheritance than he had had in 1964, taking personal responsibility for the dissolution, and being rather more generous to Heath personally than he might reasonably have been expected to be. Throughout the day his personal qualities were seen at their very best, and particularly in his buoyant visit to a shattered and tearful Transport House. Shortly before 6.00 p.m. he left 10 Downing Street to go to the Palace to tender his resignation. After he returned and had made the final farewells he and his wife left by the garden entrance and drove to Chequers, made available to him for the weekend by Heath.

Defeat is always bitter. For a man who has never known it before it has an especially harsh flavour. When it comes, as it did then, out of a clear blue sky, a totally unexpected thunderbolt, the impact is immense. Only the most harsh Conservative could withhold from Wilson admiration for such a sustained performance of dignity, good humour, and self-control. Even those who had known him longest and respected him most were surprised and impressed. When a Prime Minister leaves 10 Downing Street after defeat he cannot but wonder whether he will ever enter it again, and no modern British Premier can forget the fate of Lloyd George, who never held public office of any kind after his fall in October 1922. Time could only provide the answer to the question that troubled Wilson's friends most on 19 June and in the following days, whether he would ever fully recover the spirit and resilience which had been his supreme political quality.

His opponents and critics have had some severe comments to make on this perplexing man. But it is fair to quote the words of a critical commentator which seem to be fair and just:

His was an amazing, try-anything, Government in so many ways, exuding super-confidence when a bit of quiet competence would have done better. But how he ripped into the class barriers; and tore into every intricate problem with the enthusiastic, intellectual conviction that solutions must be about somewhere. Over six years he was brilliant, disastrous, challenging, exciting, daring, skilful, and heart-warming, and infuriating for his opponents; terrifying at times as the salesman who turned trapeze artist just to show he could defy gravity.[1]

Mr Anthony Howard and Mr Richard West have glowingly described how Wilson had entered 10 Downing Street in October 1964.[2] Heath's arrival on the evening of 19 June 1970 was considerably less dramatic, yet it was memorable in its way. On the steps he simply announced that he had accepted the Queen's invitation to form a Government, and that, 'to govern is to serve. This Government will be at the service of all the people, the whole nation. Our purpose is not to divide but to unite, and where there are differences to bring reconciliation, to create one nation.'

It was discovered that the office of his political private secretary was embellished with an empty bottle of Polish vodka and two dirty glasses. When the new Prime Minister

[1] Walter Terry, *Daily Mail*, 20 June 1970.
[2] *The Making of the Prime Minister* (London, 1965).

asked for tea (China, with lemon), it was discovered that there was none in the house, the previous occupant having had different tastes. By this time the shops had shut, but it was fortunately recalled that a Whip in the previous Administration had been known to favour such eccentricities. A package of China tea was located at 12 Downing Street. The new Prime Minister's first cup of tea took half an hour to prepare. On the previous evening someone had stubbed a cigarette on Heath's neck. On the following day a chagrined lady in the crowd in Downing Street flung a pot of red paint at him. Under such curious and somewhat inauspicious circumstances did Mr Heath enter into office. The road to 10 Downing Street is never smooth, but few have had a more difficult journey, and few indeed have arrived so unexpectedly.

It is perhaps necessary to emphasize – as there appears to be some doubt on the subject – that the Conservatives won the General Election of June 1970.[1] They won it, moreover, with the biggest movement to any party since 1945 – 4.7 per cent. Although Labour abstentions played a significant part, the Election was decided by a considerable movement of voters to the Conservatives – a movement that was, with certain interesting exceptions,[2] remarkably even across the country. Compared with 1966 the Labour vote was down by 5 per cent, and the Conservative vote rose by 4.5 per cent. It is also worth mentioning that no Opposition party has won a Parliamentary majority of such a size over a Government in normal peacetime conditions since the Liberals in January 1906.[3] It is also important to remember that this victory followed a series of overwhelming victories between 1966 and 1970 in county and borough elections. It was only slowly that the full wreckage of the high Labour expectations and confidence of 1966 could be wholly appreciated. The historian has to return to certain seismic political years – 1945, 1906, and 1886 – to find a

[1] For a different conclusion see A. Alexander and P. Watkins, *op. cit.*, also Butler and Pinto-Duschinsky, *op. cit.*

[2] See pp. 269–270 below.

[3] As the Conservative Government had resigned in December 1905, and the Election was called by the succeeding Liberal Administration, this was not technically an Opposition victory.

just comparison with the Conservative achievement, and even these do not, on closer inspection, really equal the dramatic reversal of the fortunes of the two main parties between 1966 and 1970. The Conservative revival between 1906 and 1910 is perhaps the closest equivalent in this century.

It was a considerable time before the magnitude of what had happened was adequately appreciated. The result itself was the greatest electoral surprise since 1945, as astonishing to the majority of the victors as to the vanquished. Although most of them subsequently denied the fact, very few Conservatives had seriously believed that they were going to win, and the Labour confidence was overwhelming. This commentator met only one Labour candidate who was concerned about his own result, and he had no doubts about the national result. Political correspondents to a man had predicted a Labour victory, and not all of them made amends with such wit and completeness as did David Watt of the *Financial Times*. Many turned on the opinion polls for having misled them. The polls were, after Labour, the most conspicuous casualty of the Election. 'If they wish to restore their credibility as a tool of political research,' an editorial in the Conservative *Swinton Journal* gleefully observed, 'they still have much to explain' – a phrase that was an echo of one used by Wilson in his first television interview on the morning of 19 June. The examinations and explanations were very swiftly put in hand, but no amount of explanation could meet the essential point that only one – ORC – had got the winner right.

It is quite impossible to determine with any satisfying precision why people vote as they do, and all the attempts that have been made to reach this conclusion have merely emphasized the basic fact. Even abstention is a difficult matter to quantify. It can best be seen as the result of total apathy, or ignorance, or resentment with all politicians, or disillusionment with the party for whom the elector previously voted; it can even be personal dislike of individual candidates. Abstention can be a positive decision, and does not necessarily represent laziness, inefficient party organization, or apathy with the political process. (It is also important to recall that abstention can be involuntary, as in the case of people who were disfranchised by being on holiday in June 1970).

The first point to make of the 1970 Election is that, despite the low turn-out the issue was not simply decided by Labour abstentions, as Wilson claimed. It is important to point out that the Conservative vote in 1970 (13,144,692) was actually higher (if only marginally) than the Labour vote of 1966 (13,066,173). The important statistic was that the Conservative vote was up by nearly two million on 1966, while the Labour vote fell by slightly under one million. The small fall in the Liberal vote (2,327,457 to 2,117,638) was of less significance than the jump in the Welsh and Scottish Nationalist vote to 481,812, which would appear to have been substantially taken from Labour. Another statistic of importance is that although the percentage of the electorate who voted was lower in 1970 than 1966 (75.8 per cent to 72 per cent), the actual number of voters rose by over one million. It does not require a very detailed analysis to reach the conclusion that a substantial number of new voters and former Labour voters must have voted Conservative or for Nationalist candidates when they were available. The Conservative defeat of 1964 can be reasonably ascribed to massive Conservative abstentions and switches to the Liberals; the Labour defeat of 1970 was the result of a very definite capture of voters by the Conservatives. 'The pattern of voting,' as Professor Richard Rose of the University of Strathclyde has written, 'implies a significant shift in votes between the Labour and Conservative parties.'

The other feature of the results was the remarkable consistency of the pro-Conservative swing of 4.7 per cent. But there were several exceptions which emphasize the point made on page 267 that the national swing is not invariable. At Rugby, a Labour majority of 409 in 1966 leapt to one of 2,955. In Berwick and East Lothian, despite the intervention of a Scottish Nationalist candidate who won 4,735 votes, John Mackintosh held the seat which he had narrowly won in 1966 and had failed to win in 1964.[1] In Portsmouth West, despite a shift in population that was generally considered to be greatly to Labour's disadvantage, Mr Frank Judd's 1966 majority of 1,227 was reduced only to 955, a barely perceptible swing to the Conservatives of 0.1 per cent. In Brentford and Chiswick,

---

[1] In this constituency the importance of a stable electorate and considerable local publicity to the Member of Parliament appear to have been vital factors. A private poll conducted before the Election disclosed that 85 per cent of those interviewed knew Mr Mackintosh's name and his party.

where Mr Michael Barnes was defending a majority of 607 votes, it fell only to 513.[1] There were several other exceptions from the national pattern, of which perhaps the most remarkable was the capture of the Western Isles by a Scottish Nationalist, who unseated the Labour candidate who had held the seat since 1935. Nonetheless, these examples are interesting because they are in such contrast with the remarkably uniform movement to the Conservatives in the majority of constituencies.

After the political commentators and the politicians themselves had recovered from their astonishment, many explanations of the result were attempted. In the main, these divided themselves into those who, like the former Conservative chairman, Lord Poole, declared that the Conservative majority had always been present and had been missed by the opinion polls, and those who detected a late swing to the Conservatives during the campaign. If the latter interpretation were correct, then a very strong blow would have been struck against the almost hallowed political dictum that Election campaigns never seriously affect the result.

The case in support of a late swing to the Conservatives brings us back to the opinion polls, and particularly to the achievement of ORC in being the only poll to predict a Conservative victory. The ORC explanation is emphatic. They were very uneasy about their own and other polls, and were 'running scared' in Humphrey Taylor's phrase; they polled longer than their rivals, and made a substantial adjustment in their final prediction to meet the late swing that they had detected in their re-interview with a sub-sample of 257 electors; ORC also adjusted correctly for differential turnout.

To support their case for the late swing ORC point to the fact that the final re-call showed a definite erosion of Labour and Liberal support between the weekend of 13–15 June and the eve of poll (16–17 June). The small sample of 257 in fifty constituencies showed twenty-two changes, and a definite swing to the Conservatives. If correct, this predicted a national

---

[1] Here, there is definite evidence that the coloured immigrants in the constituency tipped the balance in Mr Barnes' favour. Both Mr Barnes and Mr Mackintosh had been excellent constituency Members.

movement of approximately 700,000 voters. ORC also point out that, had they not conducted the eleventh-hour re-interviews, their final prediction would have been a forecast of a 3 per cent Labour victory – very close to the predictions of NOP and Harris. ORC also point out that post-poll surveys conducted by themselves, Gallup, NOP and Marplan, confirmed the late swing theory. ORC are also fair in emphasizing that their specially commissioned polls for the Conservatives showed that the public attitudes towards the parties on the economy shifted very sharply in the final week, and that it seems very improbable that this would have been to the disadvantage of the Conservatives. NOP also provides evidence for a late swing to the Conservatives. NOP had operated a panel system, and took three samples, which produced Labour leads of 3.2 per cent, 5.1 per cent and 12.4 per cent (this last figure, which had caused such dismay to the Conservatives, was subsequently disregarded by NOP in the light of sample defects.) During the last weekend of the campaign NOP re-interviewed a sub-sample of the first two samples, which suggested that there was no real movement away from Labour. After the Election they did a further re-call, which indicated that there had been a movement towards the Conservatives, albeit a much smaller one than had actually occurred.

It must be recognized that the polls – including ORC – have a very deep vested interest in the 'late swing' theory. If they can establish it, then their own reputations are not irreparably harmed; the techniques must in future be modified to cope with such phenomena, but the basic technology is still correct.

The 'late swing' theory leads to the conclusion that Election campaigns really do matter, and that the news of the £31 million deficit, the high unemployment figures, Wilson's blunder in taking up the devaluation issue, and the relative impacts of the final television speeches of the principal leaders, had a cumulative effect in winning the Election for the Conservatives. But before this explanation is accepted, it is necessary to remind ourselves that the ORC hypothesis is based upon the reinterviewing of 257 electors, and the changing of affiliation of 22 of them. These are somewhat slender foundations on which to build an explanation of a General Election in which over 28 million people voted. And we must recall that the actual result was almost exactly that which had been predicted by the much more extensive sample examined by the Conservatives since 1965. And we should also recall that if the 'late swing' theory is correct, then some 700,000 voters changed from a Labour voting intention to a Conservative vote in the last three days or so. Even allowing for a volatile electorate, a switch of this proportion at such a late stage – and a switch, moreover, not from 'don't know' to positive but from one Party to another – would have been a most remarkable occurrence.

Among the factors that the exponents of the 'late swing' theory tend to emphasize is the ending of the newspaper strike, which opened up to the Conservatives a vital medium of communication; and that, had the strike not taken place, the swing would have taken place, and been picked up, earlier. This explanation implies a degree of power to the printed, as opposed to the spoken word, in Elections that is very difficult to accept in the context of modern politics.

The 'late swing' theory has, however, been subtly amended to meet the arguments of, among others, Lord Poole, that the Conservatives had a built-in advantage throughout as a result of what had happened since 1966, that the majority was there – *vide* the Conservatives' panel figures – and that the greater Conservative determination to vote and the better Conservative organization merely confirmed the situation. The 'late swing' theorists meet this argument by accepting it in general terms, and then argue what actually happened was a 'swing back' in the last few days.

While it is clearly impossible to give a precise answer to the problem – which is an important one, because if there was a late swing of these proportions, then almost every concept of modern British politics would have to be drastically revised – it is of some value to look at one constituency and to regard it as something of a test case. It can be argued that to take one constituency out of 630 is unreasonable, but it can also be argued that one specific case has a greater relevance than theorizing on the basis of a fractional sample of the total population.

The constituency is Banbury, which has an electorate of 88,852, which makes it one of the largest in the country. In terms of industry and population it is a very mixed constituency indeed, being neither purely rural or urban. In 1966 the total vote was 60,868 (81.9 per cent), and in 1970 it was 68,737

(77 per cent). The swing to the Conservatives in 1970 was 4.9 per cent, which was slightly above the national average. Between 1966 and 1970 the Conservative vote rose from 28,932 to 36,712 – from 47.5 per cent to 53.5 per cent. The Labour vote rose from 24,529 (40·3 per cent) to 25,166 (36.6 per cent); the Liberal vote fell from 7,407 (12.2 per cent) to 6,859 (10 per cent). The increase in the total vote between the Elections was just under 8,000, whereas the increase in the electorate was some 13,500. It is not, of course, a typical constituency, but there are no typical constituencies, and Banbury serves as good as most – and better than many – for this exercise.

The source for this analysis of the Election is the detailed canvass returns prepared daily by the very efficient Conservative organization, which has been made available to this commentator. Canvass returns are normally to be regarded with suspicion, but the Banbury canvass was so thoroughly conducted, and its results so accurate, that it merits examination, particularly as the Conservative predictions of 1964 and 1966 had been extremely accurate.

The principal task of the canvass undertaken by the Banbury Conservatives was to establish whether there was a 50 per cent Conservative vote. On the 1966 experience an 80 per cent turnout could be expected (in the event it was 77 per cent) this required a Conservative vote of 35,000 to ensure victory in a three-cornered fight.

It is necessary to summarize what is a complicated and highly professional canvass, in which a total of 52,346 electors (some 60 per cent of the constituency) were canvassed.

On 12 June, after 32,660 voters had been canvassed, the Conservative vote projection was 36,800. The projections subsequently went as follows:

Date	Electors canvassed (total)	Projected Conservative (vote)
13 June	34,854	37,000
15 June	44,659	37,400
16 June	49,946	37,100
17 June	51,412	37,000
18 June	52,346	37,300

The actual Conservative vote on 19 June was 36,712 (53.4 per cent). Apart from the remarkable accuracy of the projection, the interesting feature lies in its steadiness over the last five days. If the earlier stages of the campaign are examined, the picture becomes, if anything, even more interesting. On 6 June, on the basis of a total canvass of 11,522, after making allowances for the fact that the initial canvass was probably affected by local factors, including the recent County Council elections, the projected Conservative vote was 37,000 (51.4 per cent). By 11 June, the projected vote – on 18,064 electors canvassed – was up to 41,700, but a more sober and careful evaluation on 12 June gave estimates of:

Conservative	36,800
Labour	29,200
Liberal	6,000

The final result over-estimated the Labour vote considerably – a fact which indicates a substantial gulf in this constituency between Labour voting intentions and actual voting – but the other estimates were very close to the result, which was:

Conservative	36,712	(53.4 per cent)
Labour	25,166	(36.6 per cent)
Liberal	6,859	(9.9 per cent)

While it is self-evidently hazardous to draw general conclusions from one constituency, the Banbury figures appear to demonstrate that the high Conservative vote – representing a swing of 4.9 per cent on 1966 – was there from the start of the campaign, and never wavered significantly; also, that the actual Labour vote was significantly lower than the declarations of voting intention had indicated. It is the firm opinion of the successful Conservative candidate – Mr Neil Marten, to whom I am indebted for the details of his canvass returns – that there was no movement of any significance towards the Conservatives in the campaign, a view that is confirmed by his returns. All that can be said is that the available evidence for this constituency provides no indication of a late swing to the Conservatives; that the majority existed before the campaign began, and held firm. It would be unreasonable to claim that the Banbury evidence is conclusive, any more than it would be

274

reasonable to assert that the Banbury experience was universal. Nonetheless, the advocates of the 'late swing' theory would be advised to examine the Banbury case with some care.[1]

Thus, the real evidence for the 'late swing' comes from the opinion poll organizations, which have admitted frankly that their findings are based upon the same technique as the election polls themselves. But, while a cynic might dismiss these findings on the grounds that a system which has been proved to be so fallible need not be seriously considered, the evidence is of interest.

NOP's findings were as follows:

Re-interviews with electors who formed part of the pre-election samples showed that a substantial proportion of those respondents changed their minds about how they would vote. The Conservative Party was the net beneficiary of these changes. This was the major reason why the poll incorrectly forecast a Labour victory. A higher proportion of Labour supporters abstained than Conservatives. These two factors – switching in favour of the Conservatives and differential turnout – were sufficient together to give the Conservatives a lead in our sample. Neither the changes nor the abstainers were confined to any particular age, sex, or social class group . . . All the samples re-interviewed . . . show the same sort of change. The overall effect is to produce an average swing of about 2.2% to Conservative between the weekend before the election and polling day, a swing sufficient to put the Tories in front.[2]

The NOP post-mortem also emphasized that the largest movement towards the Conservatives occurred in the higher manual worker group; that there was no significant difference between men and women in voting behaviour; and that issues of personality played a markedly unimportant rôle. The implication of the NOP findings is that about half a million voters changed their voting intention between 14 and 18 June. While this is of course quite possible, the evidence of the Conservatives' panel operation and that of Banbury must be set against it.

[1] Another example against the late swing theory is Mitcham, where the eventual result was forecast accurately by Conservative canvass returns from the outset of the campaigns. But here, again, there was a large and efficient Conservative organization, a factor of crucial importance in assessing the value of such returns as positive evidence.
[2] *NOP Political Bulletin*, October 1970, pp. 1-6.

The personal contribution of Enoch Powell to the Conservative victory was almost immediately a major topic of interest and controversy, on which there was a very substantial difference of judgement. The estimate of Louis Harris Research Ltd was that, 'although Mr Powell may have been doing damage to Mr Heath's reputation as a strong leader of his party during the campaign, we found it highly probable that on balance Powell helped the Conservative cause rather than damaged it'. Powell's admirers have pointed to the fact that he received 'between five and six thousand' letters during and immediately after the Election campaign, of which only 'about 60' were hostile.[1] Some Conservatives – particularly in the Midlands – have made strong claims about Powell's effect, particularly on traditionalist Labour supporters, and certainly one defeated Labour candidate has blamed his defeat heavily on Powellite factors. He claims that his canvass returns slumped after Powell's Northfield speech, and never recovered; but this case demonstrates the perils of over-simplified interpretations, as several leading Labour organizers would attribute this particular defeat to other factors – including the alleged deficiencies of the candidate himself and his local organization.

Even in the Midlands, where it has been claimed that Powell's influence in the Conservative gains was substantial, the evidence is far from conclusive. The average swing to the Conservatives was 5.3 per cent, which was only slightly above the national average. In Powell's own constituency the swing was 8.3 per cent and in Wolverhampton North-West it was 8.7 per cent, almost sufficient to unseat Mrs Renée Short. In Brierley Hill it was 9.1 per cent and in Cannock Jennie Lee went down before a massive 10.7 per cent swing to the Conservatives. Yet in other seats thought to be particularly susceptible to the immigration issue, and in which Powell spoke, the swing to the Conservatives was far below the national average, and in Birmingham All Saints and Rugby there were in fact significant swings to Labour (in Rugby of the order of 2.6 per cent). The evidence points to the conclusion that the identification of Powell with the race issue helped in some seats, was a disadvantage in others, and had little signi-

[1] John Wood (ed.): *Powell and the 1970 Election*, p. 19.

ficance in most.[1] The only constituency in which race seems to have had a clear significance was in Clapham, where the Labour candidate was Dr David Pitt, a West Indian. But here there were other factors, of which the most important was the fact that Dr Pitt was only selected shortly before the Election, and had not had sufficient time to establish himself. In this context, his colour was a clear disadvantage, and probably contributed very considerably to the heavy fall (11 per cent) in the Labour vote.

The evidence, therefore, is very inconclusive. Some Conservative candidates believe strongly that they were actively harmed by Powell's part in the campaign, and it was certainly the case that the Conservative swing was markedly less in areas of substantial immigrant settlement. In these areas it would appear that there was some justification in the charge of *The Times* (15 June) that Powell was 'an unmitigated liability to Mr Heath'. Nationally, this was an extreme judgement; equally extreme is the claim of Maurice Cowling that, 'whatever one may wish to believe, it is difficult to avoid the conclusion that Mr Powell's impact on the Election was great, that he made a strong appeal to many of the "ordinary people" ... and that the two-year campaign he brought to an independent climax in the ten days before the Election struck oil in places where Conservatives had not struck oil before'.[2]

The logical conclusion must be that Powell's beneficent effect on the Conservative Party was hardly more than marginal, and can only have compensated for the damage he had done by offending voters – and particularly immigrant voters – and by diverting pressure on to his nominal leader at a critical moment in the Election campaign. But it is impossible to be sure, and the logical explanation may well be wrong. It will be recalled that immigration was determined to be a major cause of concern to the 'target voter' by the Conservatives' investigations.[3] Thus, while the evidence leads him to doubt the fact, this commentator cannot state with any confidence that Powell's performance before and during the Election campaign did not

[1] Nicholas Deakin and Jenny Bourne: 'Powell, the Minorities, and the 1970 Election' *Political Quarterly*, October 1970. This article does not include the example of Brentford and Chiswick where, as has already been mentioned, the immigrant vote appears to have been heavy, and heavily Labour.

[2] Wood: *op. cit.*, p. 11.

[3] See pp. 129–30 above.

actively assist the Conservative Party. It is impossible to calculate the response – positive and negative – that Powell's fire and frenzy created.

No clear answer can be given to the question of *why* the Conservatives won the General Election of 1970. The post-election analyses that this commentator has examined tend to agree on certain points:

(1) There was a late movement to the Conservatives in the last five days of the campaign;
(2) There was no discernible difference between men and women in voting change since 1966 (which would appear to dismiss the theory of Labour women voting Conservative because of prices);
(3) Issues of personality of the party leaders appear to have been much less significant than those of policies;
(4) The Conservatives did very badly in the newly enfranchised voters, and particularly in the 18–21 group;
(5) The decisive movement towards the Conservatives was in the skilled manual worker group (the 'target voter' category).

With the exception of (1) – which this commentator, for reasons already given, cannot accept – the evidence to support these contentions seems to indicate very strongly *what* happened. As to *why* it happened, no satisfactory answer can be given. But the essential fact was that, by the beginning of 1970, and despite the encouraging indications, Labour was in a highly vulnerable position. Its record as a governing party was not good; its organization had been permitted to deteriorate; it had lost much of the bed-rock traditional support of those who had worked for the movement devotedly during the long years of defeat. Its advantage lay in the facts that it was the governing party and that its opponents had failed to exploit its deficiencies fully. Labour's partial recovery was essentially the result of the fact that 'the competence mandate' appeared to have been fulfilled. There is no question, in this commentator's judgement, that there was a real movement back to Labour in the spring of 1970, but it was subsequently clear that this was a 'ripple' rather than a 'tide' and was not as permanent or as substantial as the opinion polls and the South Ayrshire by-election result had indicated.

Did the campaign itself have any real importance? The evidence is contradictory. The Labour campaign, which had started so promisingly, collapsed in the last week for several reasons, but failure of leadership and preparation would seem to have been the most crucial. The Conservative campaign, particularly on television, was considerably better organized and directed. The Conservative organization, for all its defects in some areas, was immeasurably more efficient. All reports emphasize the greater general determination of the Conservatives to work and vote for their Party.

One feature of the Election that struck most observers was the relative lack of significance of the personalities of the respective leaders. The polls that gave Wilson a substantial lead in terms of personal popularity over Heath may well have been right, but the Election campaign did not become a 'personality contest', as some commentators had expected, and as had appeared probable at the outset. The comparison with 1945 is not really a close one, but the pattern of voting being primarily on issues and parties rather than individual leaders is common.

This is not to say that the contributions of the respective party leaders were not significant, but they were significant in a different way than in directly determining voting behaviour. Heath's outstanding achievement was that he did not lose his nerve in what was an acutely trying three weeks. He was very well served by his advisers – particularly by Barber, Fraser, and Hurd – and by his colleagues, but his personal success was one of character. It would perhaps be to overstate the case to say that his conduct was an inspiration to his Party, but his determination, hard work, and spirit was a strong corrective to defeatism.

In contrast, Wilson's performance demonstrated the physical and mental toll that nearly six years in Downing Street had extracted. In April 1970 this commentator had seen him at close range for the first time for over a year, and it was evident that the Prime Minister was a very tired man. Before the audience, the arc-lights, and the television cameras, the old spirit and verve was there; but off-stage, one saw the weariness. If he decided to take the easiest course in the campaign – which he did – this factor must have had (no doubt, subconsciously) its significance. Thus, on the straight contrast

between the two men, Heath's alertness, energy, and aggressiveness must have compensated for the fact that he lacked the
warmth of touch and expression that Wilson, at his now very
occasional best, could still display.

The final element in the personality factor was that whereas
the Conservatives genuinely – however unfairly – hated Wilson,
Labour regarded Heath with condescending contempt. Heath
and Wilson have consistently underestimated and misjudged
each other, but in the events leading up to the dissolution of
May 1970 the Labour underestimation of Heath and over-
estimation of Wilson's popular appeal had its importance in
the timing and strategy of the campaign. The conclusion must
be that the General Election of 1970 was not decided one way
or the other by popular feeling about the party leaders, but
that Heath's overall performance was of considerably greater
benefit to the Conservatives than Wilson's was to Labour.

Considerable attention has been devoted to the matter of the
timing of the Election. In retrospect, the 'economic' arguments
for June as opposed to October do not look so strong as they
did at the time, as there was in fact a healthy trade surplus for
the last quarter. But timing is only part of an election strategy,
and the real point of criticism against Labour was the management of the campaign. The fundamental error was to run on the
post-1966 record and to talk only with studied vagueness about
current and future policies. The Conservatives, in 1955 and
1959, had run on their record, but had also produced policies
for the future. All the other elements in the Labour defeat were
perhaps of less significance than this one. The surrender of the
political initiative to the Conservatives was made even more
serious by the disparity between the two major parties' organization, planning, and preparation. It is not necessary to allege
that the Conservatives waged a notably exciting, imaginative,
or elevated campaign to make the point that, when contrasted
with that of Labour, it was incomparably better conceived,
planned, and executed.

But perhaps the most serious error of all in the Labour
strategy was the conviction that it enjoyed a virtually built-in
initial advantage. The polls, the political scientists, and a
not inconsiderable element of *hubris* had persuaded the Labour
leadership that it was in the ascendant, and that it did not have
to win votes but only to hold them to be assured of victory.

They did not know that they had already lost the support of the decisive target voter on which everything hinged. It is just conceivable that an entirely different campaign might have won him back, but the Labour leadership did not realize what had happened and did not try. Thus, if the campaign itself had an importance, it was probably a negative one; by its conduct of it, Labour lost the opportunity, which was probably not great, of winning back the key sector of the electorate which it had alienated since 1966.

The Election brought no solace to the Liberals. Their total vote fell by over 200,000 despite the fact that they contested 21 more seats than in 1966. They lost seven seats, and their leader survived by only 369 votes in North Devon. Indeed, this situation had severely limited Thorpe's national efforts. Liberals came second in twenty-seven constituencies (a reduction of two on 1966); although they had put up candidates in eighty-five constituencies which they had not contested in 1966 they did not contest sixty-three seats which they had in 1966. In general, Liberal interventions seemed to have helped the Conservatives rather more than Labour.

The impact of the Welsh and Scottish Nationalists was much less than had been anticipated in 1966–7. Mr Gwynfor Evans lost Carmarthen, and Mrs Winifred Ewing lost Hamilton, both defeated by Labour; the only Nationalist victory was in the Western Isles. Plaid Cymru contested all thirty-six Welsh seats, and polled over 175,000 votes; the Scottish Nationalists contested sixty-five seats, and polled 306,000 votes. This was far from derisory, but a severe disappointment after the heady dreams of 1966 and 1967.

The 1970 General Election cannot be regarded in isolation from the events since 1966, which have been summarized in this study. It is of course, possible that the electors considered that, if they had to choose between two conservative parties, they might as well vote for the real thing. It is also possible that a significant proportion personally preferred Mr Heath to

Mr Wilson. But the most probable explanation is that there was a deeper feeling that, given a handsome majority in 1966, Labour had not justified the expectations placed in it as a competent governing party, and that the combination of erratic policies and complacency had eroded the confidence of Labour supporters and uncommitted voters. This is the most probable explanation for the *negative* aspects of the Election, and particularly the Labour abstentions. This has drawn Dr Butler and Dr Pinto-Duschinsky to the conclusion that the Election was 'an unpopularity contest'. But this cannot be the full explanation of what was – despite the relatively small eventual Parliamentary majority – a very comprehensive victory for the Conservative Party. For, viewed in the long historical perspective, the supreme significance of the 1970 General Election was that the national Conservative coalition had been revived, and that the Labour-inclined target voter had in fact voted Conservative, or had abstained. The most interesting feature was that a substantial proportion of this element of the electorate had actually moved from Labour to the Conservatives between 1966 and 1970. The new volatility of the British electorate could not mean that this movement would be permanent, but it did mean that the Conservative national coalition was still a serious and important political factor.

The 1970 General Election had confirmed that the Conservative Party's position was based on English votes. One conspicuous feature of the result was the relatively poor performance of the Conservatives in Scotland, Wales, and the North-East of England. In 1955 the Conservatives held half the Scottish seats; in 1970 they were reduced to 23 out of 71. In certain key areas in North-East England – including Sunderland and Hull – the Conservatives did very poorly. Wales – with a considerably higher turnout (77.4 per cent) than the national average – was more encouraging for the Conservatives, but a total of 7 seats out of 36 was a reminder of the Principality's basic loyalties. The Election was won in England, where the turnout was the lowest (71.3 per cent) and the movement to the Conservatives (5.1 per cent) the greatest. For both parties these figures are sobering. For the Conservatives, the evidence of their steadily declining political appeal in industrial Scotland and the North-East of England must cause considerable concern. For Labour, the long-term apprehension is that the Party may find itself in the Liberal predicament – gradually forced towards the 'Celtic fringe' for its hard support, and losing the political territory that decides elections – England. In 1970 Labour held 216 English seats; the Conservatives 292. In Wales and Scotland combined the Conservatives held only 30 seats out of 107, whereas Labour held 71. Even if Labour actually increased its strength in Wales, Scotland, and the North-East of England it could not hope to regain power unless it made substantial inroads into the Conservatives' English majority.

There is no clear answer as to *why* the British electorate voted as it did on 18 June 1970. The historian must record that 28,344,807 voters, out of a possible 39,384,364, went to the polls; that 13,144,692 voted for Conservative candidates, 12,179,166 voted for Labour candidates, 2,117,638 for Liberal candidates, 38,431 for Communist, 481,812 for Welsh and Scottish Nationalists and 383,068 for other candidates. In the new House of Commons there would be 330 Conservatives, 287 Labour, 6 Liberals, 1 Scottish Nationalist, 1 Independent Welsh, 4 Independents from Northern Ireland, and the Speaker. The Conservatives won 74 seats and lost 8 on the pre-Election figures; Labour recovered ten, and lost 70; the Liberals lost seven seats. There, in hard statistics, are the results of the 1970 General Election. The student of contemporary politics can only record the result, and hazard opinions as to why that result occurred.

After the Election one embittered commentator wrote that, 'the manner in which the Election campaign was conducted by the leadership of both parties was deplorable. Never has there been such complacency, narrowness of outlook, and personalization of issues. Never has there been such public boredom and cynicism. Not since the time of Baldwin and Chamberlain has there been such a failure to educate and prepare the public for the problems ahead.'[1]

These are harsh strictures, and it should be remarked at once that there can never have been a modern General Election upon which similar epithets were not delivered – invariably

[1] *Political Quarterly*, July 1970

from the losing side. But these charges require some examination and discussion.

The issues of a General Election are created less by the politicians than by the context in which they have to operate. The Conservative leader certainly did not wish immigration and Powell to become issues, and yet they were, for a short time, forced upon him. The economy was certainly a major issue, and it can be argued with some force that it transcends all others in its relevance to Britain's future. Thus the manner in which the economy had been run by Labour and could be run by the Conservatives was a genuine, and crucial, issue. The fact that the debate degenerated as the campaign progressed into personal charges and a certain trivialization of the complex subjects – shopping baskets and jumbo jets – cannot dispute the main point, that this was *the* issue.

As for 'boredom and cynicism', the relatively low turnout – 72 per cent – gives some statistical support, but the fact remains that the total vote was the highest since 1951. And, despite the fine weather, attendances at the meetings of the major party speakers were high. There certainly seemed to be boredom at the outset, but this seemed to disperse quickly, and public interest and involvement was high in the last week. And abstention, as has been emphasized before, is not necessarily an indication of apathy.

Cynicism is a highly subjective matter. The British attitude towards politicians has tended to be irreverent for some time past, and a healthy scepticism for political promises need not be interpreted as cynicism. Nonetheless, the whole style of British politics in the 1960s had been such as to breed a cynicism with the political process which must be regarded as both justified and disturbing.

It is on such matters that statistics of the education, background, occupation, and age of politicians cease to have any real significance. The credibility of a public man is something highly personal to himself, and one of the most striking features of the 1960s was a general decline of confidence in the trustworthiness of politicians. Seen in this context, the skilful tactical operations of the Macmillan and Wilson Governments assume a less attractive significance. For, if confidence in the political process withers away, what is left? There were many indications in the late 1960s that this confidence was under strain. Governments elected on a certain programme, with certain undertakings then calmly abandoned or amended them, and refused to be deflected by the only form of constitutional protest open to the citizen – by-elections and local government elections. Governments must govern, and it would be absurd to claim that they should slavishly follow opinion polls, by-election results, or other temporary manifestations of unpopularity. But when there is a massive and sustained emphasis of the popular mood there are dangers in a Government and a political system that appears to be taking little notice. The frustration thus created can tempt people into other directions. These may be valuable and constructive – and the rise of *Shelter* and community social groups (a remarkable and significant development in the 1960s) are good examples. But they can also be more vehement and more violent, and the slow but steady increase in the use of violence in the 1960s was an ominous, but significant, novelty in British politics. When there is confidence in the political system, violence or the threat of violence – usually euphemistically described as 'direct action' – is counter-productive. But when that confidence falters – as in 1911–12, 1919–20, for a brief period in the 1930s, and in the late 1960s – a different situation emerges. The real significance of Peter Hain's campaign against the South African cricket tour was the conviction that passive, polite, 'constitutional' protest was ignored, and that the only way to jerk the attention of politicians to a major issue of this nature was to use intimidation.[1] The flare of enthusiasm for Powell in 1968 was another indication of this impatience with a remote, insensitive, and distant political oligarchy. Similarly, the plight of the homeless had to be graphically demonstrated in forcible seizures of houses. No doubt, there were sinister elements eager to exploit such situations, but the context and the atmosphere have to be created. And they are created by governments and politicians who confuse determination with arrogance, and who fail to see the crucial difference between a refusal to be stampeded by waves of popular emotion into courses they know to be wrong and a refusal to take heed – *between elections* – of public feeling.

Here we must face one of the salient problems of British politics. Despite the virtual universality of the franchise, the poli-

[1] Peter Hain: *Don't Play with Apartheid* (London, 1971).

tical centre of the nation remains in London – and in a very small part of London. Unless he is exceptionally sensitive and careful, the politician becomes increasingly obsessed by the movements and twists of 'the Westminster square mile', by the 'ups' and the 'downs', the 'ins' and the 'outs'. Slowly, but inexorably, he becomes mentally remote from the world outside, to the point when he reads opinion polls, by-election results, and newspapers as though they were messages from afar, which he interprets in his own fashion. And thus, without being at all aware of the fact, he is slipping quietly away from political reality. The shock at Westminster when the pro-Powell dockers marched was but one example. Another occurred when the Labour Government refused to implement the proposals of the Boundary Commission. Conservative MPs were convinced that this would create shock-waves of revulsion throughout the country. Perhaps it should have, but the knowledge that one lot of politicians appeared to be taking an unfair advantage over another lot of politicians left the electorate wholly unmoved.

This development of popular detachment from, and disillusionment with, London politics was not, of course, wholly the responsibility of the Labour Government. It had been growing in the final period of the Macmillan Government and in the short-lived Home Administration. It faded in the 1964–6 Labour Government, but revived sharply after the 1966 July Measures. One form that it took was the turning to Nationalist candidates in Scotland and Wales – which proved to have been a temporary movement. Another was in a refusal to become actively political – and one indication of this was the fall in Party membership, and particularly in the Labour Party. Another form was the increasing popularity of extremist organizations – the Monday Club, in its revised guise, the Maoists, the Young Liberals. Although entirely non-violent, the well-planned and vigorous campaigns to save Stansted airport from being developed into the third London airport and to legalize abortion – both extra-Parliamentary movements with subsequent Parliamentary support – had their message. Thus, if Parliament did act, it was only in a reactive sense; it tended to follow, rather than lead. And by 'Parliament' we necessarily mean 'the Government'. Many activists found, as had the Suffragettes, that courteous presentation of a good case had little impact, whereas more vehement action – preferably with television cameras present – got better results.

Thus, although we can see few indications of boredom with politics and society in the 1960s, we have indications of cynicism with a system that seemed increasingly remote, and increasingly obsessed with its own tactics and machinations. And it is clear that this cynicism was a major contributory factor towards Labour's decline in public esteem, and its eventual defeat. For it lost touch not merely with its own supporters, but with its former image of the people's party, the compassionate party, and the sensitive, democratic party.

It is inappropriate to treat politics in an episodic manner; it is a continuing process in which a myriad of elements are involved, and, although the political struggle has its highly dramatic characteristics, it is a drama without an end. Furthermore, events far beyond the control – and often the comprehension – of politicians are remorselessly changing the environment in which the politician has to operate. It has already been emphasized that, far from being the master of destinies, as he is so often portrayed, the politician is usually the helpless victim of forces in whose creation and development he has played no part whatsoever, and which in a free society are dominated by factors which are not really susceptible to the control and influence of a Government. Sometimes these forces assist a politician; on other occasions they sweep him away. Thus, what political commentators often deride as blunders or laud as master-strokes are usually actions, often taken on inadequate evidence and taken hastily, whose wisdom or the reverse cannot be assessed until these other forces have come into play. The modern British politician, far from being a man of power, is in fact usually painfully impotent.

The most serious misconception of recent years in British politics has been to forget this elementary situation, and to regard the haphazard and highly unpredictable profession of politics as a scientific exercise, in which there are rules, norms, and patterns which, if closely followed, bring success as well as comprehension. The close attention given to public opinion polls is but one instance of this; the remarkable proliferation of journals and books devoted to proving that politics is a science is another. It has become highly unfashionable to admit that no one has the faintest idea about why people vote, or do not vote, in a particular way, or that no one can hope to assess the impact of Election campaigns on the electorate. If the General Election of 1970 taught anything, it emphasized that *ex post facto* rationalizations of previous Elections are poor guides for the future, but it is doubtful whether this uncomfortable lesson has yet been absorbed.

While all this must be emphasized, and firmly emphasized, there is much to be learned from the events of 1964–70.

For the Labour Party, the most important lesson of all is that – if it is to regard itself as a governing Party – it must address itself to the vital importance of prior preparation for Government, a lesson that must go right through the Party and not be confined to its top echelons in the Parliamentary Party. The lesson of 1964–70 had also been painfully learned in 1945–51, but had not been subsequently taken to heart. Attitudes and principles, in short, are not enough. Labour learned much as a governing Party, but much of it need not have been learnt so laboriously and so unnecessarily in office.

In part, this particular failure may be regarded as endemic to the Labour Movement, which is obsessed by the importance of committees and of talk. The Conservatives dislike committees, and are more interested in results than debates. There tends to be, accordingly, a briskness and speed about the Conservative approach which has its defects, but is at least not so time-consuming and exhausting as the methods instinctively preferable to Labour. As a Labour Minister subsequently wrote:

> The Cabinet are dealing with decisions which should be taken by Cabinet Committees; the Committees with decisions which should be taken by individual Ministers; the Ministers with decisions which should be taken by civil servants.[1]

This was one of the factors that left the Conservatives less physically and emotionally exhausted after thirteen years in office than Labour was after six. Another element was the Conservative skill in grooming promising young men for office and regularly replacing their seniors. The importance of this

[1] Article by Mr Reginald Prentice in the *Political Quarterly*, April–June 1970.

talent spotting is very considerable, and resulted in the Conservatives making much better use of what ability they possessed than Labour achieved. Wilson proved himself to be a 'bad butcher' of inefficient Ministers; he was also not sufficiently alert to the importance of bringing on the most talented of his younger men. Several who were given junior office often appeared to have been chosen for idiosyncratic reasons in which talent appeared not to be the dominant consideration, and the obsession with balancing all factors – personal loyalty, long service in the Movement, equitable geographical distribution, and ideological differences – seemed to have more significance. There were, of course, some exceptions, but the fact that they *were* exceptions is the important point. The Labour Government consistently carried too much dead wood; some is perhaps inevitable, but there are limits; the Labour Government consistently exceeded them.

And while there is no need to become obsessed by matters of organization, the importance – and quality – of the Conservative research machinery must be emphasized. In office, such machinery is principally of value to back-benchers; in Opposition, it is crucial for the whole Party. The kind of research facilities – and, which is even more important – the research *approach* that the Conservatives have created, has no real parallel in the Labour Party, and this must be accounted a very serious failure of intelligence and imagination. If it is not corrected, Labour will continue to lurch into Office without any serious conception of what it is going to do and how it is going to do it.

Labour's qualities as a governing party stemmed from its intellectual capacity, loyalty – if often heavily strained – to the leadership, and its skill in improvization. Its deficiencies were principally the result of a serious failure in preparation for Office, in a certain impatience at working at the sources of problems and providing real solutions, in a preference for appearance rather than substance, and in being too ready to become submerged in administrative detail. If Labour were to learn from its failures and were to utilize its resources more sensibly, the resultant challenge to the Conservatives would be a very formidable one. Wilson's principal contribution has been to make the Labour Party *think* of itself as a governing party. But it is still left with the dilemma of how it is to *be* a more effective governing party, and how it is to reconcile its attitudes to the hard business of national administration.

The Conservative Party should be concerned by the factors that made a man of the calibre of Sir Edward Boyle leave politics; why an element such as the Monday Club has expanded so dramatically; and why Powell aroused for a time such intense enthusiasm. It still remains a minority party, and its survival still depends upon its ability to contrive to continue to recruit substantially from Labour. And it is not necessary to accept Powell and his various creeds, nor to endorse wholly the attitude expressed by Quintin Hogg, quoted on page 142, to underline the point made by Angus Maude in 1965 that the portrayal of Conservatism as a more efficient group of technocrats is not enough. There was about the Conservative Party in the 1960s what can best be described as an ever-increasing coldness. The animosity towards Butler was less against him personally than what he represented. His objective in 1945–50 had been, as has been emphasized, to establish a Conservative philosophy that was 'viable, efficient and humane'. The Conservatives in the 1960s gave the clear impression of having decided to ignore the last theme. Humanity in politics does not consist merely of providing tax reductions and improved social benefits for the young, the elderly, the infirm and the unfortunate; it should be a central theme in a modern political philosophy. There were many indications in the 1960s, and after June 1970, that it was no longer a central theme in the new Conservatism.

Another disturbing trend has been towards what must be loosely described as the revival of 'anti-intellectualism' in the Conservative Party. The Party, no less than the country, urgently requires men and women of first-rate brains, not necessarily as candidates or MPs but involved in its activities. It is a striking feature of British politics in the 1960s that, with very few exceptions, the Conservative Party failed to attract many people of this calibre; even more alarming, from the Conservative view, is the fact that many have been positively alienated. Many of the policy documents produced by the Conservatives between 1966 and 1970 were designed for eventual Government action; this was undoubtedly necessary, but there was a marked absence of the intellectual quality and depth of the comparable documents published between 1945 and 1951. And here we may remind ourselves of the unique contribution made to post-war Conservatism by Lord Butler.

Two of the most marked features of the Conservative revival in the late 1940s and early 1950s had been a distinct movement to the party in the universities and the remarkable popular success of the Young Conservatives. In the 1960s, in contrast, there was no movement of any significance to the Conservatives in the universities – indeed, all indications suggest that exactly the opposite occurred – and the Young Conservatives, despite strenuous efforts to breathe new life into the movement, actually declined in numbers. On foreign and defence affairs, an area in which the Conservatives are supposed to have a superiority over Labour, the Conservatives failed to make use of the considerable expansion of research and thought in the universities. Labour showed itself very willing to commission outside bodies to undertake research studies over a wide area of public policy, while – quite properly – reserving the right to adopt or even ignore them. The Conservatives failed to appreciate the possible benefits of utilizing the expansion in advanced research that has taken place in Britain in the 1960s. The Labour Government deliberately encouraged and cultivated involvement in public affairs by some of the best minds in the country, even when it knew that the political bias of many of them was hostile to the Labour Party. The establishment of University Readerships in Defence Studies by Denis Healey is but one example of what can be done to generate the kind of research and thinking which Government Departments, as a result of time and other pressures, cannot undertake.

Conservative suspicions of 'intellectuals' and 'the intelligentsia' places it in danger of forfeiting not only much goodwill but also much ability. In this context we may recall the comment of George Orwell: 'The English will never develop into a nation of philosophers. They will always prefer instinct to logic . . . but they must get rid of their downright contempt for "cleverness".'[1] This criticism is equally valid today, and has particular relevance to the Conservative Party.

The Conservative Party exists because it is based on a certain conception of life, and a certain conception of Britain. It eschews ideology, because ideology is limited and narrow. It appeals to common sense, reality, and scepticism. But, like all

[1] George Orwell: *The English People* (London, 1947).

serious human confederations, it must have an objective that is not definable in strictly materialist terms. Patriotism is not enough; efficiency is not enough; pragmatism is not enough; certainly the seigneurial assumption of the right to govern is not enough. Despite their remarkable revival and Election victory, it was difficult to accept that they had succeeded in determining the needs of the 1960s.

The Conservatives must also consider with care the comparisons between 1955 and 1970 set out in the Nuffield study of the 1970 Election.[1] The net movement to the Conservatives in the United Kingdom in this period was 0.1 per cent. In the South-East Region it was 1.1 per cent; in the South-West 2.2; in East Anglia 3.6; in the East Midlands 2.8; in the West Midlands 2.9. In Yorkshire, the North-West, and the North-East there were net movements to Labour of 0.5, 2.3, and per cent respectively. In Wales there had been a net movement to the Conservatives of 1.9 per cent; in Scotland, a net movement to Labour of 5 per cent. If the large cities are examined, it will be seen that in the period 1955–70 the Conservatives can only record a net movement towards them in Bristol (0.6 per cent), Leicester (3.1 per cent), and Stoke on Trent (1.6 per cent). The figures for London, Glasgow, Birmingham, Liverpool, Manchester, Edinburgh, and Hull are hostile to the Conservatives. It could be argued – to employ the metaphor again – that the 'ripples' between 1966 and 1970 gave the Conservatives much ground for optimism and encouragement, whereas the 'tides' over a fifteen-year period provided less encouraging indications.

Thus, looking at the 1970 Election in a larger perspective, this observer is reminded of the letter written by the young Winston Churchill after the Conservative victory in the General Election of 1900:

> I think this election, fought by the Liberals as a soldiers' battle, without plan or leaders or enthusiasm, has shown so far the strength, not the weakness, of Liberalism in the country.[2]

The General Election of June 1970, viewed coldly in the context of all that had preceded it, had demonstrated the

---

[1] Butler and Pinto-Duschinsky: *op. cit.*, Appendix 1, pp. 356–7.
[2] R. Rhodes James: *Rosebery* (London, 1963), p. 418.

strength of Labour in Britain – a strength which not even an inadequate Labour Government had fully succeeded in eroding. The dilemma of the political future of Britain lies essentially in whether Labour can build on and exploit effectively these foundations, or whether the Conservatives, with their superior dedication and organization, can preserve their position as the minority party which wins Parliamentary majorities.

A study of this nature has been difficult to undertake and even more difficult to accomplish. Many of its conclusions are tentative. Others will undoubtedly prove to have been inaccurate or superficial. Some may be subsequently regarded as valid. As was emphasized at the outset, the student of contemporary politics is inevitably to some extent a participant, and his judgements are subjective. If he is entitled to these judgements, so is the reader entitled to reject them.

It will be evident that this commentator does not contemplate the political history of Britain in the 1960s with much elation. It was a decade in which so many hopeful indications of the late 1950s proved false that although it was not a decade of disaster, it was one of disappointment. To blame 'the politicians' in entirety would be unreasonable, and false. But they must carry their responsibility.

The 1960s had opened with so many expectations, which were largely unfulfilled. So we drifted, unhappily. Sometimes we voted Labour; on others, Conservative; on others, Liberal; we flirted with fringe movements; or we stayed at home. Thus this nation, with its formidable potentialities, its remarkable assets of intelligence and character, and its still-substantial wealth and influence, passed through the 1960s with few catastrophies but with few achievements. The drift towards insularity, introspection, and parochialism, evident in the late 1950s, was dismally accelerated. Spirit, enterprise, and imagination seemed to be conspicuously absent. The erosion of the standards of public life and of personal conduct was not reversed. A pall of stagnation hung gloomily over the nation. The late Lord Nuffield, just before his death in 1959, described Britain as 'a nation in semi-retirement'. This sombre description seems applicable to the period we have been examining. But perhaps it was only an interlude. And we may profitably recall the warning of de Tocqueville:

Without ideas and leaders, a people cannot truly be said to exist.

Select Bibliography

Alexander, Andrew and Watkins, Alan: *The Making of the Prime Minister* (Macdonald, 1970).

Brittan, Samuel: *Steering the Economy* (Secker & Warburg, 1969).

Burgess, Tyrrell (ed.): *Matters of Principle: Labour's Last Chance* (Penguin, 1968).

Butler, David and King, Anthony: *The British General Election of 1964* (Macmillan, 1965); *The British General Election of 1966* (Macmillan, 1967).

Butler, David and Pinto-Duschinsky, Michael: *The British General Election of 1970* (Macmillan, 1971).

Butler, David and Stokes, Donald: *Political Change in Britain* (Macmillan, 1969).

Butler, Lord: *The Art of the Possible* (Hamish Hamilton, 1971).

Collins, Sidney: *Coloured Minorities in Britain* (Lutterworth, 1957).

Daniel, W. W.: *Racial Discrimination in England* (Pelican, 1968).

Deakin, Nicholas: *Colour, Citizenship and British Society* (Panther, 1970).

Foot, Paul: *Immigration and Race in British Politics* (Penguin, 1965); *The Rise of Enoch Powell* (Penguin, 1969).

George-Brown, Lord: *In My Way* (Gollancz, 1971).

Hodder-Williams, Richard: *Public Opinions Polls and British Politics* (Routledge and Kegan Paul, 1970).

Howell, David: *A New Style of Government* (Conservative Political Centre, 1970).

Hutchinson, George: *Edward Heath* (Longmans, 1970).

Jenkins, Peter: *The Battle of Downing Street* (Knight, 1970).

Kitzinger, Uwe: *The Second Try: Labour and the EEC* (Pergamon, 1968).

Lapping, Brian: *The Labour Government, 1964–1970* (Penguin, 1970).

Lester, A. (ed.): *Essays and Speeches by Roy Jenkins* (Collins, 1967).

Powell, Enoch: *Freedom and Reality* (Batsford, 1969).

Rose, E. J. B.: *Colour and Citizenship* (Oxford University Press, 1969).

Roth, Andrew: *Enoch Powell – Tory Tribune* (Macdonald, 1970).

Stacey, Tom: *Immigration and Enoch Powell* (Stacey, 1970).

Uri, Pierre (ed.): *From Commonwealth to Common Market* (Penguin, 1968).

Utley, T. E.: *Enoch Powell – The Man and His Thinking* (Kimber, 1968).

Wilson, Harold: *The Labour Government, 1964–1970* (Weidenfeld & Nicolson and Michael Joseph, 1971).

Wood, John (ed.): *Powell and the 1970 Election* (Elliot Right Way Books, 1970).

Index

Wilson, Harold—*cont.*
235; campaign, 237–8, 239–40, 242–3, 249–50, 258, 259, 260–1, 279–80; Conservative recognition of his qualities, 242; tiredness and loss of touch, 260–1, 279–80; defeat, 264–6; his achievement, 266, 289
Wolverhampton: coloured immigrants in, 152, 154, 179, 182, 245; Powell speech (June 1970), 246
Wolverhampton *Express and Star*, 160
Wolverhampton North-West, 1970 swing to Conservatives, 276

Wolverhampton South-West, Powell as Member for, 167, 276
Wood, David, 237
Wood, John, 191*n*, 276*n*, 277*n*
Woodcock, George, 68
Woolton, Lord, 93, 112, 126
Worthing, 213

York, Heath speeches (Sept. 1968), 208, Wilson speech (April 1970), 227
Yorkshire, swing to Labour (1955–70), 292
Young, George K., 191*n*, 206
Young Conservatives, 210, 291
Young Liberals, 223, 225, 286